Ethics i

Ethics in Comedy

Essays on Crossing the Line

EDITED BY STEVEN A. BENKO

ETHICS AND CULTURE
Series Editor James M. Okapal

McFarland & Company, Inc., Publishers
Jefferson, North Carolina

This book has undergone peer review

Library of Congress Cataloguing-in-Publication Data

Names: Benko, Steven A., editor.
Title: Ethics in comedy : essays on crossing the line / edited by Steven A. Benko.
Description: Jefferson, North Carolina : McFarland & Company, Inc., Publishers, 2020 | Series: Ethics and culture | Includes bibliographical references and index.
Identifiers: LCCN 2020040874 | ISBN 9781476676418 (paperback) ∞ | ISBN 9781476640976 (ebook)
Subjects: LCSH: Wit and humor—Social aspects. | Wit and humor—Moral and ethical aspects.
Classification: LCC PN6149.S62 E84 2020 | DDC 809/.917—dc23
LC record available at https://lccn.loc.gov/2020040874

British Library cataloguing data are available

ISBN (print) 978-1-4766-7641-8
ISBN (ebook) 978-1-4766-4097-6

Front cover image © 2020 Fer Gregory/Shutterstock

Printed in the United States of America

McFarland & Company, Inc., Publishers
 Box 611, Jefferson, North Carolina 28640
 www.mcfarlandpub.com

For my wife, Sarah, who makes me laugh.
For my children, Kate, Allison, Ryan, and Thomas:
I hope you laugh, but only at the right things.

Acknowledgments

Something never comes from nothing, so I would like to acknowledge the people who have nurtured this project along the way. This work is undergirded by support from Meredith College administrators who encouraged my interest in comedy and ethics with generous travel support and research grants: Matthew Poslusny, Garry Walton, and Sarah Roth, thank you.

Rebecca Duncan, everyone should be as lucky as I have been to have a colleague who listens, shares ideas, and supports them as much as you have supported me during my time at Meredith. You listen to every idea and provide invaluable feedback. As if you were not busy enough, you selflessly volunteered to review and proof these essays, greatly improving the quality of the book. Thank you for your time and skill.

Ellie Jones, one of the great pleasures of this project has been your emergence as a conversation partner and co-writer. You demonstrated ambition, insights, skills, and knowledge beyond your years. I am glad that your efforts will have this material form to preserve many fun and interesting conversations and to serve as evidence of your growth as a writer and research. Elena Blackwelder, Scout Burch, and Raynor Dail, thank you for your help with the final corrections; you earned more than two dinners.

And of course, my family, friends, colleagues, and students who encouraged me during this project, listened to my ideas, and gave me feedback and advice: Mike Runy, Andrew Ball, Victoria White, Hayden Hains, Amy Hruby, Shannon Grimes, Margarita Suarez, Cynthia Edwards, Julie Schrock, Cece Toole, Tim Hendrix, and Mark O'Dekirk. Erica Rogers, you encouraged this project the best possible way: with laughter.

It goes without saying that this work would never have come together without support from my wife, Sarah. Writing about the social nature of comedy and laughter, and the possibility of becoming a better person through both, makes you want to laugh with others. No one makes me laugh the way you do, and there's no one I want to laugh with, or be better for, more than you.

That's right! That's right! That ain't right!
—Dave Chappelle, *Undercover Brother*

Table of Contents

Introduction

Steven A. Benko

Picking an example of offensive comedy to frame the intertwining of ethics and comedy ought to be as easy as shooting fish in a barrel. Comedy has never been more prevalent: live, or shared across a variety of platforms and mediums, there are more comedy specials on more networks, streaming channels, and the internet. Comedy has also never been more relevant. Comedy is how people get their news, share their politics, religion, and also their very strong feelings about movies, TV shows, and cats. The infiltration of comedy into all aspects of life has meant that one can find jokes about any topic. Racist jokes. Sexist jokes. Jokes that mock religion. It's an embarrassment of riches. So why is it difficult to pick a joke as an example? So far, this book is only 160 words old and it might not age well, if at all, if words 175–419 made the rest of the book impossible to read (the punchline was, "The Aristocrats!"). The editor and contributors to this volume feel strongly that this is a book that should be read. Instead of starting out with something that offends for the sake of offense, thinking about what humor and laughter are, or defining the work they do in culture (and the inability to reach any final conclusions about that), is the most productive launching point when speaking about an ethics of comedy.

But why put the two together? Why ethics and comedy? One reason is because both are uniquely human. Robert Provine's *Laughter: A Scientific Exploration* locates humor and laughter as part of human evolution and development. There are physical and physiological similarities between non-human and human laughter, but those similarities do not amount to much. If you tickle a monkey or chimpanzee (our evolutionary ancestors), their breathing will change and they will produce a "play face": "mouth open, upper teeth covered, lower teeth exposed," and they will emit "a breathy pantlike sound" that is close to something like laughter (Provine 77). The intensity of the expressions and panting is relative to the intensity of the stimulation.

1

What chimp laughter and human laughter have in common is rhythm: chimp panting and human laughter occur at a regular rhythm but at different speeds. The similarities end there. One difference between chimp panting and human laughter is that chimps can express only one syllable per respiratory cycle (monosyllabic exhalation) while humans can express multiple syllables per respiratory cycle (polysyllabic exhalation):

> Chimpanzee laughter is locked into the cycle of breathing with one pantlike laugh-sound being produced per exhalation and inhalation. Chimps are unable to chop an exhalation into the discrete 'ha ha ha's of human laughter. What elevates this distinction in laugh-form above footnote status is that it reveals a fundamental inability of chimpanzees to modulate an exhalation, a critical condition for the production of humanlike speech. Humans laugh as they speak, by the virtuosic modulation of sounds produced by an outward breath [Provine 85].

Provine's conclusion is that laughter and speech emerged alongside other evolutionary developments like bipedalism which changed how humans breathe. If Provine is correct, then laughter resulted from some of the earliest developments that separated humans from their primate forbearers. The change in human breathing allowed for a different laugh sound, but also the development of speech. As speech became more complex, so did laughter: as human brains developed so did the complexity of what would produce laughter. So while there may be physiological similarities between human and non-human laughter, the continuities end there. While there is continuity between humans, chimpanzees, and apes, non-human animals do not laugh, play, or joke with the same intent and sophistication that humans do. If non-human animals are laughing, we do not yet know what they are laughing at. And we do not yet know if they know what they are laughing at. However, humans can know what they are laughing at. The questions the contributors to this volume are wrestling with deal with the moral rightness and wrongness of that laughter. Humans can laugh, but should we?

Human laughter is a behavior, like other human behaviors, that becomes more complex as humans grow and mature: infants laugh at peek-a-boo games, toddlers at exaggerated pratfalls, children at silly word games, sullen teenagers laugh at nothing (though this might be a sign of an ironic disposition), and adults can laugh at images and complex word play. Laughter, then, is a complex trait shared by all humans that did (and still does) mature and become more sophisticated as humans grow and develop. What makes laughter unique as an object of ethical analysis is that it is not always an intentional behavior: it is difficult, if not impossible, to will oneself to perform an authentic and sincere laugh. While making someone laugh, or at least attempting to, is an intentional (and difficult) action, laughter is spontaneous and uncontrolled. What makes an ethics of humor and laughter so ripe for analysis is that where humor can be deliberate and intentional behavior, laughter is often not. Humans laugh before they realize what they are laughing at. Yet, laughter is thought to be revelatory of character. No one would fault a dog for getting excited and showing that excitement by panting or jumping up and down. But, it is possible to train dogs to moderate their excitement so that it occurs within the bounds of certain acceptable behaviors: no jumping on humans when they approach; no pulling on the leash when a squirrel or rabbit comes into view. So it is with humans: we laugh unreflectively, almost instinctively, yet morally appropriate laughter is bounded on all sides by cultural pressures that dictate what is appropriate or inappropriate to laugh at. Making matters more complex is the fact that the borders of this area are always shifting; we routinely enter spaces where cultural norms governing appropriate and inappropriate laughter are suspended and anything goes. Laughing at a sexist joke at work is problematic; laughing at the same sexist joke told among friends might be less problematic; laughing at that same sexist joke in a comedy club is even less problematic. Not laughing at it (while everyone else does) might make someone feel self-conscious and excluded from the group. Making sense of these gray areas and making sense of the lines that comedians cross is one of the goals of this volume.

Humor and laughter, like ethics, are both personal and social. The lines that comedians cross are not drawn or crossed in isolation. First, every theory of humor is built on a social foundation: superiority theory, relief theory, and incongruity theory each posit a shared set of cultural facts that jokes either uphold or disrupt. Superiority theory, problematized by Aristotle, but best explained in the work of Hobbes and Descartes, posits that laughter comes from the enjoyment of putting down one person or group for the benefit of another: "laughter expresses feelings of superiority over other people or over a former state of ourselves" (Morreall, "Philosophy"). When comedians downrank one group of people to show their superiority to another, they draw from shared histories, traditions, institutions, attitudes, beliefs, practices, etc., to (re)draw the social map that maintains in-group/out-group boundaries. Relief theory posits that social attitudes, norms, practices, or values can be so repressive that their subversion through humor provides psychological relief and benefits. In incongruity theory broadly construed, laughter results in a sudden but pleasant psychological shift:

> This approach to joking is similar to techniques of stand-up comedians today. They speak of the *set-up* and the *punch (line)*. The set-up is the first part of the joke: it creates the expectation. The punch (line) is the last part that violates that expectation. In the language of the Incongruity Theory, the joke's ending is incongruous with the beginning [Morreall, "Philosophy"].

In order for there to be laughter the surprise must interrupt and pleasantly alter the laugher's projection of what happens next. The social dimension of incongruity theory is that conceptual schemas and frameworks can only be violated if they are shared. If laughter reveals what the joke teller shares with their audience, then it is also true that laughter indicates what the audience shares with each other. The relationship between comedy and social inclusion and exclusion, the labeling of a group of people, and the reification of class distinctions challenge ethicists to think more deeply about the ethics of speech acts, as well as the response to those acts.

Though laughter of superiority, relief, and incongruity are inherently social, laughter and its moral meaning are also individual and personal. Each of the theories of comedy are a form of play: normal and conventional uses of words, language, manners, customs, meaning, and identity are suspended, even if only temporarily. In humans, play is complex intentional behavior that has social meaning and consequences for all involved. Just because it is play does not mean that it is beneficial or enjoyed by all. Though play is social, and has social meaning and consequences, it is still individual behavior. Moral evaluation of that behavior—from either the joke teller or the butt of the joke—is a natural part of exploring the meaning of comedy: most of what we laugh at is wrong or inappropriate behavior that reveals something about the character of the individual.

Robert C. Roberts opens his essay "Humor and the Virtues" wondering what is meant by the compliment "she has a sense of humor." What is it that a person with a sense of humor senses? The virtue that Roberts most closely associates with sense of humor is "perspectivity" meaning the ability to adopt the correct perspective in or about a given situation. Relative to superiority theory, correct perspectivity would be appropriately ranking or down-ranking the butt of the joke so that one's feeling of superiority were warranted and could be justified. Correct perspectivity relative to relief theory would mean not just enjoying the feeling of being released from the obligation to repress certain thoughts or desires but that these thoughts and desires ought to be released; their continued repression is wrong and harmful. More than anything else, failed comedy teaches that not all thoughts or desires ought to be expressed. Laughter at incongruities is more complex because it requires seeing differently than one sees, even if only for a moment. With the right kind of perspective on the situation set up in the joke the audience can enter into the world of the joke and adopt, even if only temporarily, the attitudes, beliefs, dispositions, and values of a group. Doing so allows them to sense the incongruities between their own individual values and the values of the group, and from an outsider's perspective, maybe grasp the gap between what the group professes and what they practice. In this way, the perception of incongruity (which is the precondition of laughter) is similar to ethical analysis and reflection: the thinking through of the gaps between what is and what ought to be. When laughter becomes part of the experience of the incongruity, the gap between what is and what ought to be is given a moral evaluation: if the gap is a criticism of the status quo, then laughter is a critique. If the gap is a suggestion of how things ought to be, then laughter is both a critique and an endorsement of that suggestion. Ethics is similar in that it is the ability to look at a situation from another perspective and understand the gaps between what is and what ought to be.

It could be argued, then, that what a sense of humor reveals about the individual is their relationship between what is and what could or ought to be. Roberts does not go this far. Instead, he argues that a sense of humor is a "disposition to enjoy a certain range of incongruities as such" (Roberts 128). Here, enjoying feeling superior, or the feeling of relief, or the perception of incongruities means being able to do something with them: think about them, explore them, and push at their limits to see how far they deviate from what should be the case. But for Roberts, this is only temporary. Laughter is a moral holiday from one's normal sense of right and wrong:

> To appreciate the humor you must have the capacity to "enter into" the world of the racist, the sexist, the bigot. But this is all the sharing of perspective that is needed to appreciate phthonic humor; it is not necessary to be confirmed in that perspective, to be an endorser of it, to be a believer in it. Amusement, even more than standard emotions, has this belief-independence about it [Roberts 137].

Laughter as a moral holiday implies that one neither comes nor goes from this moral holiday with problematic baggage. To claim that laughter is an "as if" perspective taking enables the suspect defense that someone was "just joking" or that what one laughed at was "only a joke." Both of these claims, which are meant to inoculate the joke teller and laugher from charges of classism, racism, ableism, ageism, sexism, etc. (or some combination of them), deny that these are powerful social forces that ought to be eliminated. Further, the claim that it was "just a joke" defangs these attitudes by saying that they can be enjoyed (temporarily) if one could have the right perspective about them. None of the essays in this book adopt or defend the "just joking" position. Instead, the point of the book is to show that one is never just joking and that just joking is incredibly complex and difficult. While some may enjoy the privilege of being believed that excursions into these attitudes are merely a moral holiday away from tolerance, acceptance, and empathy for others, there are others for whom there is no respite or holiday from their negativity and toxicity. Having the right perspective, then, is a long-term project. A person with a good sense of humor does not treat humor and laughter as a moral holiday. As the essays in this volume suggest, the social dimensions of humor require that a good sense of humor be a moral journey.

If humor is the occasion for laughter that ranks and down-ranks, or suggests alternative ways of thinking and being that are closed off or denied, or is the catalyst for disrupting entrenched ways of thinking via the creation of incongruities are also a critique of the gap between the status quo and something better, then what ethics adds is a vocabulary for discussing the meaning and moral value of that laughter. Ethics adds to humor a way to address this complexity without reducing it to a single principle or theme. An effort at an ethics of comedy or ethical analyses of comedy is not meant to arrest this undecidability. Instead, thinking about how different approaches to moral and ethical decision making can be applied to humor, as the essays in this volume demonstrate, charts a path through this undecidability and provides clarity even while recognizing the complexity of the subject matter. This book explores the moral rightness or wrongness of that laughter, asking about what the joke construction says about the joke-teller, what claims can be made about the audience members who do and do not laugh, and the effect of that laughter on the butt of the joke.

Laughter, Ethicists and Ethics

If there is a thread, then, that runs through the essays that run through this volume, it is that humor is something to be wrestled with. The authors in this volume take seriously that humor, when it punches down, does more harm than good. Conversely, each of the authors believes that humor, when punching up or speaking from a marginalized position, is a powerful tool that can shed light on—and in some instances correct—social injustices. To advance these claims, Jennifer Marra begins by rejecting arguments that humor and laughter be evaluated either in terms of subjective enjoyment or aesthetic appreciation. Humor is an activity that reveals the joke teller's world at the same time that it shapes the audience's. Put another way, telling a joke is an opportunity to think and to represent for others the content of that thought. Marra's position is that if humor represents an activity of the mind, then joke telling can be held to the same intellectual and moral standards as any other symbolic form of communication: is it true? Is it inclusive or exclusive? Was the thought deliberate, intentional, multi-perspectival, and rigorous? Having considered and given a moral value to those factors, the familiar criteria of what makes something praiseworthy or blameworthy can be applied to the joke: was it inclusive or exclusive? Marra lays the groundwork for what many of the authors of this volume will say: a joke does not get a pass for being a joke; if anything, given the role that jokes play in culture they deserve extra scrutiny. Shouta Brown calls this effort by joke tellers to avoid this scrutiny the "comic loophole." The comic loophole usually takes the form of the "I was just joking" or "it's just a joke" defense. An ethics of comedy treats comedy as an opportunity to invite people into a conversation that they would otherwise avoid. But where does the responsibility for ethical comedy lie: in the actual joke, the audience who does or does not laugh, or in the joke teller?

Robert R. Clewis responds by fleshing out what a Kantian approach to humor would look like, arguing that the ethics of humor is in the joke teller's intentions. Kant's relevance cannot be overstated: he is one of the first to articulate what comes to be known as "incongruity theory," the idea that what provokes laughter is the perception of a cognitive dissonance that provokes laughter. Clewis fills an important gap in Kant scholarship by asking "what would Kant laugh at?" The conclusion is not as straightforward as one would expect (or hope for) from the person who authored an ethic that finds moral rightness in consistency and the absence of exceptions. But this just shows that humor can be so slippery and complex that consistency of intent might be the most one can ask for. Liz Sills takes a different approach to sussing out rules that might apply to humor: if what frustrates the effort to establish an ethics of comedy is the different social positions separating joke teller and audience, is there a possibility for an ethics of comedy in a society where everyone is both equally positioned and shares the same worldview? This is not a mere thought experiment; Sills sees in the cartoons published in the Carville *Star*—the publication of the National Leprosarium of the United States in Carville, Louisiana—as an opportunity to think about the relationship between humor and justice in a community where all the members are similarly situated. This allows Sills to consider the relationship between humor and appropriateness in light of the theory of justice articulated by John Rawls. If Clewis locates the moral appropriateness of humor in the intent of the joke teller, Sills places more of an emphasis on how the joke teller's social situation encourages (or discourages) morally appropriate humor. It is more likely that in a just society humor will be just. If humor is not just, then there are mechanisms for redressing the problems that result from morally inappropriate or blameworthy humor.

As much as the essays in this volume explain the why and how of an ethics of comedy, it is possible to read against them for answers to the question "why not?" When Sills points to the absence of social stratification as the reason why just humor could exist in the Carville community, that is also an answer to the question of why an ethics of comedy is difficult outside such a unique social scenario. Steven A. Benko uses a Levinasian approach to ethics to explain the how and why of an ethics of comedy. Morally problematic humor can be avoided if the joke teller has the right intentions, but their intentions must be more than avoiding offense. From a Levinasian perspective, the intent must be to avoid violence against the other. Just comedy, then, recognizes in the laughter that comes from incongruity the possibility of opening up new ways of being. The social stratification that Sills sees as largely absent from the Carville community can be overcome through humor that extends community to the other, and that the other accepts the invitation by laughing too. Overall, these attempts at an ethics of comedy recognize how complex humor is. Humor comes from different places, in different forms, for different reasons, having different effects on the joke teller and the audience. These approaches to an ethics of comedy become an occasion to think more about humor without exhausting all the possibilities of what can be thought or said about the moral appropriateness or inappropriateness of humor.

Laughter, Gender and Race

The essays in the second section narrow the focus of the ethical investigation by addressing the role of gender and race in laughter. The essays that focus on gender show how far the study of humor has come from arguments about whether women can be funny. Instead, they address what happens when women are allowed to be funny and how social debates about gender and sexual behavior are played out in humor. More than just being fodder for jokes, the anger and tensions of the #MeToo movement animate humor and become occasions for asking who gets to tell jokes. These show how complicated humor can be when laughter intersects with controversial social topics or people. While there remains too much humor that rehashes tired tropes and stereotypes, these essays point to new directions for humor dealing with gender and race. At the same time, they show how complicated race and gender remain as topics of humor.

Rebecca Krefting wonders, given the uncomfortableness that comedy and laughter can produce, which rhetorical strategies comics employ in order to make the audience comfortable with offensive speech. When we wonder how offensive or racist comedy persists, the answer is in the deft and nuanced ways that comedians ingratiate themselves to their audience in order to soften the blows that their jokes will land. As Krefting points out, though, these rhetorical strategies work for comedians who want to punch up as much as they have worked for comedians who have punched down. Difficult truths land softer if they come from a positive place, so comedians who begin at the margins can use these strategies to move themselves, and perceptions of people who are similarly situated, closer to the center.

Steven A. Benko and Eleanor Jones begin with a similar assumption: comedy has the ability to make difficult ideas easier to accept and process if they come from a positive place. Taking this one step further, Benko and Jones consider how Aziz Ansari's feminism made it possible for him to change the affective dimensions surrounding that word. But just as Ansari was making it safe to tell progressive jokes about feminism, sexual assault allegations were levied against him. In the midst of the #MeToo movement, Benko and Jones consider the relationship between how the affective atmosphere around words and people can change (and be changed on them) and how comedians, specifically Ansari, negotiate both the logical dimension of the joke as well as its emotional dimensions.

Christophe D. Ringer's analysis of how the television show *The Boondocks* addressed the accusations of child abuse and sexual assault by R. Kelly explores the complicated relationship between race and comedy. Given the lack of minority representation on TV, *The Boondocks* was a (short lived) effort to give voice to the African American experience and perspective. Despite the radicalness of the comic strip upon which it was based, the TV show was less incisive in its critique of American culture and the African American community. Ringer uses the episode on R. Kelly to show how satire can fail if it is not attentive to the lived realities of the people it is trying to critique. The larger point, then, is that similar to the way that ethical analysis must take into account the characteristics of the individual or community being evaluated, so too satire, which is perhaps the most obviously ethical form of comedy, must always be mindful of who is being satirized.

To complete the section on laughter, gender, and race, Olivia Moorer delves even further into the #MeToo controversy by using the words and logic of Dave Chapelle to think about Louis CK and the women who reported on the ways that he sexually assaulted them. The essays by Benko, Jones, Ringer, and Moorer show the ways that comedy is not a safe space from the harsh realities of cultural and professional misogyny and racism but highlight the different ways that comedians have responded to the #MeToo movement and sexual assault controversies. Further, they suggest ways forward for thinking about gender politics and race.

Laughter and Late Night

No venue for viewing comedy has become more relevant in recent years than late night comedy. Humor has always had a home on late night television, but *The Daily Show with Jon Stewart* transformed late night humor from being politically relevant to being politically important. While a number of works review how Stewart, and then Stephen Colbert, transformed the late night comedy landscape, the essays in this section take a different approach to late night humor. Erica A. Holberg delves into the gender debate by exploring the relationship between Freud's theory of humor (humor and laughter as safety valve releases for built up tension) by showing how Samantha Bee uses humor to talk about topics—and talk about topics in ways—that would be impossible without the good feeling of laughter to soften the critical edge. In doing so, Holberg raises the question of whether women are the only ones who can raise these moral and political questions. At the same time, Holberg challenges us to think about another question that animates many of the essays in this volume: comedy and laughter feel good, but can they do good? It is clear from the essays in the first section that there are right ways and wrong ways to do comedy and get laughs, but then what? What has changed when the laughter stops? Is a changed perspective enough, or does there need to be meaningful political, social, or economic change? Holberg's conclusion is that uncomfortableness and anger are their own motivators toward more ethical behavior.

If satire can only be successful when it is aware of its object, what is one to make of the satirist? How much of the ethical critique of satire rests on the audience's perception of the satirist? This question makes it worthwhile to revisit the essays on Ansari and Louis CK, while Cindy Muenchrath Spady chronicles the evolution of David Letterman from a virtue ethics perspective. While many comedians eschew the connection between their political jokes and personal political perspective or leanings, Spady asks a different question about one of late night comedy's most enduring institutions: David Letterman. Letterman can be considered a walking, living, and breathing satire of who a late night talk show host is supposed to be. Spady is an avowed fan of Letterman and goes on a moral journey with him, cataloguing the comedian's growth through professional and personal failures and successes. Would a more skeptical attitude toward the subject yield different conclusions about the virtues of the satirist or the need for the satirist to embody the values and attitudes they are advocating for through satire? Or, to revisit the tension caused by the "if it feels good, is it also good" dynamic, do we transfer the positive feelings from the laughter to the person who made us laugh? Instead of looking at the jokes for moral guidance, Spady thinks through looking at the host as a moral guide. Different from Spady's enthusiasm for Letterman, Shelly A. Galliah is more circumspect toward late night host Jimmy Kimmel and his forays into public advocacy. Drawing from his personal experiences, the way Letterman does, Kimmel has used experts to advocate for vaccinations and to raise awareness about global climate change. Where Spady sees Letterman as sincere, Galliah is suspicious of Kimmel's intentions and the jokester-being-serious persona Kimmel deploys when he monologues about pressing social issues. Where Letterman may have been playing it straight by acting sideways, the opposite question applies to Kimmel (and by extension, all comedians who drop their comic persona in order to advocate for a social cause): are their moments of serious just another way that they are playing it sideways for the audience? Even if being serious is an act, if the act does some good, is it wrong for the comedian to play the serious or sad clown even if only for a few minutes?

Laughter and Ridicule

In the *Philebus*, Plato problematizes laughter because of the way that it encourages vice and bad behavior. Plato worries that laughter directed at others is a form of ridiculousness: we are laughing at the weaknesses of others, enjoying their suffering, or are blind to our own faults and shortcomings. On the other hand, Don Rickles said, "you hockey puck!" But Rickles, who built a career out of being an insult comic also knew the difference between a joke and an insult, defending his brand of humor by saying that if he "were to insult people and mean it, that wouldn't be funny" (Holmes 2017). While insults can be funny, they are not always appropriate. Bergson suggested that the point of comedy was to reintegrate someone back into the moral community because their sense of self or behavior had alienated them from others. Here, an insult serves a positive moral function by restoring the integrity of the community. But an insult can just as easily exclude and marginalize people from the community. An insult can dehumanize a person, making it easier to exploit their vulnerabilities, by denying them their rights and caring less about their interests and needs.

Ralph H. Didlake and Caroline E. Compretta consider the moral worth of insults in a medical context, where people are at their most vulnerable physically, emotionally, and institutionally. But does the moral valence of insults in a medical context change when it serves as a coping mechanism in a stressful environment? Or is there a way to think about the insult that it is not about the patient per se but about larger, systemic, social injustices that are the reason why a person needs medical care to begin with. Or, as Jonathan Peter Wright wonders, is it wrong to laugh at a self-inflicted pain that was brought on to generate laughter or profit? Fail videos are videos where a person attempts to do something but, in failing to accomplish that end, ends up causing themselves embarrassment or physical pain. If the vulnerable position that medical patients find themselves in makes jokes at their expense both a violation of professional codes of conduct and manners, as Didlake and Compretta conclude, does that make laughing at intentional self-harm morally neutral and socially acceptable? If there is harm, where? Is the harm to the laugher who is taking delight in the pain of others (*schadenfreude*)? Or is the harm to the dignity and humanity of the person in the video whose folly and pain are celebrated? One of the reasons that fail videos are funny is that they allow for two forms of moral distancing: first, it is likely that the butt of the joke has had some hand in publicizing their own failure and so moral blame can be placed on them or on the society that has monetized the self infliction of pain. Second, the subject of the fail video is not present when the video is being replayed. Other than the royalties that they receive from YouTube, they never know if and by whom they are being laughed at.

The anonymity that allows for moral distancing in the case of fail videos is not available when the butt of the joke is sitting across the table. Nicole Graham interrogates the moral rightness and wrongness of insults when the offended parties are gathered in one place playing *Cards Against Humanity*. Contra some of the other essays in this volume, Graham finds that the rules of the game and willing participation of the players changes the moral valence of intent, consequences, and social transgression. There is a narrow opening for insults and offense during this game to be morally acceptable and a reiteration of the social norms and courting of taboo built into the game's design and play. While *Cards Against Humanity* may be defended on the basis of all the participants agreeing to play fast and loose with social taboos, David K. McGraw considers taboo breaking not from the perspective of rules or outcomes, but from the good or harm they might do to relationships. Invoking Nel Noddings and an ethics of care, McGraw expands the question of the social dimension of laughter and humor to include more than inclusion and exclusion. Practical jokes, which are premised on the joker and butt of the joke being in a shared social relationship, can undermine that relationship by exploiting the power dynamics between the people involved. However, if the practical joke brings the people closer together, is that not a good thing? Even if the joke looks uncaring, if the end result is a closer more intimate relationship that will allow for more care in the future, then playing a practical joke on someone might be an act of caring. While it seems difficult to imagine frightening, shocking, upsetting, or offending someone as a practical act, McGraw's essay is yet another example of the way that humor and laughter turn ethics on its head, and how an ethical analysis of comedy can only speak to the complexity of humor but never fully resolve it.

Grant Moss brings all of these questions to the fore by relating Hannah Gadsby's forceful critique of jokes as stories in *Nanette* to the role of satirical late night shows like *The Daily Show*, *Last Week Tonight with John Oliver*, and *Full Frontal with Samantha Bee*. Gadsby's critique of jokes is that the effort to generate laughter requires skipping over the pain and trauma that animates the joke. Comedians who tell jokes from a marginalized social position about marginalized people (like Gadsby) are left to repeat their trauma as a way to entertain others. This marks a return to the question of whether laughter can change (if it does change) social attitudes or behaviors. Gadsby worries that no social good comes from these jokes, and she wonders whether she should leave comedy altogether. Moss applies this same critique to late night news shows which mine the horror show that is contemporary American politics and society for laughs. Moss cautions that while the goals of these comedians and satirical shows are ethically laudable—they speak truth to power on a nightly basis—they might also be the opiate that is dulling the masses from doing something meaningful about their pain. While it might feel good to make people laugh and that laughter might serve as an important (and maybe necessary) coping mechanism, what if making the audience not laugh is the right or better thing to do?

∼

The essays in this volume share a common belief about the importance of comedy in society but also a desire to see it mean more than "just joking." Comedy and ethics share the same perception of incongruity: the gap between what is and what could be. When ethics adds "ought" to comedy, the perception of incongruity goes from being cognitive dissonance to moral and ethical dissonance. It is fair to say that the authors of these essays share a common desire to see the good in comedy. That good can be in the person or persona of the comic. Or, it can be in the intentions of the comedian who is trying to do something in addition to making people laugh. Or, that good can be in the change in how the audience organizes their world so that there is more room for those who have been marginalized or excluded from the community. None of the authors of this volume think that it is ever just a joke because there is always the possibility that with more care, more thought, and more concern for the other that it could be a just joke.

Works Cited

Holmes, Dave. "Don Rickles and the Lost Art of the Insult." *Esquire*, 11 Oct. 2017, www.esquire.com/entertainment/a54363/don-rickles-lost-art-of-the-insult/.

Morreall, John. "Philosophy of Humor," *The Stanford Encyclopedia of Philosophy*. Winter 2016 Edition, Edited by Edward N. Zalta. https://plato.stanford.edu/archives/win2016/entries/humor/.

_____. *Taking Laughter Seriously*. State University of New York, 1983, pp. 60–61.

Provine, Robert R. *Laughter: A Scientific Investigation*. Penguin Books, 2001.

Roberts, Robert C. "Humour and the Virtues." *Inquiry: An Interdisciplinary Journal of Philosophy*, vol. 31, no. 2, 1988, pp. 127–149.

PART ONE

Laughter, Ethicists and Ethics

Toward an Objective
Ethic of Humor

Jennifer Marra

There are three positions one could take when asking moral questions about humor: a subjective position, an exemption position, or an objective position. A subjective position would argue that you simply can't determine whether a joke is right or wrong without taking the specific circumstances, persons, and/or reactions into account. An exemption position would be to say that humor is a special mode to which normal moral rules don't apply, and, therefore, there can be no such thing as a right or wrong joke. An objective position would be to say that moral standards can be universally applied to humor, and that those standards do not rely on detailed specific facts of the humorous event.

In this essay, I will argue that an objective approach is the only justifiable means of making moral claims about humor, and then I will introduce a way to begin the hard work of developing such an approach. My methodology is based upon my understanding of humor as a "symbolic form"; that is, a unique perspective through which we understand ourselves and our world (Marra, "Humor"). This perspective has a special purpose for human culture—it gives us the opportunity to question our default beliefs, reveals errors in our judgments, and helps us break out of absent-minded habits of the mind (Marra, "The Phenomenological"). In other words, I understand humor as something which interrupts "epistemic viciousness" such as laziness, closed-mindedness, and arrogance (Medina). Humor helps us struggle toward liberation by performing this special cultural function, and in this way is an important piece of the larger human story (Cassirer, *An Essay*). Embedded in this understanding are moral implications: first, for humor to perform its function, it must not encourage epistemic viciousness, and second, for humor to join other symbolic forms in the struggle for liberation, humor must not idealize an oppressive culture.

The Trouble with Subjective and Exemption Approaches to Humor

Scholars and comedians alike tend to favor subjective or exemption approaches to moral questions about humor. A subjective approach argues that humor is a matter of taste. My sense of humor, and, therefore, what I think is moral and immoral when it comes to jokes, is specific to me. I might find a joke funny that you find offensive—neither of us is right or wrong, per se; we just have different preferences when it comes to comedy. With this approach, it's not necessarily the *joke* that holds moral content, it's really more a matter of the person telling the joke, the person hearing the joke, the context in which the joke was told, or a combination of these factors. For example, say I tell the following joke:

I like my beer like I like my violence: domestic.

From a subjective perspective, to determine if this joke is ethical or not would require us to go beyond the joke itself. A subjectivist would consider the fact that I, the person telling the joke, am a woman. I surely wouldn't be making fun of violence against women or trying to demean myself, a woman, in the telling. They would also consider whether I have experienced domestic violence—if I or someone close to me has, it is likely that the subjectivist would determine that I would never seriously find such a thing funny, so I'm not doing anything morally wrong in telling this joke. But if a man told the joke, the subjectivist could question the moral intent simply because the males are typically (though certainly not always) the perpetrators, not the victims of, domestic violence. The subjectivist may also ask those who heard the joke to make the determination. If the joke was heard by women or victims of abuse, then the subjectivist would ask if the audience was upset by it. If they weren't, then the joke caused no harm and, therefore, was not unethical. If they were upset, then the joke did cause harm and from an ethical standpoint should not have been told.

It doesn't seem that a subjective approach can really help us determine whether or not the joke itself is moral—rather, the reception of the joke, or the identity of the person telling it, seems to be what retroactively determines its moral value. And if this is the case, then it may be impossible for comedians to write a joke that is immune to offense from someone somewhere, unless they somehow identify with every marginalized group at the same time or tell the joke only to audiences who have never been marginalized, violated, oppressed, or upset.

But there is a further problem from a subjectivist position. It is illogical to claim that the same joke can be moral in one case and immoral in another. How can one action—the telling of this joke—be moral when I say it to the right audience, but immoral if I tell it to the wrong audience? It's the same joke, after all, and I perform it the same way. If the act of telling the joke can be moral in one context and immoral in another, then the *joke* can't be what is determining the action's moral value. Rather, it is the *audience* that changes the moral value. And if the moral value of the joke is dependent upon the audience, then the *audience member* is the moral agent here. But if the audience member is the moral agent, then the audience member is responsible for the moral value of joke. And if that is the case, then we would never be justified in placing moral blame on the joke's teller—the blame can only be justly placed upon the audience member who, necessarily, must have *chosen* to perform the act of feeling offense at the joke. Of course, this conclusion is absurd. Calling someone a crude name is the action of the teller, regardless of whether the teller reports that he or she intended to cause offense. But for the subjectivist, the teller just has a different sense of humor than the audience, and both parties are entitled to their respective preferences. Because neither preference can hold any more moral value than would the preference of ice cream flavors, there would be no ethical reason for the teller to limit his jokes to any preference, and furthermore no moral responsibility to do so.

The problematics of subjective approaches push us to an exemption approach. If it's impossible to tell a joke that won't offend someone, and we couple offense with moral blame, then perhaps it's best to understand comedy as the sort of thing that should not be understood as having any moral value at all. This approach is very popular among comedians. For example, in a 2013 debate moderated by *Totally Biased* host W. Kamau Bell, comedians Jim Norton and Lindy West argued for and against the right of the comedian to tell jokes about any subject, and specifically rape, without fear of negative repercussions. Norton took the former position, articulating a common argument about the nature of humor and its role in human life. Norton claims that life is full of very serious and very tragic events and that human beings need relief from these pressures in order to maintain psychological well-being. Comedy must remain a socially acceptable way to get that relief, and censorship or condemnation of comedy will rob audiences and comedians alike from crucial and necessary psychological relief. We should grant comedians the moral leniency to joke about even the most serious subjects without fear of monetary or social condemnation in order to preserve the very important social function they provide, because there is no *real* harm that comes from jokes. In sum, this position states that comedians should be exempt from moral blame insofar as they are cultural contributors who perform the unique and important psychological service of providing relief from the overwhelming seriousness of life.

This approach also has flaws. Either (1) it provides a special moral exemption for one particular group of people, comedians, or (2) it provides an exemption for anyone insofar as they serve the practical function of providing comic relief. If it is the first, the argument itself is inconsistent, for it claims both that comedians have tangible effects on their audiences (they feel relief), and that comedians have no tangible effects on their audiences (nothing said causes any harm). But research has shown that it is the former that is correct: humor really *does* affect the way we think. Alice Isen's studies have repeatedly shown that humor primes the creation of in- and out-group affiliation: those being laughed at and those doing the laughing (Isen, "An Influence" and "Some"). Drucilla Cornell and Kenneth Panfilo explain, "languages actually create different worlds" (Cornell and Panfilo 27), and the language that we use in jokes to designate others creates concepts about those others that influence, if not determine, the way we think about them. Scholarship regarding the effects of cultural shifts in humor have been documented by historians, sociologists, and philosophers alike, including Mel Watkins' *On the Real Side: A History of African American Comedy from Slavery to Chris Rock* (1994/1999), Steve Lipman's *Laughter in Hell: The Use of Humor during the Holocaust* (1991), and, more recently, Johanna Gilbert's *Performing Marginality: Humor, Gender, and Cultural Critique* (2004) and Rebecca Krefting's *All Joking Aside: American Humor and its Discontents* (2014). Lindy West, respondent to Norton in the debate above, explains, "I'm sure sixty years ago there were some 'hilarious' jokes about black people, and comedy was way more overtly racist sixty years ago, and it's not a coincidence that life was more hostile and dangerous for black people." Just because the jokes are "hilarious," she argues, doesn't mean that they didn't have effects on the way that others thought about and treated the butts of those jokes. And, as Gilbert notes, comedy can be (and has been) weaponized for a particular end and can create or destroy feelings of connection with individuals or groups: "Whether performing in a comedy club or out stumping for votes, humorists engage in a power play with real or imagined targets, entertaining audiences as they promote agendas" (Gilbert 13). Intentional or not, the effects of the jokes we tell go beyond the laughter they may inspire. To pretend that they don't, as the exemption argument seems to want to do, is simply incorrect. West summarizes the inconsistency of the exemption argument beautifully: "You don't get to say that comedy is this sacred, powerful, vital thing that we need to protect because it speaks truth to power … and then also be like, 'well it's just a joke, language doesn't affect our lives at all'" ("Totally Biased").

If we don't want to fall into the inconsistency of the "comedians are morally exempt" claim, then we can go with the latter claim that anyone who provides comic relief is morally exempt. But this is counterintuitive. Granting someone a moral exemption so long as she can claim that she is "just joking" is tantamount to handing out a "get out of ethics jail free" card. Most, if not all, of us are guilty of back-peddling on an offensive comment by claiming that we were just joking. We try to erase the harm caused by the comment by saying that it was all in jest, and we feel upset when others retain their offense anyway. Most, if not all, of us have also been on the other side and refused to excuse the comments of another based on their claims that they were just joking. And it's not just that we don't believe that the comment was a joke, it's that we feel justifiably upset *even if it was*. The joke crossed the line, we would say, and therefore we hold the person morally responsible for telling it. So while the exemption argument may be popular, it doesn't correspond to our actual lived experiences. Either the position applies only to comedians, and the whole argument is a contradiction, or it applies to everyone, and the "just joking" tag doesn't affect the harm or offense caused.

That leaves us with only one remaining approach—the objective position. An objective position states that there are instances of humor which are morally wrong, regardless of the particular circumstances in which they occurred. We would be able to determine beforehand if a joke should be told, rather than wait to see the reaction of the audience, by which time it would be "too late." Furthermore, it is only through an objective approach that we would ever be morally justified in holding each other accountable. If comedy is merely subjective, then we have no just foundation, that is, no *good reason*, to punish the "insult comic" bully; her behavior falls perfectly in line with her particular comedic tastes, and those tastes happen to be different from those of her victim. Her victim has no legitimate cause for complaint—the bully's preference in comedy may be different, but we have no objective measure against which we could possibly determine whether that taste is morally blameworthy. In other words, without an objective method by which we can judge the morality of jokes, we have no legitimate justification to punish someone, or even be upset with them, for telling an offensive or harmful joke. But we ought to be able to place blame on the bully for picking on a classmate, even if the bully argues she was "just joking" and didn't mean any harm.

I will argue that both the *idealization* guiding the use of humor and the *function* of that humor can guide us toward an objective ethical approach. I suggest that we ask two questions: (1) what is idealized in the joke? and (2) what is the functional aim of the joke?

Theory: Symbolic Forms and Idealization

Ernst Cassirer summarizes his philosophy of symbolic forms in his 1944 book *An Essay on Man*. Here he explains that art, language, myth, and science, among others, are distinct perspectives through which we make sense of our world. Humanity expresses itself through these symbolic forms in unique ways, and this expression is what we call culture. As Cassirer puts it,

> Human culture taken as a whole may be described as the process of man's progressive self-liberation. Language, art, religion, science, are various phases in this process. In all of them man discovers and proves a new power—the power to build up a world of his own, an "ideal" world.... All these functions [of each symbolic form] complete and complement one another. Each one opens a new horizon and shows us a new aspect of humanity [Cassirer, *An Essay* 228].

While each form struggles toward this ideal in its own way, each means of expression is in harmony with the others. That is, each form has its own particular part to play in the human story, which ultimately aims toward an ideal of freedom, even as we find ourselves constantly failing to meet this end. Cassirer considers his philosophy of culture to be an ongoing project, and while he does not list humor among the forms himself, his work leaves plenty of room for forms that he could not investigate in depth himself. For this among other reasons, I argue that humor ought to be counted among these forms, and that humor has its own unique role to play in culture's ideal end.

Humor's principle function, that is, its unique role in the human struggle for liberation, is to reveal and disrupt epistemic vice. Epistemic vices, as explained by José Medina, are ways of thinking that prevent the possibility of learning; they include arrogance, laziness, and close-mindedness (Medina 23). Scholars like Lydia Amir go further than myself in arguing that humor can lead to the development of epistemic virtues, serving the moral function of *reversing* these vicious habits, specifically regarding development of self-acceptance and self-liberation, "gradually freeing oneself" from imprisoning attitudes of oneself and others (Amir, *Rethinking* 122). And while we know that freedom for humanity is an ideal goal, and one that may be impossible to attain, humor is one way we can struggle toward it.

The notion of operating on an ideal, even if we know it is unattainable, is not a new idea. In Kwame Anthony Appiah's *As If: Idealization and Ideals* he writes: "Once we come to see that *many* of our best theories are idealizations, we will also see why *our best chance of understanding the world must be to have a plurality of ways of thinking about it*" (Appiah x, my emphasis). That is, it makes sense that something as ordinary as humor can provide us with insight into the world, even if we don't tend to think about it as having serious impacts or implications. When it comes to understanding how ideals can help us in terms of morality, Appiah explains, "the idea that a thought might be useful for some purpose other than mirroring reality invites us to consider what that purpose is ... and whether it is good or evil" (4). He writes that we "will need to have many pictures in the long run.... And whenever someone proposes replacing one of our many pictures with a better picture, it will always be a good idea to ask Vaihinger's question: 'Better for what?'"

(111). And later, "we need to ask not just what false claims a theory treats as true, but also for what *purposes* this idealization occurs" (115, my emphasis). Even if an ideal is unattainable, I can still submit that I should behave *as if it were* "because the world will be better if all or most of us act as if it is so" (133). He says that we do, in fact, operate in this way, "because most of us do want to make the world better, even if we aren't always clear about how that is it be done" (135). And indeed, this impulse is, for Cassirer, the human story itself. We cannot but posit an ideal to which we struggle, and culture struggles toward freedom.

Idealizations are only useful, Appiah contends, insofar as they make a practical difference in action (135). Morally speaking, this means that what we present as our ideal world is ultimately inconsequential if it does not have some sort of effect, on a large or small scale, upon the actions of those around us. For example, when I teach my children to say "please" and "thank you," I am idealizing a world in which they are always polite, grateful, and kind. That is the reason I teach those words to them. This idealized world, while impossible to actualize (no one is ever *always* polite, grateful, and kind), is morally valuable when I act upon it and it is acted upon by others. It becomes a morally *praiseworthy* idealization when the children behave in alignment with this ideal. But the same cannot be said for an ideal which guides my teaching of children that they should slap those who mock them. The ideal that I am projecting here is one in which justice is violent and instantaneous. When I teach my children to hit others, I teach them that, in an ideal world, violence is the only way to stop people from behaving in ways that they don't like, and that they are justified in deciding whose actions deserve their punishment. This would be an ideal that is morally *blameworthy* when my children act on it.

These two points, that humor functions to reveal epistemic viciousness and that idealizations have moral value when they are acted upon, ground the questions that I suggest can serve as the starting point for an objective ethic of humor. While Appiah works from idealizations to actions, I want to take the "As if" understanding to work from the action, a joke in this case, to an understanding of the posited ideal. I wish to ask the "to what end?" question of humor. This question has two parts: (1) is the joke idealizing a liberated world (the aim of culture) (2) with curious (epistemically virtuous) people? The question considers whether the telling of the joke encourages the ideal to which it aims, specifically in regard to whether it fulfills the function of humor by making us pay attention to things we ordinarily ignore. This approach is objective because it doesn't require us to have any information about the person telling the joke or to consider the reaction of the audience to the joke. This avoids the problems of the subjective and exemption approaches we explored earlier.

Application: The Domestic Violence Joke

Let's test out the theory with the joke from above:
I like my beer like I like my violence: domestic.

To determine if this joke is ethical, we should ask, (1) is the joke idealizing a liberated world (the aim of culture) (2) with curious (epistemically virtuous) people?

First things first. The joke presents a world where domestic violence is preferred over other types of violence. Clearly, this is a picture of an ideal world that is oppressive—it dignifies domestic violence *as if* domestic violence were desirable, or at least as morally neutral as one's taste in beer. Domestic violence is treated in this joke as an inevitable part of life at best, or an enjoyable activity at worst. Based purely on content, we must answer the first part of the question—is the joke idealizing a liberated world?—with a resounding "no."

The second part of my question regards the function of humor, asking whether the world idealized is inhabited by "curious (epistemically virtuous) people." Were any curious person to think more critically about the content, they would find a host of problematic and harmful implications. The joke minimizes physical harm against others, or as John Morreall puts it, the joke would be "promoting a lack of concern for something about which people should be concerned" (Morreall 110). Because the joke encourages lazy thinking, it is promoting epistemic viciousness and is therefore acting *against* humor's cultural function. Given that we answered with a resounding "no" to both parts of my question by looking purely at the content of the joke, and not at the opinions or perspectives of the teller or audience, we can conclude objectively that the joke is ethically problematic.

This is not to say, however, that no joke with content about domestic violence, or any type of violence, will ever pass the objectivity test I present here. For example, take this joke from comedian Norm MacDonald regarding rape allegations against Bill Cosby, a comedian who not only was known for his wholesome, family friendly act, but who would also take pains to criticize comedians like Chris Rock and Eddie Murphy for using "bad words" in their sets. Here is a portion of MacDonald's bit:

My buddy said, "The worst part about Cosby was that he was a hypocrite." I said, "I don't think that was the worst part. To me the worst part was the raping. Way up high. Then the second would be the drugging. Then the third would be the scheming. But anyways hypocrisy would be way down the line, like on the fourth page.... Like I'm no expert but I think probably most rapists are hypocrites. You don't meet a lot of guys who go 'I like to rape, I don't give a fuck. I know it's not a politically correct thing to say, but I like raping.'" And you go, "goddamn, at least he's not a hypocrite." If that's the worst part of it [MacDonald].

This joke is about sexual violence against women. But, I contend, it is not a morally problematic joke.

The joke idealizes a world where harm is understood as worse than hypocrisy. It idealizes a world where everyone understands that the actions are unacceptable whether or not the actor would outwardly endorse them, and undermines the idea that hypocrisy is somehow worse than committing sexual violence. The "buddy" in the joke is intentionally taken down by Mac-Donald for holding a position which is oppressive, that is, a position which implies that rape is fine if the rapist acknowledges their actions. In the world idealized in the joke, this position is obviously false—taking ownership of the harm you do does not lessen that harm. In the world idealized by this joke, everyone understands clearly that you do not drug and sexually assault people. It is a joke that takes the harm caused by Cosby, or anyone else who perpetrates sexual violence, seriously. So we can certainly answer the first part of the question, "is the joke idealizing a liberated world?" with a "yes." This world is one where violence is wrong. Furthermore, it challenges the lazy thinking of MacDonald's friend. To think that hypocrisy is the problem with Cosby, or any rapist, is a clear indication of someone who has not thought very long or hard about the topic. It demolishes the arrogance behind the view by pointing out its absurdity and reveals a deeply problematic understanding of the situation. In this way we can answer the second half of the question regarding humor's function with another "yes." Humor is *supposed* to reveal precisely these epistemic vices. This joke, then, is morally praiseworthy on both counts.

Conclusion

Subjective and exemption approaches to ethics in humor are flawed at best and empty at worst. I argued that only an objective approach to humor would give us the tools necessary to hold comedians (or jokesters of a non-professional nature) accountable for the content they chose to perform. Without an objective measure through which to determine whether a joke is truly morally blameworthy, we're left with no choice than to write off an insulting or harmful joke as a simple difference of taste between the teller and the offended. This is particularly dissatisfying when we think of those circumstances where joking becomes a free pass to behave viciously toward others. Words do matter, and humor impacts culture. Comedians should be held to the same standards as any other cultural contributor.

An objective approach, on the other hand, gives us a universal standard against which we can measure the content of a joke. Instead of blaming the audience for getting upset over something that "isn't meant to be taken seriously," an objectivist will claim that insofar as the comedian is free to tell the jokes she pleases, the moral responsibility lies with her. I suggested that one way we can begin to develop a robust objective approach to ethics in humor is to consider the role of humor in the larger cultural picture—by understanding humor as one of many important and necessary means through which humanity expresses and understands itself. Understanding humor as a symbolic form grants us the tools to place humor alongside other forms of expression, all of which work in harmony to reach toward an ideal of a liberated humanity. Humor's special role in this journey is to reveal epistemic viciousness which prevents learning, hindering our ability to think outside of the box and beyond the status quo. When humor encourages closed-minded thought, encourages us to be lazy in our thinking, or reinforces arrogance of thought, it operates against the very function it ought to serve. When it idealizes an oppressive or otherwise imprisoned end, it works against the goal of culture itself. With these as starting points, we can begin the hard work of developing a more complete objective method of making moral judgments in humor.

Works Cited

Amir, Lydia. *Humor and the Good Life in Modern Philosophy: Shaftesbury, Hamann, Kierkegaard*. SUNY Press, 2014.
_____. *Rethinking Philosophers' Responsibility*. Cambridge Scholars Publishing, 2017.
Cassirer, Ernest. *An Essay on Man*. Yale University Press, 1944.
_____. *Language and Myth*. Translated by S. Langer, Dover Publications Inc., 1946.
_____. *The Logic of the Cultural Sciences*. Translated by Stephen Lofts, Yale University Press, 2000.
_____. *The Philosophy of Symbolic Forms 1: Language*. Translated by Ralph Manheim, vol. 1, Yale University Press, 1955. 4 vols.
_____. *The Philosophy of Symbolic Forms 2: Mythical Thought*. Translated by Ralph Manheim, vol. 2, Yale University Press, 1955. 4 vols.
_____. *The Philosophy of Symbolic Forms 3: The Phenomenology of Knowledge*. Translated by Ralph Manheim, vol. 3, Yale University Press, 1957. 4 vols.
_____. *The Philosophy of Symbolic Forms 4: The Metaphysics of Symbolic Forms*. Translated by John Michael Krois, vol. 4, Yale University Press, 1996. 4 vols.
_____. "The Platonic Renaissance in England." Translated by James P. Pettegrove, Thomas Nelson and Sons Ltd., 1953.
Gilbert, Joanne R. *Performing Marginality: Humor, Gender, and Cultural Critique*. Wayne State University Press, 2004.
Gimbel, Steven. *Isn't That Clever: A Philosophical Account of Humor and Comedy*. Routledge, 2018.
Hurley, M.W., Dennett, D.C., & Adams, R.B., Jr. *Inside Jokes: Using Humor to Reverse-Engineer the Mind*. MIT Press, 2011.
Isen, Alice M. "An Influence of Positive Affect on Decision Making in Complex Situations: Theoretical Issues with Practical Implications." *Journal of Consumer Psychology*, vol. 11, no. 2, 2001, pp. 75–85.
_____. "Some Perspectives on Positive Affect and Self-Regulation." *Psychological Inquiry*, vol. 11, no. 3, 2000, pp. 184–187.
Kramer, Chris A. "As If: Connecting Phenomenology, Mirror Neurons, Empathy, and Laughter." *PhaenEx*, vol. 7, no. 1, 2012, pp. 275–308.

_____. "Subversive Humor." Dissertation, Marquette University, 2015. http://epublications. marquette.edu/dissertations_mu/424.

Krefting, Rebecca. *All Joking Aside: American Humor and Its Discontents*. Johns Hopkins University, 2014.

Lipman, Steve. *Laughter In Hell: The Use of Humor during the Holocaust*. Jason Aronson Inc., 1991.

Lofts, Stephen. *Ernst Cassirer: A "Repetition" of Modernity*. SUNY Press, 2000.

Luft, Sebastian. "Cassirer's Philosophy of Symbolic Forms: Between Reason and Relativism; A Critical Appraisal." *Idealistic Studies,* vol. 34, no. 1, 2004, pp. 25–47.

_____. *The Space of Culture*. Oxford University Press, 2015.

MacDonald, Norm. "Norm Macdonald on Gotham Comedy Live (05/12/2016)—YouTube." https://www.youtube.com/watch?v=a3PpS8ZZouM. Accessed 13 July 2018.

Marra, Jennifer. "How to Create Dialogue Between Theory and Practice: Stand-Up Comedy's Demand for Interdisciplinary Engagement." *American Society for Aesthetics Graduate E-Journal,* vol. 9, no. 2, 2017, pp. 1–4.

_____. "Humor as a Symbolic Form: Cassirer and the Culture of Comedy." *The Philosophy of Ernst Cassirer: A Novel Assessment,* Edited by Sebastian Luft and J. Tyler Friedman, New Studies in the History and Historiography of Philosophy Series, De Gruyter Press, 2015, pp. 419–34.

_____. "Make Comedy Matter: Ernst Cassirer on the Politics and Morality of Humour." *European Journal of Humour Studies,* vol. 6, no. 1, 2018, pp. 162–71.

_____. "The Phenomenological Function of Humor." *Idealistic Studies,* vol. 46, no. 2, 2016, pp. 135–161.

McGraw, P., Warren, C., Williams, L.E., & Leonard, B. "Too Close for Comfort, or Too Far to Care? Finding Humor in Distant Tragedies and Close Mishaps." *Psychological Science,* vol. 20, no. 10, 2012, pp. 1–9.

Medina, José. *The Epistemology of Resistance: Gender and Racial Oppression, Epistemic Injustice, and Resistant Imaginations*. Oxford University Press, 2013.

Morreall, John. *Comic Relief: A Comprehensive Philosophy of Humor*. Wiley-Blackwell, 2009.

_____. *The Philosophy of Laughter and Humor*. SUNY Press, 1987.

Smuts, Aaron. "The Ethics of Humor: Can Your Sense of Humor Be Wrong?" *Ethical Theory and Moral Practice,* vol. 13, no. 3, 2010, pp. 333–347.

"Totally Biased: Extended Talk with Jim Norton and Lindy West—Video Dailymotion." Dailymotion, 2013. https://www.dailymotion.com/video/x2nuz3m. Accessed 13 July 2018.

Watkins, Mel. *On the Real Side: A History of African American Comedy from Slavery to Chris Rock*. Lawrence Hill Books, 1999.

Closing the Comic Loophole

Reframing the Aesthetics
and Ethics of Comedy

Shouta Brown

Thinking ethically about comedy can be tricky. For some, the idea of "comedy ethics" may seem like an oxymoron because it amounts to being serious about one of the most non-serious forms of entertainment. The point of comedy, they might say, is to briefly set aside the seriousness of the world for the sake of enjoyment and amusement to cultivate lightheartedness in spite of the weightiness of our regular life. If this is true, ethics—with all of its seriousness—would have no place in or anywhere near comedy.

Whenever we develop an ethical theory, we generally want the theory to include criteria for evaluating the moral rightness or wrongness of an action. Having clear guidelines for understanding what we ought to do and what we ought not to do is fundamental for many, if not all, ethical theories. Another perhaps equally important feature of an ethical theory is the identification of what compels people to behave, decide, and act in certain ways. Particularly of interest is how the ethical theory can oblige or urge people to do the right thing and hold them accountable for doing something wrong.

However, in the context of comedy, both the criteria for moral evaluation and the obligatory force that determines a person's accountability are challenged. This friction between comedy and ethics is largely due to a particular understanding of what comedy is and is not. As mentioned above, a prevailing attitude about comedy is that it is—as an activity as well as a genre of entertainment—entirely removed from seriousness. Such an attitude is revealed most frequently during those moments when a demand for accountability rubs up against a comedic product whether that product is a particular joke, a stand-up routine, or a comedy film. Someone might, for instance, criticize a comedian's joke for being a racist remark and (assuming that racist speech is immoral) insist that the comedian stop telling the joke and any similar jokes. The comedian's defense, we can imagine, can range from statements such as "it's just a joke," "you need to get a sense of humor," and "lighten up, it's all in good fun." The comedian's *just joking defense* reminds the critic what kind of thing comedy is and reverses the blame. For the comedian on the defensive, the critic is the one to blame for being offended as a result of their ignorance about how comedy should be perceived: not seriously.

The *just joking defense* challenges the fundamental features of ethical theories as it distorts moral evaluation and the determination of accountability. Typically, speech that is racist or sexist is considered morally reprehensible, and there is consensus that those who make racist and sexist remarks should be held accountable for their speech. However, racist and sexist jokes—while they have similar content to racist and sexist speech—are not always treated in the same way as other forms of racist and sexist speech. Their status as a joke grants both the joke and the joke-teller immunity from moral evaluation and accountability. In short, those who use the *just joking defense* get a pass for actions that would be considered objectionable in a plethora of contexts outside of the comedic one. I call this ethical evasion through the comedic context the *comic loophole*.

In this essay I focus primarily on the *comic loophole*, its presuppositions, and its problems. In particular, I want to show that the loophole is an extension of a particular intellectual tradition of aesthetics: an aesthetics of disinterest made famous by philosopher Immanuel Kant. Kant's aesthetics of disinterest drives a wedge between aesthetic judgments and ethical judgments paving the way for the comic loophole which requires and preserves their separation. I hope to make clear, however, that this distinction cannot be maintained as clearly as contemporary comedians and jokesters would like and that developing an ethics for comedy would require a thorough reconsideration of the aesthetic assumptions we have about comedy which—if not treated carefully—can shield comedy and comedians from moral evaluation altogether.

I want to provide a brief caveat for readers here. The following essay will include jokes or stories told by comedians that involve topics such as sexual violence (particularly rape), racism, and ethnic slurs. Understandably, these remarks may cause some offense or discomfort. Yet discussing them in this context is crucial for demonstrating the kinds of remarks that can be made with immunity due to the *comic loophole*. I hope that this illustrates why an ethics of comedy must seek to close the *comic loophole*.

Comedians and Humor Formalism

In his 1990 comedy special *Doin' It Again*, George Carlin offers his take on offensive language and how jokes relate to it. Frustrated by criticisms that comedians get for making rape jokes, Carlin defends rape jokes as he states:

> I believe you can joke about anything. It all depends on how you construct the joke, what the exaggeration is. Because every joke needs one exaggeration. Every joke needs one thing to be way out of proportion. I'll give you an example. You ever see a news story like this in the paper? Every now and then you run into a story that says some guy broke into a house, stole a lot of things, and while he was in there he raped an eighty-one year old woman. And I'm thinking to myself "Why!? What the fuck kind of social life does this guy have?" I wanna say "Why did you do that?" "Well, she was coming on to me."

Carlin's claim is that constructing a joke with an exaggeration gives the speaker the license to tell the joke. As long as the joke is constructed with an exaggeration, it is fair game. In his example, the elderly woman's age is supposedly the exaggeration that makes the rape joke acceptable. The implication of Carlin's view is that jokes about objectionable or controversial topics are not acceptable if they are not constructed properly. If the woman in the example had been a young woman, then presumably the exaggeration in the joke would disappear and no longer make it an acceptable joke, or it may cease to be a joke altogether (however, we can question Carlin's assumption that old age is an exaggeration when it comes to the issue of rape).

On the Opie and Anthony radio show 23 years later, comedian Ricky Gervais echoes Carlin's position on jokes in his response to the controversy over Daniel Tosh's rape joke targeted at a woman in the audience. "It depends on what the joke is" claimed Gervais, who later in the interview emphasized the importance of the elements of jokes such as "syntax, semantics, and rhyming." Gervais adds that "stupid people treat jokes about bad things with the same fear and loathing as intelligent people treat the actual bad thing. And they're not related. That's what humor's for: to get us over bad things."

The irony of Gervais' remarks is that they do not adequately address Tosh's rape joke that initiated the discussion. During a stand-up comedy show, a woman in the audience told Tosh that rape jokes were never funny, and he responded "Wouldn't it be funny if that girl got raped by like, 5 guys right now? Like right now? What if a bunch of guys just raped her?" (Jardin). Tosh's impromptu response to the woman in the audience hardly represents the craftsmanship to which Gervais refers when he responds to this controversial rape joke (if it can be called a joke at all). If a rape joke can be told only when it has the proper "syntax, semantics, and rhyming," as Gervais argues, then Tosh's rape joke would most likely fail to meet this standard. Gervais' claim about the non-relation between the bad thing and a joke about the bad thing appears also to be troubled by Tosh's joke. By trivializing rape, Tosh invites his audience to be amused about sexual violence as a topic rather than being amused at the cleverness of his joke construction. In no way does Tosh's joke function to help his audience "get us over bad things" through humor. Instead he encourages the "bad thing" by claiming that it would be amusing.

By shifting the acceptability of joking about a certain topic or issue to the structure of the joke itself, comedians like Carlin and Gervais prevent the identities and experiences of their audience as well as the impact of making controversial jokes from entering into the evaluation. In other words, whether or not a joke ought to be made is up to the design of the joke itself, and by extension, the designer of the joke, i.e., the comedian. Carlin and Gervais illustrate the prevalent attitude about the serious evaluation of controversial jokes: as long as it has the aesthetic form of a joke, then it's just a joke, and we shouldn't consider its content seriously. The aesthetics of comedy overrides any ethical objections against jokes because, as Gervais might say, "they're not related."

The view put forward by Carlin and Gervais could be called *humor formalism*. To reiterate, *humor formalism* is the view that the form or design of a joke determines whether the content of the joke can or cannot be communicated in an acceptable and non-serious manner. What might count as the formal features of jokes include but are not limited to exaggeration, syntax, semantics, rhyming, timing, gestures, delivery, framing, and releasing tension. Due to the ambiguity of what formal features make the controversial content of a joke acceptable, *humor formalism* can be and often is easily abused. As long as we can appeal to the way a joke is made, we can always blame the audience or listener for lacking the sense for picking up on the formal subtleties that made the statement "just a joke."

Essentially, what I am identifying as *humor formalism* is a particular aesthetic view of jokes which separates our evaluation of the content of jokes from their formal features. By distinguishing the content of jokes from their form, *humor formalism* also separates seriousness from triviality. If someone takes a racist joke seriously in criticizing it, the humor formalist can remind them that the critic does not see the whole picture. Sure, the content is definitely serious because racism is a serious issue. However, a racist joke is primarily a joke. It has the form of a joke, which is a non-serious mode of language and communication. According to the humor formalist, the critic mistakenly evaluates the content seriously without paying attention to the non-serious way that the content is packaged. The humor formalist would claim that the meaning of the content depends entirely on how it is shaped and presented. In this way, *humor formalism* subordinates content and seriousness to form and its non-seriousness, making it close to impossible to evaluate jokes morally. *Humor formalism* is, then, the aesthetic position on comedy that creates the comic loophole.

Kant's Aesthetics of Disinterest

The *humor formalism* position may have a long intellectual ancestry— one rooted in a philosophical tradition concerning aesthetics in general. In his *Critique of Judgment*, philosopher Immanuel Kant developed an extensive theory on aesthetic judgment which isolates our evaluation of beauty from that of goodness or satisfaction. Kant sought to demonstrate that when we judge that something is beautiful, we are not making a judgment based solely on preference. For Kant, beauty is not in the eye of the beholder, nor is it a quality of an object. Aesthetic judgments of beauty turn out to be based on our subjective feeling of pleasure, but a feeling that *everyone* ought to experience if they oriented themselves to the object in the right way. This means that when we make a proper aesthetic judgment, we can demand that everyone else accepts it too. To put this concisely, aesthetic judgments are based on subjective feelings that are objectively necessary for everyone.

Kant clarifies this view on aesthetic judgments when he discusses the quality of the pleasure that is involved in them. The pleasure—or "liking" as he calls it—involved in aesthetic judgments are "devoid of all interest" (45). Kant defines interest as "the liking we connect with the presentation of an object's existence" by which he means the kind of pleasure that depends on the materiality, as opposed to the formal features, of the object perceived (45). In other words, whenever we have an interest in something, we care that it exists. If the pleasure in aesthetic judgments is devoid of all interest, then in our aesthetic engagement with something we do not take into account its reality. We need only perceive how it is presented or arranged, i.e., its design or formal features.

For this reason, Kant adds that in our aesthetic judgments we focus on the inward concern of "what I do with this presentation within myself" rather than the outward concern of what I would do with the object as it exists in front of me (46). Since the liking is based merely on how I perceive the object rather than what its actual existence means for me, I am "in the least biased in favor of the thing's existence but must be wholly indifferent about it" (Kant 46). This indifferent liking, which focuses solely on the formal presentation of the object, is what Kant calls "pure disinterested liking."

To put this into perspective, let's talk about beautiful cakes. You're watching your favorite cake themed television show (assuming you do that kind of thing) and a particular cake catches your eye. It looks perfect. You're not thinking, "Oh, I really wish I had that cake so I could taste it" or "That would be the best cake for the big event I'm planning because it would really fit the decorative theme." Instead you think, "Wow. The latticework piping on that cake is flawless, and the use of icing to create that abstract design is incredible!" You have no interest in having the cake for yourself, and you appreciate it simply for its design. The pleasure you get from looking at the cake is purely disinterested because you feel it based only on its formal qualities, which have nothing to do with how it tastes or what kind of occasion it would be good for. It does not have to exist in front of you for you to take pleasure in it because the arrangement of the cake is something you can hold entirely in your mind.

However, your friend who watches the show with you might not be as keen as you are when judging the cakes. In response to your insightful evaluation of the most aesthetically pleasing cakes, your friend frequently adds comments like "Yeah, and I bet it tastes really good. I could really go for some cake. Gotta be honest, I'm a little sad I don't have a cake like that right now." Sometimes they agree with you on the pleasing appearance of the cake, yet they inevitably add something to the effect of "Wouldn't it be cool if you had a cake like that for your birthday party? Everyone would be so impressed." According to Kant, your friend would not be making pure aesthetic judgments; instead the judgments would be interested, making them different forms of judgments.

Kant's pure disinterested liking is opposed to two forms of interested liking: liking for what is agreeable or satisfying and liking for what is good. He defines the agreeable as "what the senses like in sensation" which amounts to gratification (47). The agreeable, he argues, involves an interest because it is a form of liking that depends on the presence of the material qualities of the object (48). Imagine that a few days after your friend lamented about not having a cake, she bought one, revealed it to you, and immediately took a bite out of it. She found the cake to be very pleasing. Your friend's pleasure in the cake would be an interested liking for what is agreeable, because her pleasure would be the direct result of tasting the sweetness of the actually existing cake. If the cake had turned out to be a fake that looked just as incredible but had been rock solid and inedible, your friend would have found it quite displeasing. This reveals that your friend had an interested liking only for the cake's existing agreeable qualities.

The second form of liking involving an interest is the liking for the good. According to Kant, the good is what "we like through its mere concept" as opposed to what we like merely through the senses, i.e., the agreeable (48). The concept that is necessarily involved in the good is a purpose which establishes what an object or action ought to be and provides a measure for whether or not it fulfills that purpose (49). Let's return one last time to the example about your friend. After seeing your shock as they hastily ate the well-designed cake that probably took much time and patience for the baker to make, your friend decided to do something nice for you to make up for her blunder. Being such a great friend, she bought you a cake more magnificent than the one before for your birthday party. The cake was delivered on time to the party and everyone was impressed with the cake, pleasing your friend. The pleasure felt by your friend in this scenario is an interested liking for the good that the cake served in the situation. The purpose of the cake was to impress the people at the party and to fulfill a crucial element of birthday parties, i.e., eating cake. If the cake had not existed at the party because the order was unexpectedly delayed, then your friend would not have been pleased revealing that her liking was dependent on the purpose of the cake being fulfilled.

With respect to the interested liking for the good, Kant is thinking primarily of moral goods (and not cakes). We can like an action that is morally good but only in an interested manner. If a person saves a child from drowning, we may find the rescue pleasing. However, if we saw a person fail in their attempt to save a drowning child due to their initial hesitation, we would most likely be displeased. This is because the purpose of the action was not fulfilled and we are interested in the existence of its fulfillment.

To summarize, Kant's aesthetic theory separates the pure disinterested pleasure involved in aesthetic judgments from other forms of judgment that involve pleasure based on the interest in an object's existence. A proper aesthetic judgment focuses only on the design or formal features of an object, rather than its material features. Whenever we judge something to be beautiful, we have to omit any consideration of the object's ability to gratify us through sensations or to fulfill purposes we attribute to the object. In other words, evaluations of the object's goodness or satisfactory quality are out of the picture when we make aesthetic judgments. Lastly, whenever we make proper aesthetic judgments, everyone else must accept them because they are not based on individual preference or material qualities. Everyone should experience pleasure merely from an object's formal features as long as they are oriented to them in the proper way.

So what does any of this have to do with *humor formalism*? Recall that the humor formalists claim that the form or design of a joke determines the acceptability of making a statement with controversial content. Whenever a joke is criticized for its controversial content, the humor formalists would offer the reminder that a joke is just a joke, and that it's not meant to be serious. The form of the statement reveals that it is meant to be received as a joke the purpose of which is to produce light-hearted pleasure detached from the controversial issue that it references.

This view of jokes has several parallels to Kant's aesthetic theory. First, just as the humor formalists argue that we must evaluate jokes without consideration of their content, Kant argues that we must judge objects aesthetically through the disinterested kind of pleasure they give gives us. Both views argue that in our evaluations we must remain detached from concerns about whether the object is good (or satisfying) to us. Second, both Kant and humor formalists want to focus on the formal features of the object that we are judging and disregard any other features the object has. Just as Kant separates judgments involving interest in the good from judgments lacking interest, humor formalists want to separate discussions of the ethics of making statements from a detached appreciation of the statement as a joke.

If we substitute the terms interest and disinterest with seriousness and non-seriousness, we can see the relationship between Kant's aesthetics and *humor formalism* a little more clearly. Having an interest in what the object is good for is a serious way of orienting yourself to an object, while lacking any interest in the object is a non-serious way of relating to an object. As long as you judge something with indifference or disinterest, you do not have any concern about the existence of the object and what kinds of effects it can have. Part of the strength of such a view is to isolate what is unique to aesthetic experience without corrupting our judgments about an object with our other interests in it. Imagine if someone said "I think *The Lego Movie* is a great movie. I like its political message." Such a claim may be confusing for a number of reasons. The reason that interests us, however, is the fact that the claim misses so much about what makes films great: its narrative structure, innovative or impressive effects that enhance the visual experience, the quality of the acting, and so forth. The political message seems beside the point of evaluating a film, or at least it does not seem like the central aspect of a film. If one were to judge a film aesthetically, we might hope that they would leave out their idiosyncratic opinions. Similarly, Kant and the humor formalists want to isolate what makes our aesthetic experience of something different from our other more serious concerns.

Reframing the Aesthetics of Comedy

Holding an aesthetic position involving disinterest can be quite important. So many stories in a variety of entertainment media feature terrible, immoral acts as a part of them. Violence of varying degrees motivates the stories we often enjoy. Superheroes, for instance, would be unnecessary and boring if nothing bad ever happened. If we could not distance ourselves from the violence and misfortune in these stories, then it would be near impossible to enjoy any form of entertainment.

But what happens in those instances when the terrible act represented in our entertainment crosses a line? Those who defend an aesthetics of disinterest, including the humor formalists, will likely remind you of how you should relate to the act. They will reassure you that you are just watching a movie or that the statement was meant just as a joke. You are meant to disengage from the content just enough so you can continue to enjoy the work. They take for granted that a disinterested perspective is possible.

The humor formalists in particular presuppose the possibility of a disinterested and unbiased stance toward jokes. As Gervais claimed, a joke about a bad thing is unrelated from the actual bad thing and you would be ignorant for confusing the two. This follows the idea that a joke is "just" a joke and nothing else. A racist joke, for example, is not an actual racist comment meant to communicate a racist belief or attitude. If jokes are completely separate from what they are about, then Carlin is right to say that you can make a joke about anything as long as you make it clear that it is a joke. However, this cannot be the case.

While they may not want to admit it, there is always a limit to what can be done in the name of comedy regardless of the manner in which it is delivered. Everyone has some sort of strong investment, whether it's in a set of beliefs, people, or themselves—investments that each of us prefer not have trivialized. It would be in poor taste if, for example, if we made jokes about a comedian's dying daughter. No matter how much this hypothetical comedian would defend *humor formalism*, it would be difficult to believe that they would welcome jokes about such a misfortune that is taking place in their lives. Making light of serious matters always has the possibility of crossing the line.

Whenever comedians defend their freedom to make jokes about serious issues such as rape, they reveal that they do not have the level of investment in the issue that would outweigh their desire to tell jokes about the issue. In a telling reversal, the disinterest that allows them to defend rape jokes illustrates the level of interest or investment that they have in being able to make them. Many comedians rush to defend the controversial jokes of their peers because they have a strong interest in those jokes and preserving the reputation of fellow comedians. To put it in Kantian terms, controversial jokes would not fall under judgments involving disinterest for comedians. In fact, they would fall under judgments involving interest in some good whether the purpose of the joke is to maintain the comedian's freedom to joke about whatever they want, or to cultivate a style of comedy that would bring a larger crowd into their shows for the sake of popularity, relevance, and reputation. Humor formalists have a serious interest in preserving the non-serious quality of jokes in order to ward off criticism. In other words, they are very invested in maintaining the *comic loophole* that allows them to circumvent any moral accountability for the statements they make as jokes regardless of their content.

Nevertheless, comedy does not necessarily suffer if we abandon the idea that jokes are just jokes. The alternative to comedy involving controversial jokes does not have to be a stand-up routine packed with innocent puns or dad jokes. It can be as shocking and edgy as the controversial forms of comedy while still addressing the seriousness of the issues that it takes as its topic. In his comedy special *Homecoming King*, Hasan Minhaj demonstrates a form of comedy that mixes the serious and the non-serious. Throughout the auto-biographical show, Minhaj presents a bittersweet reflection on his life as a second generation Muslim Indian-American. Highlighting the various inter-generational and intercultural gaps he experienced, Minhaj carefully builds his humorous stories around cultural conflict, immigrant hardships, and experiences with racism. His anecdotes move seamlessly among background information, jokes, and social critique. Take, for example, this story about his adolescent post 9–11 experience:

> So when 9–11 happened I was in high school. My dad sits everybody down. He's like, "Hasan, whatever you do, do not tell people you're Muslim or talk about politics." "All right, Dad, I'll just hide it. This just rubs off." We're sitting there. Phone rings. I run, but my dad beats me to the phone. "Hello?" I grab the second phone. I hear a voice. "Hey, you sand n-slur, where's Osama?" He looks at me. "You can hear me, right? You fucking dune coon. Where's Osama?" "Hey, 2631 Regatta Lane, that's where you live, right? I'm going to fucking kill you." Click. (…) We sit down. I hear "thud, thud, thud" outside. Me and Dad run outside and all the windows on the Camry are smashed in. My backpack's open. "Fuck, they stole my stuff." I reach and I pull out my backpack. Pieces of glass get caught in my arm. Now blood is gushing down my arm, and I'm pissed, I'm fucking mad. (…) I look back in the middle of the street, my dad is in the middle of the road sweeping glass out of the road like he works at a bar-bershop. (…) Zen! Brown Mr. Miyagi, just, like, not saying a word. I'm like, "Why aren't you saying something? I'm asking you, say something!" He looks at me and goes, "Hasan … these things happen, and these things will continue to happen. That's the price we pay for being here." (…) I'm like, "I'm in Honors Gov, I have it right here. Life, liberty, pursuit of happiness. All men created equal." It says it right here, I'm equal. I'm equal. I don't deserve this. But as soon as I say that…. He looks at me like I believe in Santa. "Hasan, you'll never understand." "I'll never understand? Dad, you're the guy that will argue with the cashier at Costco when he doesn't let you return used underwear. And now you want to be the bigger man? Now you're like, 'Let's be reasonable with the bigots.' What?" And then he just walks back into the house with glass in his feet. And I honestly don't know who is more right.

Minhaj's story is simultaneously powerful, serious, and humorous in a way that does not compromise the funniness of the jokes or the serious issue of racist death threats and violence. Like many other comedians, he draws on aspects of his life, yet he does not allow his life to become completely absorbed by triviality. Instead, the seriousness of the issues remains open as he moves through them with humorous commentary. For Minhaj, his jokes are never just jokes separated from the seriousness of their content. His jokes always maintain their connection to the real suffering, triumph, confusion, and happiness of the various moments of his life that he shares.

In this way, Minhaj exemplifies a fact that has always been true about comedy: comedy is intimately connected to our lives. Whether the jokes take the form of narrative or one-liners, they borrow their information, attitudes, and emotions from the mundane and serious parts of our lives. The context of jokes, therefore, is not narrowly contained in the comedic context but is rather part of a broader social context. Situated in a social context, Minhaj's jokes work to lead his audience into first-person accounts of the effects of racism and Islamophobia and to help reveal the real hardships of immigrant life that may not be obvious to many. In contrast, the social function of supporting a disinterested stance toward jokes is to identify what kinds of things we should be allowed to belittle for the sake of our amusement. If the *comic loophole's* social purpose is to allow the trivialization of otherwise serious matters based on the desire for pleasure, then its purpose betrays its very foundation. The complete separation of triviality and seriousness supporting the *comic loophole* is in fact a very serious matter.

What Does This Mean for an Ethics of Comedy?

When people can refuse to take responsibility for making objectionable and controversial jokes, it makes developing a comedy ethics seem like a hopeless endeavor. The comic loophole created by the humor formalist position disrupts any attempt at evaluating jokes from an ethical perspective. For this reason, the comic loophole must be closed in order to apply ethics to comedy. The closure of the loophole must, in fact, be a part of the comedy ethics to be developed.

One method for eliminating the loophole would involve challenging the aesthetic presuppositions that are held about jokes and comedy. The standard assumption is that jokes and comedy are inherently and absolutely nonserious. Yet, many of us are quite invested in them, especially the comedians who deny the seriousness of jokes. An ethics of comedy would most likely require a definition of jokes that illustrates how they are never "just" jokes but are instead much more.

Through jokes, comedy creates the opportunity to communicate serious issues, frustrations about life, regrets, anger, and pain but in a way that involves some level of pleasure that does not contradict the content. Topics that are ordinarily difficult for people to approach are given a new life that makes them easier to face. This is perhaps what Gervais meant when he said that the purpose of humor is to "get us over bad things." But if that's true, it's difficult to believe that humor and those actual bad things in our lives are, as he says, "not related."

When we think carefully about an ethics of comedy, we ought to keep in mind the relation between jokes and the bad things they are about. Although comedy can be powerful in communicating something heavy in a light-hearted manner, it can also fail spectacularly. In order to avoid these failures, we, as joke-tellers (professional or not) would be best served by reflection on how our jokes could influence others and how the jokes fit into the social context. The non-seriousness of comedy is a double-edged sword. Jokes invite listening even from those who would not normally lend an ear. They can open up lines of communication. However, they also have the power to trivialize and undermine. Hence, we must wield comedy *with* responsibility, not against it.

Works Cited

Carlin, George. *Doin' It Again*. Mpi Home Video, 2005.
Gervais, Ricky. "That's What Humor Is For ... To Get Over Bad Shit." *The Opie and Anthony Show*. Created by Jim Norton, 2013.
Jardin, Xeni. "Douche.0: Daniel Tosh Digs Rape Jokes, Proposes a Female Audience Member Be Raped." *Boing Boing*, 12 July 2012, https://boingboing.net/2012/07/10/douche-0-daniel-tosh-digs-rap.html. Accessed 3 January 2019.
Kant, Immanuel. *Critique of Judgment*. Hackett Publishing, 1987.
Minhaj, Hasan. *Homecoming King*. *Netflix* Originals, 2017.

What Is Kant's Theory of Humor?

ROBERT R. CLEWIS

> One day Peter Abelard was riding in a carriage with a priest.
>
> The priest suddenly exclaimed, "Look! There goes a flying ox!"
>
> "Where? Where?" Abelard asked, looking around.
>
> The priest smirked. "It's hard to believe that such an intelligent and scholarly man as you could believe that an ox could fly."
>
> Abelard paused, then responded: "It's easier for me to believe that an ox could fly, than that a priest could lie."
>
> —Kant, *Lecture on Anthropology, 1784–85*[1]

Immanuel Kant (1724–1804) is not known for his sense of humor. He is renowned for his philosophical writings, in particular the three critiques: *Critique of Pure Reason* (1781/87), the *Critique of Practical Reason* (1788), and the *Critique of the Power of Judgment* (1790). These works have been profoundly influential in aesthetics, ethics, epistemology, and metaphysics. About half a century after these works appeared, the German poet Heinrich Heine (1797–1856) claimed that Kant initiated an intellectual revolution in Germany that was analogous to the political Revolution in France (Heine 79). At the same time, Heine asserts that Kant "lived a mechanically ordered, almost abstract bachelor existence" (Heine 79). Due to such characterizations, Kant is usually considered to be boring, overly punctual, and methodical—allegedly fitting for a philosopher who offers an ethics based on maxims and principles. But when Kant was a younger man, decades before he became famous for his three *Critiques*, he was known in social circles as the elegant *Magister* (gallant teacher) (Kuehn 115). His presence is reported to have animated balls and dinner parties, and he would tell amusing stories and jokes to his classes at Albertina University in Königsberg. The philosopher, poet, and theologian, Johann Gottfried Herder (1744–1803), who attended Kant's courses between 1762 and 1764, wrote the following about Kant: "I have had the good fortune of knowing a philosopher who was my teacher…. Talk rich in ideas issued from his lips, joking, humor and wit were at his disposal, and his teaching lectures were the most amusing entertainment…. This man whom I name … is Immanuel Kant" (404). To illustrate his account of amused laughter, Kant even included some jokes in the *Critique of the Power of Judgment*.[2]

Kant's theory of humor can be characterized as a version of what is called the *incongruity theory*, but it has elements of other theories. To show this, I will explore how Kant engaged with the dominant theories of humor of his day, in particular, *superiority theory*, which he rejected, and incongruity theory, which he developed. One outcome of this analysis is that it reveals that the image of Kant as dour and humorless is misleading. Along the way, I will use Kant's jokes to help us understand his theory of humor.

Next, I will consider Kant's view of the relation between ethics and humor—a position that (building on the literature) that can be called "moderate moralism." At the very least, for Kant, when joking we should never treat people merely as a means but should treat them with moral respect. In addition, as a socializing activity, humor (carried out in a morally permissible way) creates the conditions whereby we can perfect ourselves and create a moral community. As Kant put it in *Anthropology from a Pragmatic Point of View* (1798), a handbook based on his notes for his lectures on anthropology: "Anything that promotes sociability, even if it consists only in pleasing maxims or manners, is a garment that dresses virtue to advantage" (*Kants Schriften* 7:282). Socialization is not the same as moralization, but it is a step in that direction since it creates conditions that are conducive to morality. Furthermore, and more concretely, some forms of humor can even contribute to moralization: by poking fun at vices and morally reprehensible characters who embody them, ridicule and satire can help us identify moral shortcomings and potentially help us adopt the will to avoid them. Finally, Kant's theory of humor implies that jokes that have moral content or effects on listeners are better (in that they support morality) than those that lack such content or effects. The term "moralism" seems fitting for Kant's theory on account of (a) his view of the capacity for jokes to help create the conditions in which humans can perfect themselves and (b) his claim that moral content adds a kind of value to the joke.

But the moralism is called "moderate" because it allows (within limits set by ethical principles and in the appropriate context) for some joking about sensitive matters such as race, ethnicity, sexuality, gender, age, class, and disability. When we listen to the joke qua joke, there is a frame raised around the joke in which we put to the side our ordinary (social, ethical-political) concerns for such issues. As Kant puts it in the third *Critique*, "by means of jokes and laughter a certain tone of merriment [is produced], in which, as is said, much can be chattered about and nobody will be held responsible for what he says, because it is only intended as momentary entertainment" (*Kants Schriften* 5:305).

Kant's Predecessors

First, it would be useful to examine the rival theories or potential sources for Kant's own views. Three dominant theories can be mentioned: superiority, incongruity, and relief (release) theories.

Kant was familiar with the major theories of comedy: superiority, relief, and an early version of incongruity theory (that he would come to define). In the *Critique of the Power of Judgment*, Kant mentions superiority theory before stating his own position which is closer to incongruity theory: "We laugh, and it gives us a hearty pleasure: not because we find ourselves cleverer than this ignorant person, or because of any other pleasing thing that the understanding allows us to note here, but because our expectation was heightened and suddenly disappeared into nothing" (*Kants Schriften* 5:533). In *Reflections on Laughter* (1725), Francis Hutcheson (1694–1746) criticizes the superiority theory in Hobbes and Joseph Addison. Like Kant, Hutcheson offers a version of incongruity theory. It is possible (but not certain) that Hutcheson's incongruity theory may have influenced Kant's own thoughts about humor, for Kant was familiar with his moral and aesthetic writings. Before proceeding to relief theory, it is worth mentioning two further parallels between Hutcheson and Kant. First, they both stress humor's socializing potential. Hutcheson identifies the socializing effects (and roots) of laughter. "Our whole frame is so sociable, that one merry countenance may diffuse cheerfulness to many" (Townsend 146). "It is plainly of considerable moment in human society. It is often a great occasion of pleasure, and enlivens our conversation exceedingly, when it is conducted by good-nature" (Townsend 148). Second, they both defend the idea that in appreciating humor, our ordinary social and moral concerns are bracketed. Hutcheson implies that, in humor, a reader or audience puts aside the feeling of sympathy and concern: "The reflecting on this distress [i.e., suffering and agony] could never move laughter of itself" (Townsend 147).

Relief theory emerged most prominently (after Kant) in the 19zf in the work of Herbert Spencer (1820–1903). In listening to a joke or viewing a comic situation, a sort of tension builds, and upon hearing the punchline or resolution, we let it out. Based on the passages to be discussed in a moment, it seems that Kant's account contains elements of relief theory, as Carroll has noted (*Humour* 39). If that is right, it is unclear what sources (if any) Kant may have had. However, Shaftesbury suggested that comedy releases our otherwise constrained, natural free spirits (Carroll *Humour* 38), and since Kant was familiar with Shaftesbury's writings in general, it is possible that he was also acquainting with Shaftesbury's theory of humor.

Kant's thought on humor was also likely informed by his personal friends and acquaintances. Kant was friends with literati in Konigsberg such as Johann Georg Hamann (1730–88), a literary critic and Christian theologian who wrote in a witty, idiosyncratic style, and Theodore Hippel (1741–96), author of plays such as *The Man of the Clock*—reportedly based on Kant's close friend Joseph Green, who pedantically lived by the clock (Kuehn 154), a stereotype later associated instead with Kant. It is easy to imagine Hamann, Hippel, and Kant having conversations about humor and comedy. In addition, Kant corresponded with Moses Mendelssohn (1729–86), a German Jewish enlightenment philosopher and author of reflections on laughter in *Rhapsody*, with which we can assume Kant was familiar. The similarities between Kant's account and Mendelssohn's are notable. According to Mendelssohn, laughter is

> founded … on a *contrast between a perfection and an imperfection.* The only difference is that this contrast must be *of no importance and not be very proximate to us,* if it is to be laughable … the same circumstance can appear laughable to one person and depress someone else, depending upon whether they *participate more or less in the fate of the affected person.* The foolishness of our friends commonly vexes us, pleases enemies, and *amuses persons who are neutral* [Mendelssohn 149–50; emphasis added].

Mendelssohn defends a theory of incongruity ("contrast") as well as what may be called a principle of indifference (being "neutral"), both of which Kant takes up in his own account.

The term "wit" (*ingenium, Witz*) was widely used in the German scholastic, Leibnizian-Wolffian tradition which Kant inherited. Wit here meant not so much the capacity for humor as the ability to connect diverse ideas. One finds *Witz* used widely throughout Kant's courses on anthropology (1772–96), for which he assigned sections of the textbook of Alexander Baumgarten, *Metaphysica*. Baumgarten discusses ingenuity or wit (*ingenium*) in several sections (esp. §572, §648, §649) and defines wit in the strict sense as "proficiency in observing the correspondences of things" (§572; Baumgarten 215). In similar fashion, British writers with whom Kant was familiar, in particular, John Locke (*Essay concerning Human Understanding* [Bk II, ch. II]) and Joseph Addison (*Spectator* essay No. 62), discussed wit as a power to connect ideas. While not identical to jest and joking, "wit" as such a power provides the broader context for the discussion of humor in Kant's day.

Kant's Theory of Humor: The Secret Soul of Kant's Joke[3]

While Kant's theory of humor clearly has elements of incongruity theory, it ultimately combines elements from different theories. Although there is textual support for calling Kant an incongruity theorist, his account also contains parts of a relief theory. Moreover, since he refers to a "mere play of representations," he also offers what could be called a kind of "play" theory in that the mind playfully reflects on the cognitive incongruity. Indeed, whereas incongruity theory clearly preceded Kant, the "relief" and "play" elements in his theory seem to be more distinctively his own original contributions. What is beyond doubt is that Kant rejects superiority theory.

There is ample textual support for finding elements of incongruity theory in his account. For instance, he claims that (amused) laughter is an effect resulting from the "sudden transformation of a heightened expectation into nothing" due to our apprehension of a "nonsensical" incongruity. The key paragraph from the third *Critique* reads:

> In everything that is to provoke a lively, uproarious laughter, there must be something nonsensical (in which, therefore, the understanding in itself can take no satisfaction). Laughter is an affect resulting from the sudden transformation of a heightened expectation into nothing. This very transformation, which is certainly nothing enjoyable for the understanding, is nevertheless indirectly enjoyable and, for a moment, very lively. The cause must thus consist in the influence of the representation on the body and its reciprocal effect on the mind; certainly not insofar as the representation is objectively an object of gratification (for how can a disappointed expectation be gratifying?), but rather solely through the fact that as a mere play of representations it produces an equilibrium of the vital powers in the body [*Kants Schriften* 5:332–333; emphasis modified].

Thus, it is clear that Kant thinks that amused laughter, the kind that results from humor, is a response to a perceived mismatch. Here is a second substantial passage:

> It is noteworthy that in all such cases the joke must always contain something that can deceive for a moment: hence, when the illusion disappears into nothing, the mind looks back again in order to try it once more, and thus is hurried this way and that by rapidly succeeding increases and decreases of tension and set into oscillation: which, because that which as it were struck the string bounces back suddenly (not through a gradual slackening), is bound to cause a movement of the mind and an internal bodily movement in harmony with it, which continues involuntarily, and produces weariness, but at the same time also cheerfulness (the effects of a motion that is beneficial to health) [*Kants Schriften* 5:334].

Note that this passage implies that laughter serves to relieve a built-up tension. Specifically, it is the suddenness of the joke's punchline (which contains the incongruity) that leads to the release of tension. Like Carroll, Critchley notices this point when commenting on Kant's theory: "In hearing the punch-line, the tension disappears and we experience comic relief" (Critchley 6). This mental play leads to an intense feeling or "affect," a strong emotion that momentarily overcomes the reader or audience and, if it persists for long, produces "weariness." When we laugh heartily in response to an incongruity, the body's diaphragm is being affected by the "mind," which perceives the incongruity.

As might be expected of a view that appeals to both relief and incongruity, Kant holds that there are both corporeal and intellectual elements in humor. The physical and intellectual are in fact interrelated: the bodily reaction results from the intellectual play in response to the incongruous content of the joke or comic narrative. The movements of the diaphragm cause an agreeable sensation. This is why laughter, a common sign that one is experiencing comic amusement, is healthy and restorative. In laughter, the third *Critique* states, one "can get at the body even through the soul" and can use the soul (the mind) as a doctor for the body (*Kants Schriften* 5:332). "One feels the effect of this relaxation in the body through the oscillation of the organs, which promotes the restoration of their balance and has a beneficial influence on health" (*Kants Schriften* 5:332). If we laugh vigorously, we experience an oscillation or vibration of our internal organs, which is why it can hurt when we laugh or when we engage in it a little too enthusiastically (Critchley 9). The reaction to the humorous "produces the successive movement of the mind in two opposite directions, which at the same time gives the body a healthy shake" (*Kants Schriften* 5:335).

Because of its corporeal effects and its aiming at "enjoyment," Kant calls humor an art of the "agreeable" rather than one of the fine arts (poetry, painting, etc.).

> Agreeable arts are those which are aimed merely at enjoyment; of this kind are all those charms that can gratify the company at a table, such as telling entertaining stories, getting the company talking in an open and lively manner, creating by means of jokes and laughter a certain tone of merriment, in which, as is said, much can be chattered about and nobody will be held responsible for what he says, because it is only intended as momentary entertainment, not as some enduring material for later reflection or discussion [*Kants gesammelte* 5:305].[4]

Kant's characterization of humor as an agreeable art, however, should not be taken as a dismissal of humor, for he still assigns it the term "art," and, in addition, thinks that humor can have an important social function.

A Joke's Value: Kant's Intellectualist Account

As we have seen, Kant holds that there is an intellectual play in response to a joke: the mind tries to make sense of something that appears to be "non-sensical." While this mental play with an incongruity already makes for what could be called a conceptualist or intellectualist approach to humor (especially when contrasted with the tension and energy prioritized by relief theory), there is a more direct sense in which a joke can have intellectual content: it can bring to attention cultural, social, and ethical-political issues and criticize the status quo.

Ridicule and satire often do this. By making fun of folly, Kant thinks, ridicule and satire put us in a position to improve or cultivate ourselves morally speaking. Specifically, these forms of humor can help us identify similar moral shortcomings in our own lives or help us see why we should avoid them.

From this premise, Kant makes an interesting move: his theory assigns *more* value to jokes with such intellectual content than to those without it. Writings (such as Henry Fielding's novels) that make use of contrast in order to ridicule vice, he says, "are the most peevish [*launigsten*]" and "please greatly" (*Kants Schriften* 25:506; translation modified). This "kind of contrasting is the best way," he says, since it "sharpens the mind and at the same time makes the vicious person" look ridiculous (*ibid.*). (Keep in mind, however, that not all jokes need to have intellectual-moral content to be funny. The three jokes presented in the third *Critique*—the Merchant's Wig, the Bottle of Ale, and the Happy Mourners [*Kants Schriften* 5:333]—do not have such content and are intended to be funny.) There is an ambiguity in the phrase, "the best way." Kant likely does not mean that the joke is funnier, but that it has the potential to be conducive for morality.

Let us consider an example. The Flying Ox joke (see the epigraph at the beginning of this essay) that Kant told his anthropology course does well according to this criterion, for it has a moral message. Kant commented on this joke with the following: "Even the cleverest minds can often be deceived.... An honest man is not necessarily stupid." Abelard is wiser and smarter than the priest, but he is also trusting and unsuspecting, because he himself acts from a "love of humanity." "The person who is tricked often puts up with the trickster; when he acts from love of humanity, he doesn't suspect anything bad." This may make him seem gullible—at least the first time around, "but when he uncovers the deceiver the first time, he certainly won't be deceived by him ever again" (*Kants Schriften* 25:1272). Kant appears to like this story because of its moral content, which the wit sugarcoats.

In his anthropology lectures, Kant distinguishes between superficial and profound wit.[5] Whereas *superficial* wit makes use of incongruity and "surprise of the unexpected," *profound* wit is more enduring because it appeals to reason. The former is more playful, the latter more serious.

> Trickster [*launichter*] wit means one that comes from a mind disposed to *paradox*, where the (cunning) jokester peers from behind the naïve sound of simplicity in order to expose someone (or his opinion) to ridicule by exalting, with apparent eulogy (persiflage), the opposite of what is worthy of approval—for example, Swift's *Art of Sinking in Poetry*, or Butler's *Hudibras*. Such a wit, which uses contrast to make what is contemptible even more contemptible, is very stimulating through the surprise of the unexpected [*Kants Schriften* 7:221–222; translation modified].

Similar to Jon Stewart or Stephen Colbert, Swift and Butler make the contemptible look even more contemptible in a way that can be both comically amusing and useful for social or ethical-political reform. Nonetheless, Kant attributes to Swift, Butler, and Voltaire "easy" or superficial wit, which he distinguishes from difficult or profound wit. The latter arouses admiration more than comic amusement.

> However, it is an easy wit (like that of Voltaire's), and always only a *game*. On the other hand, the person who presents true and important principles in clothing (like [Edward] Young in his satires)[6] can be called a very difficult wit, because it is a *serious business* and arouses more admiration than amusement [*ibid.*].

Superficial joking is far from inherently wrong (and may even be useful for ethical-political criticism), but it is more playful than the more serious kind. Still, the former can break down and deteriorate into its extreme form: it can become too playful, insubstantial, or cute. Thus, jokes that merely make use of word play do poorly on Kant's account. Two examples of authors who fail on this score are Abbot Trublet and Samuel Johnson.

Kant thinks that the French abbot's "Essay on Several Subjects of Literature and Morality" (1735) contains more linguistic tricks or gags than insights. In one of his lectures, Kant is reported to have said: "When one reads the Abbot Trublet's gags [*Einfälle*], one becomes so weary and tired of the excessive *bons mots*" that one prefers something that is ordinary and without taste (*Kants Schriften* 25: 388). In *Anthropology from a Pragmatic Point of View*, find a similar claim:

> Wit goes more for the *sauce*. Judgment goes for the *sustenance*. The hunt for *witty sayings* (*bons mots*), as the Abbot Trublet does so well, thereby putting wit on the rack, makes for shallow minds, or eventually disgusts well-grounded ones [*Kants Schriften* 7:221; translation modified].

Just as engaging with beauty for too long can sometimes lead to feelings of saturation and disgust, so too can a sense of weariness result from exposure to too much wittiness. Thus, Kant's theory finds fault with sayings or quips that contain "mere play" without much content.

For similar reasons, Kant finds fault with Samuel Johnson:

It is true that profundity is not a matter of wit; but in so far as wit, through the graphic element that it adds to thought, can be a vehicle or garb for reason and its management of morally practical ideas, it can be thought of as profound wit (as distinguished from superficial wit). As one of the so-called admirable sayings of Samuel Johnson about women goes...

Doubtless he [Johnson] praised many women whom he would have hesitated to marry, and perhaps he married one he would have been ashamed to praise.

Here the play of antitheses constitutes the only admirable thing; reason gains nothing by it. [*Kants Schriften* 7:222].[7]

Kant considers this to be one of Johnson's *so-called* admirable sayings. It is not in fact admirable since it does not help improve the world morally-speaking. Despite his vast knowledge of language, Johnson (a lexicographer) is unable to combine wit and reason in a balanced way.[8]

Kant seems unbothered by the implicit sexism in Johnson's saying. This raises the question of how best to characterize Kant on the ethics of humor.

Kant's Moderate Moralism

Kant is one of the most important writers on ethics of all time, and an ethical orientation runs through his entire philosophical thinking. Not surprisingly, some critics have charged his theories (e.g., this theory of the sublime) with being overly moralistic. For instance, one commentator attributes to Kant "a tendency that let him to moralize, in one way or another, any experience he valued" (Budd 84).

An ethical orientation can be found in his account of humor, too, but I do not think that Kant is guilty of over-moralizing. While there is an ethical underpinning to his theory of humor, it is balanced by the notion that there is a time and place for joking that allows humorists and the audience to say or attend to certain things that (in another context) they would not. The term "moderate" is fitting because Kant thinks we may and should listen to the joke as a joke, at a distance from the events recounted, in which case we bracket our ordinary concerns (while feeling neither threatened and nor annoyed) and listen to the joke in "an arena of playfulness" while not solving a real puzzle or genuine problem (Carroll *Humour* 36).

This does not mean, however, that joking is completely exempt from the universality test that is the foundation of his ethics and that is supposed to govern all rational agency and human action. Morality for Kant is determined by the moral law, or, to use his technical term, the categorical imperative. "There is, therefore, only a single categorical imperative and it is this: act only in accordance with that maxim [i.e., a subjective principle of action] through which you can at the same time will that it become a universal law"

(*Kants Schriften* 4:421). In other words, we should not make exceptions of ourselves when we deliberate, adopt maxims, and act. Another way to put this is to say that we should treat other people as ends and with moral respect, recognizing their dignity. "So act that you use humanity, whether in your own person or in the person of any other, always at the same time as an end, never merely as a means" (*Kants Schriften* 4:429). One may not, for instance, actually beat someone up in order to make people laugh. It is wrong to be comically amused when that amusement is at the expense of other (innocent) people, that is, if it treats them as a mere means rather than as an end.

Moralism (aka ethicism) refers to the thesis that that a joke with a morally flawed outlook is to an extent, and precisely on account of its immorality, deficient as a joke.[9] Thus, even if the joke could still be funny overall, its immorality makes it less funny. Note that there appears to be an asymmetry here: a joke with a *moral* outlook is not thereby funnier (Carroll *Humour* 106). A joke with a moral perspective may be better for practical-moral reasons and because it is (potentially) morally edifying, but it is not necessarily better as a joke (funnier). Kant's theory counts as a kind of moralism because (i) he holds that there are ethical constraints on joking (the immorality worsens the joke); (ii) he maintains that jokes can have a moral content or effect, and that the jokes that have such a content or effect are better (given their potential to promote morality) than jokes that lack it. Specifically, jokes that identify or poke fun at human folly and moral shortcomings, or that potentially support morality, have more value than ones that are merely playful witticisms.

What counts as "morality" has to meet a very high bar. Morality consists in action done for the right reason, namely, for the sake of duty, not just action that happens to comply with duty. Kant allots morality utmost import in human affairs; of all kinds of actions, actions that are morally obligated have priority over and override all other kinds of actions. Nevertheless, our social nature is important too, and Kant holds that, by bringing humans together to enjoy a shared agreeable experience, jokes have a socializing function, though by itself this does not count as a moral function. Humor can help socialize us when it leads us to feel shared pleasure in response to a story or anecdote. Kant holds that if humor and wit are used properly, they have the potential to cultivate and refine humanity. Humor is often enjoyed and experienced with fellow human beings—friends, relatives, coworkers, acquaintances, even people in a crowd. Sure, one can laugh when alone, to oneself, and even at oneself, but, in addition to relieving tension, humor can boost social bonding, creating a context that can allow us to perfect ourselves and become better people. This is not the same as direct moral cultivation,[10] but it is a step in that direction since humor helps create an amenable setting that is conducive to moral self-cultivation. It is on account of humor's socializing and moralizing potential that many of the aforementioned jokes and stories come from Kant's course on anthropology, for that course was intended to help students become globally minded, cultivated, and moral citizens.

Kant holds that some forms of jest, such as Fielding's *Tom Jones*, can satirize vice and portray folly as worthy of ridicule. As Hutcheson had put it: "Another valuable purpose of ridicule is with relation to smaller vices, which are often more effectually corrected by ridicule, than by grave admonition" (Townsend 149). Such humor criticizes and potentially corrects the presumed claims and ways of the morally reprehensible characters. Accordingly, Kant liked the Flying Ox joke because it ridicules the lying priest and praises the smart and upright Abelard. Such humor, in other words, has moral content, which adds (practical) value to the joke.

The way in which Kant's account is a kind of "moralism" deserves more elucidation. As much as he appreciates humor and wit, Kant considers wit to be "dispensable," to be controlled by reason and governed by ethical principles (the "moral law" as expressed in the categorical imperative). Joking is not a necessity, but instead is like a delicacy or luxury: "For the joke is very delicate and is only fitting for the nobleman's supper, as Rabelais says" (*Kants Schriften* 25:508). Kant extends this "sauce" metaphor in another passage: "Sound reason and understanding are like a dish of beef and mutton. They are fit only for the peasant's table. But a ragout of folly, accompanied by a sauce of wit, is fit for an Emperor's table" (*Kants Schriften* 25:1256). Humor is important, but it is only an accessory, and accessories should be used wisely and not be mistaken for the main substance.

But the "moralism" is not extreme. In order to find attend to a joke properly, for Kant, we should accept ahead of time that we are hearing a joke and listen to it as such. The story or idea we are trying to understand should not be a matter of importance to us. As Carroll puts it, we "bracket" our sympathy and moral concern (*Humour* 86). If the object or idea is something serious or of import to us, or if it affects us personally and we cannot put aside our social or ethical-political concerns, we cannot find it humorous, but instead would feel instances of the emotions appropriate to the case at hand—empathy or discomfort when learning about a stroke of bad luck, excitement or joy when hearing of good fortune, righteous anger in response to a perceived wrong, and so on. If we are having such responses to the events recounted in the joke or story, we are no longer perceiving the joke as a joke, i.e., in the arena of playfulness, and this makes it difficult to find it funny. The *Critique of the Power of Judgment* contains a joke that illustrates just this point.

> A merchant was sailing with his entire fortune from India to Europe aboard his ship. Due to a terrible storm, he was forced to throw all of his merchandise overboard. He was so upset that, that very night, his *wig* turned gray [*Kants Schriften* 5:333; translation modified].

To explain his point about indifference or the bracketing of concern, Kant then offers another, realistic version of the joke: the merchant's *hair* turns gray (*Kants Schriften* 5:333). After hearing that version, he says, we are likely to shift into a relation of empathy with the merchant. When it is only a wig and the story is "otherwise indifferent to us," we are in a better position to find the anecdote amusing and engage in a playful reflection on the joke's content. "It gives us gratification, because for a while we toss back and forth like a ball our own misconception about an object that is otherwise indifferent to us, or rather our own idea that we've been chasing, while we were merely trying to grasp and hold it firm" (*Kants Schriften* 5:333–34). This bracketing does not determine or make up the moral worth of the joke; rather, being removed from the situation is required even to be in a position to find it humorous. The joke does not create a distant attitude in the audience; comic distance is rather the condition for hearing it as a joke rather than as a report of an unfortunate event or just something bizarre.

A similar notion has recently been defended by Steven Gimbel.[11] He discusses the idea of a "play frame," which is a kind of layer that surrounds the joke telling, separating the joke world from the real world. For instance, the play frame would be thicker at a comedy club than at a cafeteria at work. At the comedy club, we are not as likely to be offended by an otherwise disturbing joke because we are in a mindset that is more tolerant of offensive jokes, especially those told by comedians about themselves or groups they identify as their own. In contrast, we are more likely to be offended by a racist, sexist, homophobic, or ableist joke at the workplace, especially those that degrade other groups. The context changes our expectations of what is appropriate. Kant might say that we are more distant, or more in the joking mindset, at the comedy club than at work. Thus, Kant's notion implies that a questionable or borderline joke could be morally acceptable in one context, while being ethically reproachable in another. For he holds that in joke telling "much can be chattered about and nobody will be held responsible for what he says, because it is only intended as momentary entertainment" (*Kants Schriften* 5:305).

But where is the line—how large is the play frame? To examine this, let us consider another joke from the *Critique of the Power of Judgment*.

> A man from India and an Englishman are at the Englishman's table in the city of Surat. When the Englishman opens up the bottle of ale, it explodes in a wave of froth. The Indian looks amazed.
> "Well, what's so remarkable in that?" asks the Englishman.
> "I'm not surprised at its getting out," replies the Indian, "but at how you ever managed to get it all in" [*Kants Schriften* 5:333; translation modified].

Some readers consider this joke to be racist. Critchley refers to this joke as (one of) "the tiresome and indeed racist examples of jokes that Kant recounts, involving Indians and bottles of beer" (6). Before we can treat this as a racist joke, it is worth asking if the joke is indeed racist, that is, immoral on account of harming, insulting, or discriminating against someone based on their ethnicity or genetic background. Recall the criteria for what would make a joke immoral: one that violates the formula of the universal law of nature, or the humanity formula. If the joke treated people from India as mere means, or induced us to accept or endorse the belief that Indians do not deserve moral respect, for instance, it would be immoral.

Yet, there may be a more innocent way to interpret the joke. First, the Indian man is at the Englishman's table (presumably to share a beer), implying that at least some kind of friendship exists between the two. If so, upon closer inspection it may be harder to accuse the contents of the joke as being racist. (Given the colonial context, it might be conjectured that the Indian man is the Englishman's servant, and that the joke implicitly accepts and endorses the unjust colonial power structure. But first, the joke simply does not call him a servant, and second, if he were a servant, it is questionable he would have spoken up that way—and wouldn't he have seen beer before?) Second, even if one is not willing to grant that reading, perhaps there is another way to interpret the joke charitably. The punchline of the joke requires the person watching the beer bottle being opened for the first time to be unfamiliar with beer. Hence the joke teller is forced by the very structure of joke to find a culture that did not have a tradition and history of drinking beer. That need not be racist, since it is not necessarily an insult or harmful to accuse someone of being unfamiliar with beer or of being from a culture lacking that tradition. Indeed, any culture could be unfamiliar with some of the practices of another culture. In any case, it seems a stretch to accuse Kant of having deliberate ill will or malicious intent toward Indians when he included this joke in the third *Critique* (Moreover, it is easy to imagine that Kant liked this joke as an illustration of how comic amusement unfolds. The exploding beer foam symbolizes the sudden reversal accompanying comic relief).

But let us leave that aside, and examine jokes that we easily agree are racist or sexist. On Kant's account, could it be ethically permissible to tell a racist/sexist joke? The short answer is no (The longer answer complicates this by appealing to the notion of a play-frame or context,[12] which allows for some joking about sensitive matters. In other words, the "moderate" aspect will modify the moralism.). It would be morally unacceptable if it were told with malicious intentions or if the joke made some slur (say, if the previous joke referred to the man as "another stupid Indian"). Generally, it is unacceptable to treat a people as a mere means and to disrespect their humanity (say insulting or ridiculing them on the grounds of ethnicity), even if it is in the course of joking. This could be summarized by invoking Kant's humanity formula: jokes that treat (actual) people or groups of people as mere means are morally wrong, jokes that treat people as ends having dignity are not morally wrong (they are permissible). Kant's account entails that we cannot joke in just any manner we please, but instead that there are ethical limits on what counts as a fair topic or subject. If we break those limits, the joke is the worse for it.

Similar thoughts apply to joking about sex, gender, and sexuality. In marginal notes from the mid–1760s, Kant appears to criticize (what we would now call) locker room humor insofar as it becomes offensive or "uncivilized." He writes: "Jokes told in the company of men only [i.e., all men] have no real life, and become uncivilized too" (*Kants Schriften* 20:21). In similar fashion, in *Observations on the Feeling of the Beautiful and Sublime* (1764) Kant deplores those who "get just as lively a joy from vulgarities and a crude joke," and he in turn praises "persons of nobler sentiment" (*Kants Schriften* 2:207). In other words, bawdy, crude, or lewd jokes—jokes that make (actual) people or groups into mere ends, for instance by treating them as mere objects or reducing them to their sexuality and sexual organs—are reproachable. They are blameworthy at the very least from the perspective of civility and etiquette, and they may even be morally reproachable as well, e.g., when they do not treat people as ends. In addition, such jokes may even violate duties toward oneself, that is, they can be self-degrading. In other words, by treating and interacting with other people merely in terms of their sexuality and sexual organs rather than in terms of their rational capacities to set and act on ends, one may be implicitly disrespecting the humanity in oneself, since one is likewise a rational yet embodied being.

I conclude with a question followed by a tentative answer. Let us grant that Kant told jokes that were morally questionable.[13] Such jokes raise an interesting question for his theory. Should we focus more on the *moralism* in Kant's "moderate moralism," or instead emphasize the moderate side to his theory? In the case of his seemingly sexist or racist jokes, is it more accurate to view those jokes as being inconsistent with his theory of humor and as violating the constraints set by ethical principles (focusing on the "moralism")? Or, reading him as being consistent, should we instead infer that such racist/sexist jokes (so long as they are not told with malicious intent) are actually compatible with his account and that they are permissible because listeners can be expected to put aside moral and social concerns when listening to a joke (the "moderate" element)? This is not an easy question to answer, but I would emphasize the moderate aspect. I think that we should adopt the view that he was being "inconsistent" only as a last resort, that is, if there is no other way of explaining his claims. But the texts I have quoted in discussing his concept of "indifference" seem to justify emphasizing the moderate element. In joking and jesting, "much can be chattered about and nobody will be held responsible for what he says, because it is only intended as momentary entertainment" (*Kants Schriften* 5: 305). Accordingly, we should probably emphasize the "moderate" nature of his account.

Meanwhile, when jesting we would do well to bear in mind our intentions, how others might interpret them, and the joke's context or frame. We should also consider whether a joke that we may be comfortable telling to or making among friends (but not strangers or mere acquaintances) could potentially be removed from its original frame, especially if the joke telling was recorded, published, or broadcasted. And if it could be so removed, it may be better simply to refrain.[14]

NOTES

1. Peter Abelard (1079–1142) was a renowned and influential French medieval philosopher and theologian. He is also well known for his love affair with Héloïse, the subject of *The Letters of Abelard and Héloïse*. Kant tells this joke in the 1784–85 Anthropology lecture, in Kant 1900–, vol. 25:1272. Page references to Kant's works are to the Academy Edition, *Kants gesammelte Schriften* (Kant's Collected Works) (1900–), cited by volume and then page number. Unless otherwise noted, the translations are taken from Kant 1992–. When not taken from the volumes in this series, the translations are by Robert Clewis, who, to improve a joke's set up and delivery, has taken some liberties with punctuation, verb tense, word order, and the like. For more of Kant's jokes, see Clewis 2020.

2. *Humor* is what comic amusement is directed at, i.e., the object of our attention when we find something comically amusing. *Wit* is a capacity for humor, that is, to elicit comic amusement. Humor can also be *found* (as when one stumbles on a funny mistake on a menu) rather than (like jokes) invented and crafted. I see "joke," "quip," "funny remark," "wisecrack," "humorous saying," "bon mot," and "witticism" as very closely related forms of humor intended to elicit comic amusement, which sometimes (but not always) evokes *laughter*. *Jokes* often have a narrative structure, and they tend to be more temporally extended than funny remarks and wisecracks. Finally, not all forms of amusement are comic (e.g., watching soap operas, completing crossword puzzles).

3. The subtitle derives from Nietzsche, who writes in *The Gay Science* (sec. 193): "*Kant's Joke*—Kant wanted to prove in a way that would dumbfound the common man that the common man was right: that was the secret joke of this soul" (1982: 96).

4. Kant says in the *Anthropology* (1798) that gossip at a dinner party should not be repeated and implies that there are (ethical) principles that govern such matters, namely, a duty not to repeat (harmful) gossip. "It is not merely a social *taste* that must guide the conversation; there are also principles that should serve as the limiting condition on the freedom with which human beings openly exchange their thoughts in social interactions" (Kant 1900–, vol. 7: 279). I would suggest that this principle, as a limiting condition, would govern statements used in humor. It would limit what we should/should not say in joking, and would specifically prevent our treating (actual) people as mere means and without moral respect. (Thus, it would make up part of the *moralism* in Kant's account.)

5. In "To the Author of the Dublin Journal," Hutcheson discusses "grave" and "serious" wit (Townsend 143). Yet unlike Kant, Hutcheson does not ascribe to serious wit any *moral* content, but rather discusses "serious" wit in order to identify incongruity as a source of humor.

6. Young's *The Universal Passion* (1725–27), a collection of seven satires.

7. Samuel Johnson is perhaps best known as the author of the *Dictionary of the English Language* (1755), the first comprehensive lexicographical work on English. Kant is here citing a line from *The Life of Samuel Johnson* (1791), written by Johnson's biographer James Boswell (1740–1795).

8. Kant's jokes can be classified into different joke types (Clewis, 2020): general incon-

gruity jokes, linguistic wordplay jokes, ethnic/racist and sexist jokes, and moral satire and ridicule. In addition, he sometimes tells vivid anecdotes to illustrate an ethical point, and while not exactly jokes, they display a kind of wit (what he would call "profound" wit).

9. I adopt the term "moderate moralism" from debates about the relation between art and ethics (Carroll 1996, 1998, 2014; Gaut 2007; Winegar 2011). In calling Kant's account a kind of moralism, I assigning him 1) the view that there are ethical constraints on what we may find funny (thus, that a moral flaw worsens the joke) 2) the claim that if a joke has a moral content or a morally edifying effect, then those ethical qualities make the joke better (ethically speaking), though not necessarily funnier. Moralism is to be distinguished from two further views of the relation of humor to morality: *autonomism* and *immoralism*. Roughly put, autonomism (aka amoralism) holds that there is no influence of morality on humor. A joke's morality or immorality has no affect on how funny or amusing it is. Immoralism holds the inverse of moralism: a moral flaw improves the joke. The more a joke violates and disrupts ethical norms, the more its value as a joke increases (the funnier it is).

10. Morality is always a matter of deliberate effort and activity, for Kant; there is no replacement for respect for the authority of the moral law.

11. While I am broadly indebted to Gimbel's idea of the play frame in interpreting Kant's notion of indifference, I do not claim to use the concept in Gimbel's precise sense.

12. One of the problems with joking via emails, recordings, videos, and Tweets, etc., is that such jest can easily be taken out of context, moving the frame from the one that was originally intended by the humorist, and into a broader public space.

13. If one in unwilling to count the Bottle of Ale joke as racist, then consider this sexist quip from the playful and highly stylized work, *Observations* (2:229–230; translation modified). "A woman who has a head full of Greek, like Madame Dacier, or who conducts thorough disputations about mechanics, like the Marquise de Châtelet, might as well also wear a beard. For that might perhaps better express the mien of depth for which they strive."

14. For comments, the author is grateful to Steven A. Benko, Mikhail Melnik, and Abigail Kennedy.

Works Cited

Baumgarten, Alexander. *Metaphysics.* Translated and edited by Courtney Fugate and John Hymers, Bloomsbury, 2013.
Budd, Malcolm. *The Aesthetic Appreciation of Nature: Essays on the Aesthetics of Nature.* Clarendon Press, 2002.
Carroll, Noël. *Humour: A Very Short Introduction.* Oxford University Press, 2014.
_____. "Moderate Moralism." *British Journal of Aesthetics.* vol. 36, 1996, pp. 223–38.
_____. "Moderate Moralism versus Moderate Autonomism," *British Journal of Aesthetics.* vol. 38, 1998, pp. 419–24.
Clewis, Robert R. *Kant's Humorous Writings: An Illustrated Guide.* Bloomsbury, 2020.
Critchley, Simon. *On Humour.* Routledge, 2002.
Freud, Sigmund. *Jokes and their Relation to the Unconscious.* Translated by J. Strachey, W.W. Norton, 1960.
Gaut, Berys. *Art, Emotion, and Ethics.* Clarendon Press, 2007.
Gimbel, Steven. *Isn't That Clever: A Philosophical Account of Humor and Comedy.* Routledge, 2018.
Heine, Heinrich. *On the History of Religion and Philosophy in Germany and Other Writings.* Edited by Terry Pinkard, Cambridge University Press, 2007.
Herder, Johann Gottfried. *Sämtliche Werke.* Edited by Bernhard Suphan, vol. 17, 1877–1913. 33 vols.
Kant, Immanuel. *The Cambridge Edition of the Works of Immanuel Kant.* Cambridge University Press, 1992.
_____. *Kants Schriften.* Walter de Gruyter, 1900–.
Kuehn, Manfred. *Kant.* Cambridge University Press, 2001.
Nietzsche, Friedrich. *The Portable Nietzsche.* Edited by Walter Kaufmann. Penguin, 1982.
_____. *Basic Writings of Nietzsche.* Edited by Walter Kaufmann, Modern Library, 1968.

_____. *Thus Spake Zarathustra. A Book for All and None.* Translated by Thomas Common, Edinburgh and London, 1909.

Spencer, Herbert. "The Physiology of Laughter." *Macmillan's Magazine.* vol. 1, 1860, pp. 395–402.

Townsend, Dabney, editor. *Eighteenth-Century British Aesthetics.* Baywood Publishing, 1999.

Winegar, Reed. "Good Sense, Art, and Morality in Hume's 'Of the Standard of Taste.'" *Journal of Scottish Philosophy,* vol. 9, no. 1, 2011, pp. 17–35.

The Justice of the Funny

Liz Sills

Funniness, in its capacity both to bring people together and to push them apart, is inextricably tied to concerns of harm and redress, that is, to justice. John Rawls tells us that justice can best be envisioned and dealt by people who view a situation through a "veil of ignorance" such that they do not know their stake in the system they effect—an "original position." John E. Seery takes that train of thought to an ultimate extreme, claiming that the veil must be such that one can truly conceptualize just human relations only if one has shuffled beyond the mortal coil and views the world from the after-life—a "final position." According to this orientation, then, we can understand the ethical implications of funny discourse better if we find a possibility for funniness in the original—or final—position. Unfortunately, these positions are usually discarded as mere thought experiments, so the prospect for any study of impartial justice in the effects of funniness seems remote.

Then again, one artifact does offer potential for real rhetorical analysis in this vein. John P. Harmon published a series of hand-drawn cartoons between 1944 and 1957 in a newspaper whose audience members had been forced to abandon their occupations as well as their family ties and to redefine themselves with an entirely new identity—a sort of ad hoc original position. What's more, most of this audience was considered terminally ill, or at least consigned to remain confined to medical care for the remainder of their lives—as much final position insight as one can afford during one's lifetime. This newspaper, the Carville STAR, was a publication based in the then-named National Leprosarium of the United States in Carville, Louisiana. Harmon's cartoons about everyday life with Hansen's Disease (leprosy) provided the colony's resident patients with some mirth in their isolated and terminal existence.

This analysis will examine Harmon's work to see what sources of funniness he probed as well as what species of funny discourse he most often drew from. His work will give us insight into what funniness might look like in an original or final position—a position that could be imagined as truly just—and therefore a glimpse into what a truly just form of funniness might entail. Although generalizing from a single case is always a little fraught, this unique case gives us some concrete play in the face of an otherwise purely theoretical field of inquiry that can bring the philosophy of humor to life in invaluable ways.

Justice in the Original Position

Using John Rawls' *A Theory of Justice* as the basis for our understanding of a just lifeworld is useful because he envisions such an extreme iteration of what a just society would look like. His is an extreme justice, one which, if it could be met, is designed to create an idyllic world of fairness and equality. L Wenar describes Rawls' aims and method thus:

> Justice as fairness is Rawls' theory of justice for a liberal society. As a member of the family of liberal political conceptions of justice it provides a framework for the legitimate use of political power. Yet legitimacy is only the minimal standard of moral acceptability; a political order can be legitimate without being just. Justice sets the maximal standard: the arrangement of social institutions that is morally best.

Rawls constructs justice as fairness around specific interpretations of the ideas that citizens are, in Wenar's words,

> free and equal and that society should be fair. He sees it as resolving the tensions between the ideas of freedom and equality, which have been highlighted both by the socialist critique of liberal democracy and by the conservative critique of the modern welfare state. Rawls holds that justice as fairness is the most egalitarian, and also the most plausible, interpretation of these fundamental concepts of liberalism. He also argues that justice as fairness provides a superior understanding of justice to that of the dominant tradition in modern political thought: utilitarianism [Wenar].

Rawls defines his parameters of social justice almost immediately in his treatise, declaring that "The justice of a social scheme depends essentially on how fundamental rights and duties are assigned and on the economic opportunities and social conditions in the various sectors of society" (Rawls, *A Theory* 7). That is, justice is equality of rights and potential. For Rawls, this distribution is something that must be decided in advance of the creation of society to ensure it functioning. That said, he admits that while people are rational, they are also "mutually disinterested," or "conceived as not taking an interest in one another's interests" (Rawls, *A Theory* 13). Given this not-quite-Hobbesian view of humankind, Rawls develops very particular parameters for the pre-societal perspective from which a just social organization can be created. He tweaks the state of nature presupposed by traditional social contract theory into what he calls "the original position of equality" (Rawls, *A Theory* 12), a condition that expresses the following attributes:

> The original position is not thought of as an actual historical state of affairs, much less as a primitive condition of culture. It is understood as a purely hypothetical situation characterized so as to lead to a certain conception of justice. Among the essential features of this situation is that no one knows his place in society, his class position or social status, nor does anyone know his fortune in the distribution of natural assets and abilities, his intelligence, strength, and the like. It shall even assume that the parties do not know their conceptions of good or their special speicla psychological propensities. The principles of justice are chosen behind a veil of ignorance. This ensure that no one is advantaged or disadvantaged in the choice of principles by the outcome of natural chance or the contingency of social systems [Rawls, *A Theory* 12].

Basically, the original position is one in which people sit down and design a just society with the benefit of the "veil of ignorance," not knowing their own place in said society, thus preventing events them from caving to their own self-interest and structuring society to their own advantage. That is, they are in an inherently just situation, and because their position is just, so are the conclusions they draw from within it. The most just society would be one created by people who justly know not their own advantage, as it were. Rawls later expounds that the society created thus would be closed—removed from other societies such that "members enter it only by birth and leave only by death" (Rawls, *Political* 12) and injustices of other societies cannot trickle in. This is not a moral justice, he points out—only a political one. But in its political nature it ensures that the structure of society is one in which citizens have opportunity to flourish.

Rawls' original position seems like an extreme thought experiment. Another scholar, however, opines that it is not extreme enough. John Seery, in *Political Theory for Mortals*, almost out-Rawlses Rawls. Cornell University press, the volume's publisher, summarizes Seery's mission as follows:

> Seery offers a new conception of social contract theory as a framework for confronting death issues. He urges us to look to an older tradition of descent into an underworld, wherein classic theorists consulted poetically with the dead and acquired from them political insight and direction … by rereading the politics of death in Platonism, early Christianity, and contemporary feminism. Building on those traditions, he proposes a new, constructive image of death that can serve democratic theory productively. Reconsidered from the "land of the shades," social contractarian theory is sufficiently altered that, for example, a pro-life Christian and a pro-choice secularist might be able to strike common ground upon which to discuss abortion politics [Cornell University Press, 2018].

Seery observes that the most just social contract would arise not from a primitive pre-societal position but from a mortal post-society one—a "final position" occupied by ghosts or "shades":

> The Final Position is also a position of near-perfect freedom, because the shades can finally be forthcoming with one another.... They are free to discuss everything and anything without consequence—at least no consequence in the sense that a superintending providence will weight their words and reckon their deeds. History, for them, is over. Their only real constraint is that they must now coexist with one another. The past becomes the basis for discussion. Hence they tend to hold each other, and themselves, accountable for actions in their past lives. A god does not judge them; no votes are taken. But the shades are not divested of all decency and responsibility simply because they are dead. They are capable of feeling emotions, they are capable of evolving in their understanding of the past, they make gains in knowledge, insight, and emotional maturity [160–61].

The advantages of the Final Position include an ability for the shades to have conversations as small as an interpersonal exchange or as vast as a debate throughout the entire society. There is no time limit in the eternity of the afterlife, so everyone may discourse for as long as they please. Seery also points out that whereas a naturalist "state of nature" or "original position" bespeaks a kind of universalism that seems unlikely to be attained in actual practice, the Final Position allows for individuality among shades and presupposes that they are accountable to one another more than to any kind of mutually understood cosmic tranquility. He directly rebuts Rawls as he elaborates his stance:

> Critics complain that Rawls mobilizes an idealized, tendentious version of personhood, or that the theory abstracts the individual into a hopelessly disencumbered self, or that his theory of justice is overly regulative, too crude and clumsy to respect persons and society in their full diversity and complexity. Shades in the Final Position, by contrast, retain knowledge of their past lives in their full former colorings. Hence there arises in the Final Position none of the problems associated with the veil of ignorance [Seery 164].

In short, while the notion that one must be removed from society and the potential for personal gain to truly envision justice still stands, Rawls finds that one must also have experience with the stakes of societal personhood to understand the importance of a just structure.

Of course, all of this theorizing seems rather frivolous. If we are to believe these scholars, we must also believe that we, as members of a fully operational society, are too blinded by our own self-interest to know what true justice might look like. (By the same logic, we would not be able to conceive of a notion of just funniness.) We have an idea of justice, but we also have an understanding that we can't have it and the whole notion seems relegated permanently to the realm of the Platonic forms. As scholars of comedy and humor we are left with little hope for imagining a world in which mirth could be fair or equal opportunity. Fortunately, the artifact we are about to examine gives us some hope for a real-life application of a justly created society in which people actually did find things funny, meaning that perhaps laughter is not always precipitated by superiority or inequality. To explore this potential, we will travel together to south Louisiana to explore a small society that seems surprisingly faithful to the principles outlined by Rawls and Seery.

Carville, Louisiana

From the late 1800s until the early 1960s, Carville, Louisiana, housed the only quarantine and treatment facility for patients of Hansen's disease (leprosy) in the continental United States. (Another colony at Kalaupapa Hawaii operated during roughly the same time frame but served mostly the indigenous Hawaiian population, which carries a high genetic susceptibility to the disease [Wong].) Located less than thirty miles south of the state capital of Baton Rouge, Carville was once the site of the idyllic Indian Camp Plantation on the banks of the Mississippi River. Leprosy had flourished in the bustling seaport of New Orleans since the late 1700s, but when the disease resurfaced in the 1880s the state legislature leased the plantation's former main house, slave quarters, and outbuildings in an attempt to isolate and care for patients.

Leprosy has been cognized in a frame of terror and contagion since Biblical days, and fear of its effects was so pervasive in South Louisiana at the time the Carville colony was founded that it was referred to as *la maladie que to nommes pas*, or "the disease you do not name" (Gaudet 4). This reputation stems from the fact that progress of the disease is, when left untreated, deforming and debilitating. It began, often, with the patient discovering patches of numb and/or discolored skin. They might also develop ulcers and lose their eyebrows or eyelashes. Since there was no real treatment for leprosy during much of the heyday of the Carville colony, patients there expected that they would eventually lose the use of their hands and feet, especially because the disease leads to the disintegration and reabsorption of digits. (Some patients found that their nasal cartilage was reabsorbed as well.) Many patients became wheelchair-bound, an outcome all the more common because the disease often led to blindness (CDC). In short, being sent to Carville was not a sunny outlook.

In the midst of medical progress toward effective treatment for Hansen's disease, people living at the colony were subjected to an existence completely devoid of hope. Residents were legally quarantined there until the 1960s, meaning that opportunities to leave the grounds were difficult if not impossible to come by. Previous relationships were lost overnight once patients were isolated at Carville; as if the quarantine were not enough, families were often so ashamed of the stigma of leprosy and fearful of contracting it themselves that they never made contact with their affected loved one again. Bragg describes the experience of Betty Martin, a patient who lived the vast majority of her life within the confines of the Carville colony and who, like many residents, changed her last name after her arrival to protect her family from the shame of her condition:

> The debutante disappeared 68 years ago, removed from New Orleans society like a piece of chipped china. A car pulled up to her house and carried her away, 60 miles up the dark River Road to a hospital compound guarded by tall fences and discretion.
>
> Nuns in white robes and stiff winged hats took the young woman inside to join the sick, the crippled and the anonymous. Back in New Orleans the neighbors wondered what had happened to Betty, the beautiful 19-year-old daughter of a proud family, but the secret gathered dust [Bragg].

Martin's experience was not atypical among her Carville peers. In the early days of the colony patients were dropped off by boat, in the later days by car, but the result was always the same: utter exile, despite the fact that many were only miles from their original homes, families, and workplaces. In the decades before drug therapies were developed, patients understood that a diagnosis of leprosy was a painful death sentence to be served in prolonged and complete isolation. Every patient at Carville had to pass through a period of profound trauma upon their arrival that marked a significant break in their understanding of themselves and their life, a break Gaudet points out that nobody was ever able to regard with any sense of lightheartedness or humor.

On the other hand, Gaudet, whose chronicle *Carville: Remembering Leprosy in America* remains one of the outstanding narratives about everyday life for patients at the colony, also observes that "the recurring humor in … Carville stories is striking. However despairing the circumstances, most of the narrators eventually saw sources of laughter in their situation, calling to mind Anatole Broyard's statement about his own life-threatening sickness: 'Illness is not all tragedy.… Much of it is funny'" (24). Once they had become acclimated to everyday life at the colony, patients often began to find some dark humor in their situation, leading to a spirit of jest about the disease that created a universal Carville common reality. When residents hosted their own Mardi Gras celebrations, for example, they prominently featured armadillos (who were being used as test subjects in Hansen's Disease treatment experimentation) on their floats and doubloons. Patients found amusement in wordplay as well as images: White remembers his confinement to Carville in terms of a terrible pun:

Three men were sunbathing on a shuffleboard court. Another man was zipping around the grass on a small, motorized four-wheeler pulling a trailer full of garbage bags. He drove the vehicle in my direction and stopped in front of me. He turned off the engine and let out a loud howl like a coyote.
"You know they got lepers here, don't you?" he said.
"I've heard."
"And you're a convict, right?" he asked.
"I guess so."
The man smiled and said "Then that makes you a lepercon!" [White 11].

Once the colony became a well-established treatment facility, it tried to allow this sort of lighthearted spirit to flourish as much as possible in the everyday lives of patients. The grounds were home to recreational opportunities in addition to shuffleboard and Mardi Gras parades, including a casino and a golf course. These activities were not escapes, per se, since the patients partaking in them were suffering from various stages of disfigurement and the golf course was located within spitting distance of the Carville cemetery. The point, though, is that moments of happiness were not impossible to come by even in such fatal surroundings. There was truly a sense of happy community—even society—within the Carville fences.

Perhaps one of the greatest bits of evidence that such a spirit existed is found in the Carville *STAR*, a magazine founded in 1931 by resident patient Stanley Stein as a mimeographed newsletter (Gaudet). The publication circulated both inside and outside of the hospital such that by 1967 it had reached a 10,000-strong readership (La Societe). Although the magazine incorporated a great diversity of content, one of its most remarkable features was a series of cartoons written and drawn by patient Johnny Harmon. Having spent three years at Carville in the 1930s after which he was released because his symptoms were so mild, Harmon re-entered the colony as a long-term resident in 1941 when his symptoms could no longer be concealed. Eventually becoming something of a Carville celebrity (and a prominent face of Hansen's Disease to the outside word), Harmon became involved with the *STAR* as a photographer and eventually also began writing funny comics for the paper under the alias J.P. Harris. These brief instances of comedy and humor take the sometimes uncomfortable facts of life at Carville and expose their lighter side, giving residents an outlet for laughter (or at least a smile) in their quarantined exile. As such, Harmon's *STAR* cartoons give us a unique opportunity to examine how comedy and humor might work in a situation where people have been robbed of most of their former outlets for self-interest (although they still remember them) and left to create their own society that functions in the constant reality of death—in short, something very much akin to Rawls' Original Position read through Seery's Final Position.

Harmon's STAR Comics

If we could exist in a condition that was so removed from everyday self-interest that we would have the capacity to envision a truly just society, would we laugh? Funniness, after all, is often the product of difference between people or of perceived threats to social stability (Epp 55). What's more, it is usually considered to be inextricably related to our self-possession: consider Smith's observation that

> The ancient philosopher said "Know thyself," but in the contemporary world the equivalent injunction is "Laugh at thyself." …humor is able to mediate between the paradoxes inherent in the contemporary idea of selfhood and the conflicting demands of psychological versus social modes of being … it is not surprising that in America today, the sense of humor has become the paragon of virtues. In this cynical age, we do not necessarily expect courage, honesty, industry, or loyalty from other, but a sense of humor is nonnegotiable [158].

In short, as anyone who ever got picked on at recess in elementary school can tell you, the precepts of funniness and the precepts of justice often seem to operate as ships in the night. But the residents of the Carville colony still managed to laugh together, as illustrated in the lepercon joke. This apparent dichotomy can make a big difference for our understanding of humor, thus prompting a closer examination of Harmon's *Carville STAR* cartoons to see what exactly people who are essentially living in the Final Position might be able to laugh about.

The archives of the *STAR*, fortunately available for free as part of the Louisiana Digital Library, date back to Harmon's permanent re-entry to the colony in 1941. The National Hansen's Disease Museum now located at the former colony also houses a display of Harmon's comics. (Both archives were used in this research: the images below were captured from the latter by the author or the former from the digital archive.) An examination of these resources reveals two major veins of funniness in Harmon's cartoons: the universal physicality of everyday life, and the conundrum of beginning again in the Final Position. Whereas people who are still mired in the self-interest of their subjective position in society might be more inclined to laugh at the misfortune of those with Hansen's Disease, Harmon's cartoons tend less toward ridicule of gravity and more toward egalitarian topoi.

Physicality

Consider the cartoon, published in the *STAR* in August 1945. Harmon depicts two men (both of whom appear to be in fairly robust health) chatting while one of them is on his way to see one of the colony's recreational film

The realities of life in south Louisiana without air conditioning affected patients' lives as much as their medical conditions did (The Carville *Star*, August 1945).

screenings. The bystander assumes that his friend is hung-over (a not uncommon occurrence in a facility that contained a casino and from which patients occasionally "escaped" through a hole in the fence to go drink at a nearby community bar) because he is carrying a fan and a block of ice. It turns out, though, that this patient is simply over-prepared for the lack of air conditioning in the movie theater. The material reality of the diversion was that it was physically uncomfortable, and patients who read this comic could laugh together at this shared inconvenience.

A similar spirit applies to an August 1944 installment of Harmon's cartoons that deals more directly with the symptoms of Hansen's Disease.

In another instance of standing and observing passers-by (one gets the

Even the pain of medical treatment could be addressed cheerfully with observational funniness (The Carville *Star*, August 1944).

impression that the flaneur was not an uncommon figure at Carville), two men who are again apparently in good health and wearing fashionable clothes discuss their colleagues who are walking around with one fist in the air. Eventually referred to as the "Promin Salute," the gesture is indicative of an individual who has just received a shot of Promin, a drug that was a popular and effective treatment for Hansen's Disease at the time but was also quite painful to receive. Again, the "Salute" reflects a common inconvenience—not a horror, not a disparity, but a condition of everyday life with which the paper's subjects can easily identify.

Beginning Again in the Final Position

As Seery establishes, one is not removed from one's trademark individual proclivities in the Final Position, and one still has memories associated with life in an unjust society. (This is evident at Carville nowhere more than in the period of intense trauma almost all patients experienced upon their arrival.) In short, you're still you even if you're only a shade of you, and the patients at Carville were very much still themselves, with memories of their origins and their former larger communities.

Harmon addresses these identities and proclivities in his cartoons as well, often ludicrously but sometimes with a wistful air. Take, for instance, his illustration to accompany an article about dating at Carville in the February 1946 issue of the *STAR*:

But all I wanted was a place to put a few dishes!

Carville residents could not escape the confining gender expectations of their era (The Carville *Star*, February 1946).

The image features the sorts of Thurberesque relations between a man and a woman that one might find in many 1940s periodicals. The man provides, the woman demands, and in return the woman performs traditionally feminine duties. The text of the article itself accents these relations:

There is only one woman to every three men in our patient population and when Dick stuck his big toe through a hole in his best socks he said, "I've got to do something about this," and he had no intentions of learning the intricacies of darning. To further aggravate an annoyed chap he hit three days in a row of stew, hash and goulash as the fare in the cafeteria. Thumbing through the pages of the Sears-Roebuck catalog [the patients's primary shopping venue] Dick began mumbling, "First off, I've got to order a red neck tie to match these socks. This little Sally from deep in the heart of Texas is some looker—and I bet she can cook and sew, too" [6].

The situation is so deeply enmeshed in the broader 1940s culture that it seems downright sexist to a modern audience. The man reifies the gender roles of the time because he wants someone to cook and sew for him and therefore considers dating a fellow patient. Is it a just situation? Absolutely not. But it is predicated on a memory of injustice—and in Harmon's cartoon the female figure seems to harbor a similar memory, because she is taking advantage of the new situation to make life easier for herself than it might have been on the outside. The Final Position in action, one might say—the characters are able to mitigate past injustices in order to create a new life for themselves similar to their vision of normalcy and desirability but also liberated, at least to some degree, from more intolerable circumstances.

A less laugh-out-loud funny comic, but one that certainly illustrates the spirit of the broader society, was published as the cover of the *STAR* in July 1945:

" . . . . . WITH LIBERTY AND JUSTICE FOR ALL."

The patriotic fervor of the World War II years left some residents wistful for life on the outside (The Carville *Star*, July 1945).

The National Hansen's Museum notes regarding this image that patriotism at Carville was quite high during World War II, but at the same time resident patients understood that theirs was an entirely different species of American-ness. Hansen's Disease patients were not currently eligible to vote, they could not leave the colony to enlist in the military, and they could not share the tribulations of their relatives whose lives were otherwise intertwined with the war effort. Harmon's comic expresses the feeling of impotence that comes in the Final Position when one can remember one's old allegiances but cannot act on them.

Harmon's cartoons, while no less whimsically funny or mirthfully thought-provoking than comics have the potential to be, reflect a reality that is busy considering a just social structure, albeit on a small scale. They provoke us to laugh at everyday foibles rather than at individual failures—they are comedy, not humor, in that way (Burke 39). They also acknowledge the society from which they came while reflecting upon it, exactly as a just contemplation of social structures is meant to do. This combination of laughing in the moment and laughing forward provokes us to begin to imagine what a more just species of funniness has the potential to look like.

Conclusion

Although the Carville Final Position-esque society was distant from more mainstream socialization, we must remember that the newspaper's identity as an agent of mass media meant that colony cartoons did not operate in a vacuum. What Berger observes of reproductions of fine art holds true for all images, even (and especially) funny ones: "The meaning of an image is changed according to what one sees immediately beside it or what comes immediately after it. Such authority as it retains, is distributed over the whole context in which it appears" (29). That is to say, images are contextual. People from the "outside" who read the *STAR* probably interpreted the funniness with a degree of revulsion or pity by dint of their lack of Hansen's. People from the inside may have read the comics with some mind as to how they would be interpreted by people on the outside. The rhetoric of the images affected both groups differently, and engendered polysemous interpretations of their meaning.

Our analysis here is not meant to function as an authoritative statement, therefore, about the effects of the Harmon *STAR* cartoons, nor have we identified any sort of categorically "just humor" that can be understood as such beyond the Carville situation. The nature of social justice as we have defined it precludes us from doing that, and from coming up with much by the way of generalizability. But if the society created from the original or final position can be understood as just, then the funny artifacts created in the original/final position of the Carville colony might be understood similarly. What this tells us is that funniness might have the capacity to exist in just conditions, even in the most extreme iterations of justice-as-fairness such as those proposed by Rawls and Seery. We commonly acknowledge superiority as one of the primary sources of laughter, and also tension reduction (Meyer). In a world populated by soon-to-be shades whose memories of their past lives are as real as they are distant, though, just funniness seems to stem more from human foibles, from everyday exchanges, and from common, whimsical sociocultural associations. Now, this is not an observation of vigilante humor seeking to redress wrongs, e.g., satire—that would be moral justice, and what we're after here is a broader political justice. What we see here is that *ceteris paribus* there is a way to laugh together without stratification, which in contrast with how we normally conceptualize funniness is remarkable news indeed.

WORKS CITED

Berger, J. *Ways of Seeing.* Penguin Books, 1972.

Bragg, R. "The Last Lepers: A Special Report; Lives Stolen by Treatment, Not by Disease." *The New York Times*, 1995, http://www.nytimes.com.

Burke, K. *Attitudes Toward History, Third Edition.* University of California Press, 1937.

CDC. "Hansen's Disease (Leprosy)." *Centers for Disease Control and Prevention*, 2017, http://www.cdc.gov.

Cornell University Press. "Political Theory for Mortals." *Cornell Press*, 2018, http://www.cornesspress.cornell.edu.

Epp, M. "The Imprint of Affect: Humor, Character, and National Identity in American Studies." *Journal of American Studies*, vol. 44, no.1, 2018, pp. 47–65.

Gaudet, M. *Carville: Remembering Leprosy in America.* University Press of Mississippi, 2004.

La Societe des Quarante Hommes et Huit Chevaux. "Carville Star." *Forty and Eight*, 2016, http://www.fortyandeight.org/carville-star/.

Mitchell, W.J.T. *What Do Pictures Want?* The University of Chicago Press, 2005.

Rawls, J. *Political Liberalism.* Columbia University Press, 2005.

———. *A Theory of Justice.* The Belknap Press, 1971.

Seery, J.E. *Political Theory for Mortals: Shades of Justice, Images of Death.* Cornell University Press, 1996.

Smith, M. "Humor, Unlaughter, and Boundary Maintenance." *The Journal of American Folklore*, vol. 122, no. 484, 2009, pp. 148–171.

Wenar, L. John Rawls. *Stanford Encyclopedia of Philosophy*, 2017, http://plato.stanford.edu.

White, Neil. *In the Sanctuary of Outcasts: A Memoir.* Harper Perennial, 2010.

Wong, A. "When the Last Patient Dies." *The Atlantic*, 2015, http://www.theatlantic.com.

Otherwise Than Laughter

Levinas and an Ethics of Laughter

STEVEN A. BENKO

Laughter and ethics are both social phenomena. Laughter is easier in a group setting and contributes to in-group/out-group dynamics. Ethics, as the effort to identify morally praiseworthy and blameworthy behaviors toward other people, is also social (Morreall, "Humour" 69). But where ethics is the effort to discern the right from wrong or the praiseworthy from the blameworthy, laughter is often occasioned by transgression but a transgression that might not be wrong or blameworthy. Indeed, humor is complicated because humorous transgression, offense, and inappropriateness are often praiseworthy, depending on one's perspective. The problem of perspective invites, if not anarchy, then at least relativism: who is authorized to say that a joke, prank, or skit has gone too far and crossed the line? For Lockyer and Pickering, editors of *Beyond a Joke: The Limits of Humor*, lacking a belief in the line, or at least being unwilling to accept someone else's drawing of it, is problematic because "if we accept that we should never draw a line between what is acceptable and what is offensive, then we can accept that anyone can say anything about other people, however malicious or laden with bigotry, and that they may do so with impunity" (Lockyer 16). It would follow, then, that there is a need for a line, but uncertainty about who gets to draw it and where it ought to be drawn.

While there are those who argue that there ought to be no limits on humor, others argue that historical events such as the Holocaust, violence against women and rape, stereotypes that further marginalize vulnerable populations, and a particular word that starts with 'n' are too wrong to be joked about. But people will joke and will offend, and, for that reason, it is essential to understand how, why, and when humor crosses the line. On the other hand, calls for restraint in the name of respect for the experiences and feelings of others slide into self, cultural or legal censorship. An ethics of humor and laughter is concerned with these questions because laughter is (supposed to be) enjoyable; laughter feels good. But is it a moral problem when those good feelings come at the expense of other people? Because we have all seen the pain on the face of someone harmed or wronged by a joke we cannot simply declare the work of an ethics of comedy too demanding, throw up our hands, and walk away from our responsibilities to and for others. Instead of thinking of the line that separates good (ethical) humor from bad (unethical) humor as somehow external to us, we ought to begin with the idea that what constitutes the line between good and bad humor is our orientation toward other people: what we see when we face them and how we understand our responsibility for that visage.

Ethics and Incongruity Theory

Incongruity theory, which posits that laughter erupts when one is pleasantly surprised by the sudden turn of a joke, can be analyzed from a variety of moral perspectives. Both a Utilitarian and Virtue Ethics approach to comedy of incongruity are useful for identifying and assessing, respectively, the nature of that violation and the potential harms that can come from humor that offends or a jokester who lacks the virtues of discernment and sensitivity to know when a joke would cross the line. In comedy of incongruity, a Utilitarian approach would have to be able to balance between the pleasant feelings caused by incongruity and whatever harms might come from the punchline that caused that pleasure. How would these have to line-up in order to speak with finality about the moral rightness or wrongness of the joke or laughter? Would it have to cause more harm than pleasure (fewer people laughed than not) AND the punch-line furthers harmful attitudes or stereotypes? But what if it the punchline furthered harmful attitudes or stereotypes but more people laughed (found pleasure) than not? The endless combinations of funniness relative to harm show why a Utilitarian framework fails to adequately address an ethics of comedy.

A Virtue Ethics approach would focus less on the outcomes caused by the incongruity but would instead determine moral praise or blame relative to whether the incongruity was in or out of character for the joke teller. This raises a host of questions that reveal the limits of a Virtue Ethics approach to humor, most obviously: if incongruity was in keeping with character, then it would not be incongruity. If incongruity were in keeping with character, then moral praise and blame would fall not on the punch-line or the effect on its targets, but on the character of the joke teller. The vice of racism is being judged more than the joke, and one does not need the example of a joke to judge racism as vile. Worse still, incongruity would allow a person to hide behind their character to avoid accepting responsibility for the consequences of their joke or what their joke might reveal about their character. How many times has a person avoided accepting moral responsibility for a racist or sexist joke because, they claim, they are not racist or sexist?

Both of these approaches do not adequately address an essential feature of comedy of incongruity: the presence of the surprise as not-yet-said within the conceptual schema of the joke teller and laugher. To understand the not-yet-said of the joke, it is necessary to understand how the brain anticipates and then processes the incongruity. Rod Martin describes the cognitive processes of comedy of incongruity this way:

> while we are hearing the setup of a joke, a schema (or script) is activated to enable us to make sense of the incoming information. However, information in the joke punch line does not fit with the schema, causing us to search for another schema that will make better sense. This second schema typically gives an altogether different (and even contradictory) interpretation of the situation, rather than just a slightly modified perspective. The second script does not completely replace the first one, however, so the two are activated simultaneously [Martin 86–87].

Studies have shown that in order to be perceived as funny, the interruption has to be obvious enough to be related to the joke and cannot be so obtuse as to have nothing to do with the original line of thought. To make this point, Martin cites a study by Wyer and Collins which concluded that "elicited humor is greatest when an intermediate amount of time and effort is required to identify and apply the concepts necessary to activate the alternative schema. If it is too difficult or too easy to find the second schema, less humor will be elicited" (Martin 87). In comedy of incongruity, when the joke starts, the punch line exists as a possibility within an ever narrowing field. There are many different incongruities that the joke teller can settle on, but, having settled on one, she has essentially chosen one not-yet-said possibility and made it real by stating that it could be, should be, or is the case. Laughing, then, is an admission that the state of affairs described in the punch-line is at least as possible as the state of affairs in the set-up for the joke, but the key point is that the punch-line was always there. Each punch-line that gets a laugh is a redescription of the current state of affairs: having laughed, the audience member is testifying that the punch-line can replace current habits, behaviors, or attitudes.

Comedy of incongruity reveals that the alternative frame or script is an un-said or not-yet-said within the laugher's conceptual schema. The surprise of comedy of incongruity is this not-yet-said being said, a not-yet-thought being thought. Replacing one conceptual schema with another, comedy of incongruity is a comedy of interruption—one state of affairs is interrupted then redefined or replaced by another. While the Utilitarian consequences of interruption are important, as are the virtues of the person who does the interrupting or endorses that interruption with their laughter, just as interesting and important are the conclusions that can be drawn from an ethics of interruption. An ethics of interruption applied to comedy of incongruity raises questions about the relationship between the said and not-yet-said, about the perpetuation of cognitive schemas and the ethics of calling them into question. Finally, an ethics of interruption asks if all attempts at humor are ethical. Laughter prompted by the perception of incongruity requires an ethic grounded in the same sort of alterity and interruption that prompts that laughter in the first place. While Emmanuel Levinas is more known for an ethics of otherness that focuses on the relationship between the subject and Other, his distinction between the Saying and Said in *Otherwise than Being* is an accurate description of what happens both cognitively and socially in comedy of incongruity and can better address the ethical questions raised when someone is offended by humor.

Levinas, Art and What Humor Must Do

To make an ethics of comedy from the work of Levinas is no small thing. As many of the authors who contributed to *Comedy Begins with Our Simplest Gestures: Levinas, Ethics, and Humor* (edited by Brian Bergen-Aurand) pointed out, art, generally, and humor, specifically, are problematic for Levinas. William Paul Simmons explains the problem of humor and enjoyment in Levinas by pointing to passages in *Totality and Infinity* where Levinas connected enjoyment with the perpetuation of the ego that is the root of violence against the other: "The movement to self in enjoyment and happiness marks the sufficiency of the I.... The I is, to be sure, happiness, presence at home with itself," and "only in enjoyment does the I crystallize," and finally, "In enjoyment throbs egoist being" (Levinas, *Totality* 143, 144, 147). Julia Lane writes in "A Clown in Search of Ethics" that Levinas's problem with representation was that its artificiality stifled the encounter with the actual other that inaugurated responsibility and substitution. She writes:

> Because they are simply spectators in the world as represented by art, audience members are called to participate in an experience that absolves them of their responsibility to hear and respond to the call of the Other. And yet these calls do not cease, and the spectator's "real world" responsibilities are not truly erased so much as they are ignored in favor of participation with the artwork [Lane 166].

When Levinas compares art to something that one should be ashamed of ("There is something wicked and egoist and cowardly in artistic enjoyment. There are times when one can be ashamed of it, as of feasting during a plague"

[Hand 142]). Lane takes him to mean that "when we are consumed by pleasure in reaction to a piece of art, we can forget that we bear a responsibility beyond the fulfillment of our own pleasure" (Lane 166). The general theme of these two concerns is that art and humor prevent the subject from recognizing its responsibilities.

In order for an ethics of comedy to be Levinasian than what happens in the telling of the joke, as well as the resultant laughter, must be more than a metaphor for how Levinas defines responsibility and substitution. In order for there to be a Levinasian ethics of humor then there has to be something about humor and laughter that prompt the subject (here, the laugher) outside of herself and toward the other. Humor and laughter have to undo the subject in a way that moves him toward responsibility. Here, the joke becomes an occasion for acting ethically and accepting responsibility for the other, or, alternatively, reasserting one's ego and doing violence against the other. Understanding and participating in humor (both jokes and laughter) as moments where responsibility for the other is a choice that the humorist and laugher can make prevents all parties from avoiding their responsibility with claims that it was "just a joke" and gives ethical weight to the phrase "just joking."

Incongruity, the Saying and the Said

Comedy of incongruity presents the option of responsibility for the other: the way that the incongruous punchline interrupts and violates the conceptual schema, disrupting, dislocating, and replacing it, so too the Saying is a possibility lurking beneath the surface of the Said that erupts onto the scene and replaces the Said with something new. In *Otherwise than Being* Levinas attempts to move beyond ontological language by explaining how Otherness emerges in the encounter with the Other in a way that does not reduce otherness to a theme (this was the critique of *Totality and Infinity*). For Levinas, the Said can consist of any statement with a settled or agreed upon meaning; Critchley defines the Said as a "a statement, assertion, or proposition (of the form S is P), concerning which the truth or falsity can be ascertained ... the content of my words, their identifiable meaning, is the Said" (Critchley, *Ethics* 7). In *Otherwise than Being* the Saying is the subject's exposure to the Other, and the ethical question is how the subject responds to the Other's approach:

> The saying is my exposure—both corporeal and sensible to the other person, my inability to resist the Other's approach. It is the performative stating, proposing or expressive position of myself facing the Other. It is a verbal and possible also a non-verbal ethical performance, of which the essence cannot be captured in constative propositions [Critchley, "Introduction" 16].

As a verbal act, the Saying emerges within the Said and restates it to unsettle it. Critchley writes that Saying, even if it is appears via a non-verbal performance, has "to show itself within a more complex discursive structure"—the Said—and that the Saying is not a bracketing of the Said. Levinas writes that the reduction of Saying to Said "could not be effected simply by a parentheses which, on the contrary, are an effect of writing. It is the ethical interruption of essence that energizes the reduction" (Levinas 44). The reduction of Saying to Said is ethical if there is a "continual contestation of the Said. The Saying shows itself within the Said by interrupting it" but Saying does not replace the Said (Critchley, *Ethics* 164). Saying remains as a residue within the Said. The Said is unavoidable but its totality is relativized by the presence of Saying—and possibility of another Saying—within the Said (Critchley, *Ethics* 165). Recall that in comedy of incongruity laughter only occurs if the deviation from the conceptual schema only occurs if the incongruity is familiar enough to be recognizable, but different enough to be surprising. Here, Saying would interrupt the Said and destabilize it by indicating that alternative meanings are always already present but suppressed by the Said. The interruption of the subject's schema is accomplished via an irony that unsettles the laughter's world and reveals the ethical significance of multiplicity, a surplus of meaning, and that any sense of closure is temporary at best.

Laughter emerges from an incongruity that was always a possibility within the schema shared by the humorist and laugher. Lane quotes Critchley who says that the origin of humor is in the disjunction "between the way things are and the way they are represented in the joke, between expectation and actuality" (Lane 182). In this way, humor provides new ways of looking at how things are and showing how they might be by revealing that it is not necessary for things to be the way that they are. When the comedian punctures the schema with a moment of incongruity, the integrity and soundness of the schema is violated; this is the Saying erupting in the Said, relativizing it, and destabilizing it. This intrusion of otherness calls the subject into question: how will they respond? If they are on one side of the line and substitution is on the other, how does the subject know whether to cross a line now that a line has already been crossed?

In comedy of incongruity, laughter is the effect of the interruption of the Said by Saying. What I have called the not-yet-said in comedy of incongruity is the potential for the schema, the Said, to be interrupted and called into question. Here, calling into question means that the world organized and made intelligible by the schema can be said otherwise; things in the world can be understood in another way. Brian Bergen-Aurand elaborates on this point in "Knock Knock/Who's There?/Here I Am Exposed...." Jokes are occasions to look again at mundane habits and experiences and see them differently. Jokes that attempt humor in incongruity suggest alternative ways of being: "Jokes show me the other side of things, prompt me to other ways of looking at things, things I have come to take for granted" (Bergen-Aurand 87). If the schema is the Said in that it contains propositional truth claims about the world and the subject, laughter is the reaction to the interruption by otherness. That interruption brings the joke teller and the laugher into contact with each other and otherness: "Jokes are jokes precisely because they alter reality in unexpected ways that affect the other by calling her to respond. They intend toward the other, so to speak, and in their intention expose me to the other" (Bergen-Aurand 93).

Laughing at Myself / Laughing at Others

Incongruity exposes the subject to their own otherness: laughter is spontaneous and uncontrollable and is the moment that the subject has become other to himself. Robert Bernasconi writes in "You've Got to Laugh: Levinasian Laughter and the Subjectivity of the Subject" that it is ethical (and in a Levinasian sense, necessary) to laugh at oneself first (with others). Here, laughter is both a physical and psychological loss of control: one loses control over oneself, and what remains from before the laugh is a question. Writes Bernasconi, when the subject laughs at herself she goes a distance from herself, from her ego. He cautions that not all laughter "can be described as a relation analogous to exceedance," but "Levinasian laughter is a form of exceedance because it answers the need to escape without my losing myself altogether" (Bernasconi 30). How Handwerk describes the impact of irony on the subject is relevant here: the coherence of the subject is called into question and left "constitutively unfinished and incoherent" (Handwerk 3). Adrian Peperzak writes, "the Other's face (i.e., any other's facing me) or the Other's speech (i.e., any others speaking to me) interrupts and disturbs the order of my ego's world, it makes a hole in it by disarraying my arrangements without ever permitting me to restore the previous order. For even if I kill the other or chase the Other away in order to be safe from an intrusion, nothing will ever be the same as before" (Peperzak 20). Laughter that makes the subject let go of himself—see himself differently than before—is "a shameful laughter" that "interrupts our pathetic self-aggrandizement [and] self righteousness of those who take themselves too seriously" (Bernasconi 32). This laughter is the first step toward recognizing the responsibility to the other.

Laughter from comedy of incongruity reveals the proximity of the Other (or Saying) in every Said. Saying, Levinas writes, "is the proximity of one to the other, the commitment of an approach, the one for the other, the very signifyingness of signification," and, in what can only be called ironic understatement continues, "perhaps because of current moral maxims in which the word neighbor occurs, we have ceased to be surprised by all that is involved in proximity and approach" (Levinas 5). Proximity reveals the presence of the Other as Saying and the presence of the Saying within the Said. Saying, as an interruption of the Said, dislocates the subject by revealing the violence of the subject's spontaneous freedom to make a world. Levinasian ethics is a critique of freedom and spontaneity: it is "the critical putting into question of the liberty, spontaneity and cognitive emprise of the gap that seeks to reduce all otherness to itself" (Critchley, "Introduction" 16). If the ethical question of enjoyment was whether the pleasure of laughter would make the subject reject responsibility for the other in order to enjoy the pleasure that is both the privilege embedded in the already existing schema and security that comes from remaining familiar to oneself, it can now be answered: "humor brings the figure of the hostage to the language of enjoyment, the face, and proximity" (Stock 62). It does so because of the asymmetry that exists between the joke teller and the audience: the audience is hostage to the joke teller and she is the catalyst of the violation of the schema (Said) via incongruity (Saying):

> Humor has its hold, it is the other under-the-skin; I am an other who can be immobilized by my vulnerability, even to enjoyment. Surely laughter can be faked, or I could doubt my own reasons for laughing, of I can come back, worrying even, about *why* I found something funny that I no longer do (or still do!).... Laughter is a form of proximity in the way that it indicates the ethical valences, stakes, and risks of saying.... The subject of saying does not give signs, it becomes a sign, turns into an allegiance. Beyond laughter there is an ethicality to humor that rests under my skin as a basic exposure to the humor of the other [Stock 67].

Levinasian ethics, notoriously difficult to read and (to some) perform is often defended as being as simple as opening a door for another and saying "After you!" In a Levinasian ethics of comedy, the question, just as simple and no less profound, is "Do you laugh, too?" (Stock 67). This simple phrase asks whether the butt of the joke is laughing at himself and if, as a result, they have been dislodged from themselves. If they are laughing too, then the joke teller and the object of the joke are in community. However, it would be a violence against the butt of the joke to laugh at them if they are not laughing, too. To laugh at them when they are not laughing is to reduce them to a theme, to reiterate Saying. The joke teller laughing at herself has become one-for-the-other; the butt of the joke laughing at themselves have become otherwise than they were.

Saying and the Said are not just about interruption of the conceptual schemas the subject uses to make truth claims about him/herself and the world. The interruption of the Said by Saying calls for an ethical response to the Other who is the occasion for that interruption. That ethical response is not in the sum total of the harm done by that laughter; consequentialist ethics does not apply here. In the effort to make someone laugh, comedy of incongruity is a more intentional and deliberate performance of Saying that makes every attempted joke and laughter an ethical moment. The question is not whether a joke or laughter harms some more than others or if it crosses a line that someone practicing the right degree of sensitivity or situational awareness would know how to avoid. A new set of concerns appears for those interested in the ethics of humor and laughter. The nature of the Said is to resist the Saying; a truth that gave itself up would not be true for long. Laughter, as an interruption of the Said, is an occasion to ask about the content of the conceptual schema that was just interrupted. Where did it come from? Why did it endure? What needed to be repressed in order for it to remain true or useful? What methods, tactics or strategies were employed for it to endure? The ethical moment that laughter is the effect of occurs in an instant, maybe outside of time, and is quickly reduced to a Said. The question then becomes, "what has just been said?" or "what new theme has emerged?" Beyond that one can ask about the violence of that new conceptual schema and for whom is it a violence against.

Perhaps the most interesting question is about the nature of laughter itself. Questions of whether that laughter is harmful or malicious and excludes or marginalizes people, or whether that laughter is sincere or open and invites people to a community can be subsumed under the question of whether that laughter admits to and invites the possibility of another Saying to interrupt this new Said. Is it a laughter that invites further incongruities? Is it a laughter that is open to the possibility of another interruption of Otherness and another Other? If it is a laughter that maintains the interruption of ordinary discourse—a laughter that the Said could not recover from—and the butt of the joke is laughing, too, then it is an ethical laughter. Frances Degnin suggests that laughter "might succeed in maintaining an interruption that ordinary discourse would recuperate" (Degnin 37). This would be, as Levinas puts it, a "laughter which refuses language" (Levinas 8).

A laughter that refuses language is the response of one who has been disrupted by Saying. Responding to Saying, one is responding to the Other whose approach is the occasion for the interruption of the Said by Saying. For Levinas, "Saying states and thematizes the said, but signifies it to the other, a neighbor, with a signification that has to be distinguished from that borne by words in the said. This significance to the other occurs in proximity. Proximity is quite distinct from every other relationship, and has to be conceived as a responsibility for the other" (Levinas 46). Laughter reveals the proximity of Saying within the Said and the subject's proximity to the Other person who is signified by Saying. In Levinas, Saying is an intrusion of otherness that the subject is responsible for recognizing if violence against the other is to be avoided. Therefore, the encounter with the other is an ethical encounter that the subject performs in relation to his/her disposition toward otherness but is enacted toward Others. The Other, though is encountered as a trauma and a wound. The form of the wound is, first, the interruption of the subject's possession of the world and, second, is the recognition of the subject's violence against the Other.

Where Saying is the wounding intrusion of the Other into the world of the subject, denial of this wound takes the form of violence against the Other that reduces the Other to Same or Saying to Said. Reframing the Other as the Same would deny the reality that the subject has been affected and changed by the encounter with the Other. The subject is formed and re-formed in the encounter with the other, different from the moments before the encounter with the other because they had not yet recognized the irreducible uniqueness of the other. To recognize that uniqueness the subject must become responsible for the Other's spontaneity or freedom by becoming one-for-the-other.

How Is Any of This Funny? How Is Any of This Ethical?

If the encounter with the Other is a trauma that leaves the subject wounded and dispossessed of his/her world, how can there be laughter? How can laughter from incongruity be a Saying that interrupts the Said if the incongruity is supposed to be a pleasant or a delightful surprise? Laughter occurs spontaneously and is an admission that there has been a suppressed surplus of meaning within the Said. The expression of this surplus meaning is experienced as incongruity and is delightful. However, the surplus of meaning need not always call into question the Said, it can just as easily reinforce it. When that surplus is expressed it can enlarge the Said, repeating and reinforcing its violence against the Other. For example, laughter at racist humor that reinforces stereotypes is laughter of incongruity—there is some surprise in the joke—but it does not alter the perspective of the laugher, it reinforces it. Suppressed by the Said is doubt or skepticism about the truth of that schema (that all people of one race are alike but people of another race are not). This incongruity does not penetrate the Said. Reinforcing the schema, it becomes more difficult for Saying to penetrate the Said.

Conversely, the interruption of Saying into Said can be experienced as pleasant or delightful surprise because one can enjoy thinking of something familiar in a new way. Or, one can feel relief that a truth that they have not yet been able to articulate has been spoken. Here, we must recognize the privilege and the power of the comedian to say things that others cannot.

Additionally, one can be surprised and find it delightful that someone else's Said is being disrupted and a particular conceptual schema has to be re-Said. For example, comedian Bill Hicks tells a joke about being accosted by two men who were offended by his jokes about religion. In Hicks's telling of the encounter, two men with thick Southern accents approach him after a performance and say, "Hey, we don't like what you were saying about Jesus." Hicks chortles and replies, "Yeah well, forgive me." Hicks's rebuke is an attack on religious ignorance, hypocrisy, and those who would threaten violence to defend a pacifist. His succinct reply is surprising and can be experienced as delightful—especially for one who has been experienced the violence of religious intolerance. Because the joke works on many levels at the same time—Hicks is literally asking the men for forgiveness, ironically pointing out that he knows more about Jesus than they do, and rebuking them for their lack of commitment to the principles of their religion by pointing out how demanding those principles are—it can be an example of ethical humor in the Levinasian sense described here if the men confronting Hicks laugh, too. The joke is an example of bisociation and how the constant reverberation of ideas continually generate new meanings (in this example, what it means to forgive). Do the men who confronted Hicks leave with a new definition of forgiveness or grace? Have they become other than themselves? Ethical laughter remains ethical if it retains the possibility to unsettle what has already been unsettled. Eventually, the saying has to settle down ("Anarchy cannot be sovereign, like an *arche*. It can only disturb the State—but in a radical way, making possible moments of negation without any affirmation" [Simmons 136]).

A further obligation is required though: to be truly ethical in the Levinasian sense, one must be prepared to hear that joke from the perspective of one who hears it differently. Simmons identifies this as a moment of solidarity: "When called to this deeper responsibility, the ego not only must respond directly to the other but must work in solidarity with the other in a sustained way to take on the system that has marginalized the other" (136). Laughter, however ethical, cannot be a violence against another other. For laughter to be ethical, Saying must reverberate within the Said and make closure and finality impossible. That would mean admitting the possibility contained within every attempt of humor that it is not funny to one someone, not the majority of someone's who hear the joke. Laughter interrupts a conceptual scheme and reveals its violence by bringing to light what was hidden within it. Any new conceptual scheme is at least a potential violence against some other. Ethical laughter is awake to the possibility that the Said could be heard another way. Unethical laughter, in the way that I have described it, both is that violence and uses laughter to perpetuate it.

Ethical laughter reveals my obligation to the Other. Saying is never far, perhaps closer, than Levinas imagined it was. If laughter reveals the presence of the Other, then the subject must admit, first, the violence against the Other that is unavoidable in the freedom and spontaneity of consciousness. Second, the subject must recognize that the desire to laugh at the incongruous is a desire for interruption. To want to laugh is to risk laughing at oneself, to risk being wounded, and the wound might be the price the subject pays for the pleasure of laughter. Laughter then can become an occasion to bear the burden of a new truth that must become the subject's truth. But every attempt at humor and every laugh has the potential for violence that one must accept responsibility for. The question is how to make humor an ethical interruption. Here, the social role of humor would be responsible critique, the taking up of the voice or perspective of those who cannot be heard in the Other's conceptual schema. Hearing and responding to them might be difficult, but taking up that responsibility through laughter might make the effort delightful and surprising.

WORKS CITED

Bergen-Aurand, Brian. "'Knock Knock/Who's There?/Here I am, Exposed….'" *Comedy Begins with Our Simplest Gestures: Levinas, Ethics, and Humor.* Edited by Brian Bergen-Aurand, Duquesne University Press, 2017, pp. 83–97.

Bernasconi, Robert. "You've Got to Laugh: Levinasian Laughter and the Subjectivity of the Subject." *Comedy Begins with Our Simplest Gestures: Levinas, Ethics, and Humor.* Edited by Brian Bergen-Aurand, Duquesne University Press, 2017, pp. 21–32.

Critchley, Simon. *Ethics of Deconstruction: Derrida and Levinas.* Second Edition, Edinburgh University Press, 1999.

_____. "Introduction," *The Cambridge Companion to Levinas.* Edited by Simon Critchley and Robert Bernasconi, Cambridge University Press, 2002.

Degnin, Francis Dominic. "Laughter and Metaphysics." *Philosophy Today.* vol. 39, no. 1, 1995, pp. 31–46.

Hand, Sean, editor. "Reality and Its Shadow." *The Levinas Reader.* Blackwell Publishing, 1989, pp. 129–143.

Handwerk, Gary J. *Irony and Ethics in Narrative: From Schlegel to Lacan.* Yale University Press, 1985, pp. 3.

Lane, Julia. "A Clown in Search of Ethics." *Comedy Begins with Our Simplest Gestures: Levinas, Ethics, and Humor.* Edited by Brian Bergen-Aurand, Duquesne University Press, 2017, pp. 163–184.

Levinas, Emmanuel. *Otherwise Than Being Or Beyond Essence.* Translated by Alphonso Lingis, Duquesne University Press, 1998.

_____. *Totality and Infinity: An Essay on Exteriority.* Translated by Alphonso Lingis, Duquesne University Press, 1969.

Lockyer, Sharon and Michael Pickering, editors. *Beyond a Joke: The Limits of Humour.* Palgrave MacMillan, 2009, pp. 16.

Martin, Rod A. *The Psychology of Humor: An Integrative Approach.* Elsevier Academic Press, 2007, pp. 86–87.

Morreall, John. "Humour and the Conduct of Politics," *Beyond a Joke: The Limits of Humour.* Palgrave MacMillan, 2009, pp. 69.

Peperzak, Adriaan. *To the Other: An Introduction to the Philosophy of Emmanuel Levinas.* Purdue University Press, 1993, pp. 20.

Simmons, William Paul. "Levinas's Divine Comedy and Archbishop Romero's Joyful Laughter." *Comedy Begins with Our Simplest Gestures: Levinas, Ethics, and Humor.* Edited by Brian Bergen-Aurand, Duquesne University Press, 2017, pp. 123–139.

Stock, Timothy. "How Humor Holds Hostage: Exposure, Excession, and Enjoyment in a Levinas beyond Laughter." *Comedy Begins with Our Simplest Gestures: Levinas, Ethics, and Humor.* Edited by Brian Bergen-Aurand, Duquesne University Press, 2017, pp. 61–81.10.

PART TWO

Laughter, Gender and Race

Minority Report

Joking About the Other

Rebecca Krefting

Introduction

Fairly standard for the venue even on a Tuesday night, I was tightly sandwiched between a friend and a stranger at the Comedy Cellar in New York City. One drink into the two-drink minimum, Jessica Kirson, a white Jewish lesbian took the stage. I had seen her only in small doses on television, five to seven minutes maximum, so this stage performance took me by surprise. That night her comedy was feisty, fast-paced, and aggressive; she had the audience rolling with laughter seconds after taking command of the microphone. About halfway through her fifteen-minute set, after making fun of Jewish folks, a group to which she belongs, she moved on to a story about ordering Chinese take-out. The audience responded most favorably to her impressions of the Chinese-American restaurant staff that positioned them as alternately inscrutable and ignorant. Cultural idioms and language barriers have long been the stuff of comedy in the U.S., and Kirson cashed in on such cultural differences that night. She is not alone, and the frequency of jokes that target and end up disparaging marginalized identities, or what I will also refer to as the Other, indicate their commercial viability.

Peddling divisiveness and prejudice that appears authentic is not generally good for business. Comics defend questionable jokes by citing intentionality. If the intent is to be funny, not harmful, then comics should have a right to share the joke. Stand-up comedy has a unique built-in mechanism for challenging reproach, i.e., "It's just a joke." Joanna Gilbert writes that "humor simultaneously advances agendas and disavows its own impact" (57). Assuming comics' intentions are good renders moot any criticism leveled by fans and/or fellow comics that some jokes *do* harm and are themselves hateful reinforcement of the most insidious beliefs we have conjured about Others. It is a conversation stopper and stifles serious inquiry into how and why jokes ridiculing marginalized communities continue to proliferate and meet with such success. And they do. Rhetorical strategies for joking disparagingly about race, sexuality, and other indices of identity are plentiful and cleverly crafted to mitigate audience disapproval and instead evoke pleasure. In general, the use of these tried and true linguistic mechanisms ensures positive audience reception. Herein, I identify a broad array of rhetorical strategies used to broach topics about identity and examine how stand-up comics navigate discussions and portrayals of the Other in their performances.

The invaluable scholarship of Raúl Pérez and Simon Weaver frame this project, in which I identify the ways that stand-up comics can and do joke about marginalized identities. I broaden current scholarship on the topic to be inclusive of multiple (and intersecting) identity categories. There is no single identity or confluence of identity categories—male, female, black, Jewish, queer, wealthy, or differently abled—from which such humor originates. There is also no single target or mode of attack. Comics employ these strategies in order to introduce bigoted beliefs about minorities. These strategies demonstrate the rhetorical patterns that make bigotry acceptable, which could include but would certainly not be limited to prejudices based on race/ethnicity, sexuality, religion, class, ability, nationality, and gender. Joking about Others can be done in ways that reinforce stereotypes and stock characters but can also be done in ways that challenge those stereotypes, for instance by deploying charged humor, a type of humor aimed at confronting social inequalities while simultaneously stoking cultural community and offering solutions for redress (Krefting). This is where possibilities for subversion abound.

Mapping Rhetorical Strategies

When it comes to joking about identity in the latter 21st century, the content and intent of the comic performer are characterized by ambiguity. This makes the task of interpreting jokes all the more difficult and offers comics greater leeway for dodging accusations leveled by listeners. To that effect, Giselinde Kuipers writes: "The polysemy of a joke makes it impossible to say with certainty which function it fulfills or what the joke teller meant: humor is by definition an ambivalent form of communication" (9). Humor exhorts ambivalence because it exists within a play frame—a comic may or may not mean what he says and audience members may or may not agree with a joke's premise just because they are laughing. Within comic frames exists coding mechanisms, what I am calling rhetorical strategies that cue audiences when it is appropriate or acceptable to laugh. Simon Weaver examines the ways racism abounds in British humor, paying attention to recent coding mechanisms for joking about the racial Other. He argues that racist humor is successful for a couple reasons: "First, there is the placement of cultural racism in a comic frame that is not serious and so, to employ Freud's terminology, an expression of tendentious discourse with a lower level of social disapprobation. Second, the rhetorical devices of humour provide key coding mechanisms which confuse and multiply meaning and interpretation, and so help to hide racism" (Weaver 104). Comic frames work to situate who does and does not get the joke; it is only funny if you have the requisite knowledge—social, political, cultural, etc.—to successfully interpret the joke (Eco). Comic frames allow for bigoted joking because it is always just a joke and coding mechanisms exacerbate uncertainty about the appropriate way to interpret it.

Common Sense Strategies

Raúl Pérez identifies what he calls the *"racial common sense* strategy— that is, acknowledging the pitfalls of engaging in discourse 'about a group you don't represent'" ("Learning" 488). More specifically, I argue that this entails a number of strategies that make allowances for jokes about Others, including: (1) establishing ally or insider status, (2) prolepsis or contextualizing jokes enough to position the comic as aware of and sympathetic to histories of oppression/subordination; this is preemptive work that identifies why listeners may be offended in order to ameliorate the offense before it happens, and (3) linguistic choices that establish a homogenous audience willing to assent to the premise of the joke. These strategies can be used independently of one another or in concert with any other strategies.

Stop me if you've heard this one: "My best friend is gay or black or Asian or Jewish…" This lead-in to a joke is perhaps the most familiar and popular rhetorical strategy used as preamble to jokes about minorities. These and countless other similar introductions to audiences signal a comic's quasi-insider status, that he exists in proximity to the group in question reassures listeners that he has a right to say what he is about to say. Black stand-up comic Malik S uses his gay brother as fodder in his routines:

I'm not gay but my brother's gay. My brother's in Miami so I called my brother. I was like: "N-slur, you need to move out here. There's so much dick out here for ya [*laughter*]." And my brother's really gay. I ain't making this shit up. He's a flight attendant so you know I ain't lying, ya know [*laughter*]. These dudes just walking around [*in a higher octave lisping voice*]: "Peanuts, peanuts!" [*laughter*] … My brother so gay he texts in cursive. I'm like, "how you text in cursive, goddamn?!" [*laughter*]. But one thing about gay dudes, you got to give them props. They always got money. You've never met a broke gay dude, have you? If you meet a broke gay dude, it's his first week, he just started, that's why. That's why [*laughter*]. His paperwork ain't go through yet [*laughter*].

Positioning himself as familial insider, close to, but not "of" the group, the audience grants Malik an allowance to make fun of his brother. But his brother is not the only butt of this joke—all gay men are—and the source of humor derives from stereotypes circulating about gay men: fey affects, pre-occupations with sex and money, and pink-collar professions that immediately identify queer men entering the field, e.g., nursing, teaching, and administrative work. Positing degrees of intimacy with the targeted group can justify what comics pass off as benign derision, particularly when situated in a comic frame.

The second strategy, prolepsis, or situating oneself as anti-bigoted before and/or after joking about an Other, reduces the likelihood of negative feedback from audience members. Herein, the comic operates in "anticipation of criticism" (Weaver 105). For example, this may entail bookending such humor with disclaimers situating the comic as anti-racist and knowledgeable about the legacy of racism, even as they make racist jokes. white stand-up comic Bill Dawes does precisely this, citing his own relationships with black women (signaling proximity) then criticizing his father for racist beliefs.

See, it's fucked up because my first girlfriend was black … and uh … she still is. But I grew up in a very racist area called the United States [*laughter*]. And my dad was … my dad's a Republican. Spoiler alert! Racist [*laughter*]! … My dad told me—I swear this is true, I'm just sharing with you guys—my dad said: "You know, Bill, in the Bible, God separated the races. He didn't think that white people should commune with black people." [*Whispers softly*] My dad told me that; that's fucked up right? That's weird. I know that's awkward [*laughter*]. [*Resumes normal voice*] First of all, the Bible is black, and there's proof in it that Adam and Eve were also black. You know Eve was a black woman. And I'm not just saying that because she was made from a rib [*sounds of disapproval from the crowd*]. NO! That's not—[*laughter; points to the Laugh Factory sign behind him, then gives middle finger to the crowd in a sweeping gesture from side to side*]. I'm saying because she was a strong, independent woman! She was in the garden, she was hungry. She saw the apple. She took it [*reaches for imaginary apple and bites into it*]. [*Assumes a sassy feminine voice*] Give me that apple, snake! [*Resuming normal voice*] It wasn't a white … you know it wasn't an Asian, even. An Asian would've eaten the snake [*laughter*]. [*Assumes an "Asian" accent*] Oh, put some duck sauce on that serpent. Gonna be delicious! Sweet and sour serpent! One special, number thirty-nine [*laughter*].

Prolepsis offers information about a comic's ideological leanings and confronts potential counterarguments in advance of telling a joke that could be read as insensitive. Here, Dawes positions his father's beliefs about interracial marriage as racist, and when the audience audibly objects to his claims that

Eve was a black woman because she was made from a rib, he attempts to recover by insisting Eve was black *because* she "was a strong, independent woman." Not a single objection can be heard following his mimicry of an Asian woman. He primed the audience for this joke's success while also cashing in on the public's high threshold for mockery of the Asian Other.

The third common sense strategy for entertaining audiences with jokes about groups to whom you don't belong establishes the audience as homogenous, like-minded enough to appreciate the jokes being dispensed. Comics achieve this through the "use of the verbal cues or 'keys' that signal[s] to the audience that they [are] a 'group'" and through oscillation between serious and humorous modes of discourse, remind listeners that any insults leveled are merely jokes (Pérez, "Rhetoric" 81,85). About this strategy, Pérez argues: "These strategies [work] to homogenize the audience while insulting them, and creat[e] a 'community of laughter' that [will] tolerate racial and ethnic ridicule" ("Rhetoric" 85). Verbal cueing remains a choice way of framing the performance as all in good fun amongst a community the comic works hard to establish as ideologically congruent. Repeated use of "you know," instead of "I know," continually draws the audience into collusion with the joke's premise, reinforcing and increasing the likelihood of positive responses. Use of plural pronouns establishing a "we" help to do that work; more importantly they delineate *us and them*.

Self-Deprecation Tactics

The use of self-deprecating humor or negative self-presentation functions as a way to level the power between audience and performer and suggests that if comics can make fun of themselves, then viewers should be willing to do the same. Self-deprecation usually draws from deficiencies in the following areas: cultural ignorance, intellectual failings, and social faux pas. These shortcomings communicate that the comic is neither smart nor culturally savvy enough to be politically correct. This can play out in a variety of ways, but commonly comics will employ self-deprecation as a platform from which to engage in negative other-presentation. white stand-up comic Chris D'Elia has made a career of employing this rhetorical strategy, ostensibly making fun of himself in order to make fun of Others without engendering animosity.

> I want to be black. I think that would be cool, just because then I'd get to wear whatever the fuck I wanted to. You know what I mean? black people—like I get clowned for what I wear—these shoes—[*assumes disapproving voice*] "Nice fucking dumb shoes, bro." [*Resumes normal voice*] I want to be black, man. black people could wear anything. If I was walking down the street, and I saw a black dude in full camouflage

gear sucking on a pacifier, with like, fake wings on his shoulders, [*laughter and clapping*] wearing—wearing a safari hat with a dildo sticking out of it. [*laughter*] Well, I would not look at that dude and be like: "What the fuck is wrong with that asshole?" I would just be like: "Oh, I guess he knows some shit I don't know. Fuck it." [*laughter and cheering*]. black dudes. They're the only race in the whole world that can wear cartoons on their shirt. Not only is that cool, that's some hardcore gangster shit [*laughter*]. Right? A black dude will roll up on you and be like: [*assumes voice of black gangster*] "Hey, what up, motherfucker? Owee, partner. Fuck y'all player. Haha, fuck y'all motherfucker. Y'all better recognize that's Dora the Explorer, motherfucker [*laughter*]! Yo, act like that shit ain't Charlie Brown right quick [*laughter*]! Say that shit. Buh-buh-buh-Blue's Clues, motherfucker [*laughter*]! Say that shit, J-Bro! Watch where it get you, motherfucker! That shit lay you six feet deep, player" [*makes cawing noise, three times; laughter and clapping*]!

Coding whiteness as awkward and bland, D'Elia appears to compliment black men as natural repositories of cool but his impression resuscitates beliefs about black men as brutes or savages. The price of insulting a black man's fashion choices could be a verbal altercation or even physical violence laying "you six feet deep." This rhetorical strategy appeals to comics who occupy dominant categories of identity because it acknowledges privileged identity categories but recasts that privilege with the illusion of inferiority. Employing self-deprecation from a dominant position seldom has the impact of impugning an entire race or sexuality. A white comic is not automatically assumed to be a spokesperson for her race; nor are the actions and beliefs of a heterosexual comic considered generalizable to all heterosexuals. Comics from marginalized communities may also employ self-deprecation. The added danger is that doing so doubles as mockery of them *and their communities*. Thus, self-deprecation may be interpreted differently coming from bodies marked/self-identified as Other.

When belonging to the category of Other, establishing membership is one way of obtaining audience approval for insulting jokes; self-deprecatory humor, even more so. After all, the comic is targeting her own community. For those belonging to a minority group, a simple reference to her belonging is sufficient foundation for joking about themselves and the groups to which they belong. Sierra Katow uses her mixed-ethnic background to lob arrows at herself, simultaneously demeaning her ethnic heritage and cashing in on stereotypes about Asian-Americans more generally.

And when it comes to dating … the Chinese part of me is like: "Oh, Sierra, find a nice Chinese boy to date." And then the Japanese part of me is like: "No, no, no, find a nice Japanese boy to date." Right, and then the American part of me is like: "I don't know, they're all yellow to me" [*laughter*]. Just pick one. There's like a bajillion of you guys. You do the math cause you're typically better at that, so [*loud laughter*]. Thank you, thank you…. I also don't speak either language. I only speak English. So, it's pretty weird. I'll go to like a Chinese restaurant and they're always coming at me speaking in their tongues [*laughter*]. And I'm just like: "Sorry, no hablo Ching-glais! [*laughter*]. [*Continues miming confusion*] Ahhhh, what?" Yeah, but you know they judge me cause they think that I'm a little less Asian cause I don't speak Asian. Yeah, and it hurts, feels a little awkward so I figured if that ever happens again I'm just gonna leave. And then drive away and crash into seventeen cars and be like: "Who's the Asian now, bitch? [*laughter*]. It's me!"

There is no mistaking this millennial's disdain for preserving, let alone observing, Chinese and Japanese cultural traditions, respecting ethnic values related to outmarriage, or knowledge of customs and languages. Further, the joke reinforces stereotypes about Asians—good at math, bad at driving— without a hint of irony. Katow's solution to being a bad Asian resides in fulfilling widely held stereotypes. And, as so often happens in the treatment of ethnic groups that are simultaneously racialized for the convenience of categorization (e.g., you are no longer Filipino, Vietnamese, Thai, or Indonesian; rather, you are raced as Asian), she collapses any cultural distinctions among Asians by calling them "yellow" and stating that she doesn't "speak Asian" (Tuan). While the focus is on the ways in which she fails in her performance of Asian-ness, the real target becomes Asian Americans, and occupying ingroup membership forecloses audience dissent.

Complimenting the Other

Praising an Other proves a valuable decoy for practicing negative Otherpresentation or reinforcing harmful and narrow perceptions of marginalized communities. Ralphie May, a white stand-up comic who gained a massive following before his untimely death in 2017 at the age of forty-five, boasted his ability to not be politically correct, but just "correct." He often impersonated racial minorities, making humor out of their cultural differences and just as frequently positioned himself as anti-racist and minorities as communities to be admired. This rhetorical footwork granted him permission to mock Others, as he does in the following bit about Mexicans.

I don't think the people who have made this law [*referring to anti-immigration legislation*] up have really thought it all out, you know? Think about it, folks. If we get rid of all the Mexicans, not for nothing, how are we gonna move? Everyone I know uses Mexicans. white people, black people, Mexicans use Mexicans, ok? I'm not talking about well-nourished American Mexicans with good bone structure and proper nutrition. I'm talking about the little mojados [*slur referring to Mexican undocumented immigrants*], the ones who sneak over the border that you get at the Home Depot, three for $50, or for $100 twelve of them will show up with three old ladies, an abuela, and two tías, ok. And it takes 'em seventeen minutes, seventeen minutes and they move all your stuff out of the house on one pickup truck. One! An upside-down pyramid, they stack it. It's incredible! Amazing engineering, amazing! No rope.

No rope! They just throw the littlest Mexican up on top and he holds down two mattresses and a coffee table. It's incredible [*laughter and applause*]! ... And these old ladies they're cleaning everything. And you're standing in the former shell of your house going: "Why are we moving? This is amazing! [*laughter*]! It was our crap that was messing this house up!" [*laughter*]. Man, Mexicans are amazingly clean. It's funny, when I did that joke, I was telling this joke and, you know I tell people that's where the term "spick and span" comes from [*audience signals shock: "ohhhhh"*]. Look it up! Look it up! Cause Mexicans are so clean, see? See first you think it's gonna be a racial slur then it turns out to be a racial compliment. Now who's prejudiced? [*points to the audience*] Not me. I love Mexicans. I was doing this joke in Orange County California about a month and a half ago, and when I did it a white lady stood up and said [*dons a high pitched voice*]: "We have to get rid of all those Mexicans, they're ruining our country!" And I was just amazed at her racism, you know?

One wonders why May was surprised by the woman's racism. He had just performed a bit that reinforced her existing beliefs about Mexicans as non-natives exploiting U.S. resources. May's joke functions as complimentary of Mexicans and Mexican-Americans while also invoking anti-racist sentiments to reassure audience members that the joke is all in good fun. He distances himself from racism, turning the charge of racism onto his audience when they respond unfavorably to his use of a term used to disparage Mexicans. May imagines that linking an oft-used pejorative to cleanliness undermines the power of the racial epithet and transforms it into a compliment. Invoking compliments, criticizing the audience members vocalizing opposition, establishing himself as anti-racist, and diverting to an example of actual racism (someone else's response after telling that joke)—the confluence of all these strategies lets him off the hook and ensures warm reception of this joke.

Distancing Mechanisms

Most jokes invoke multiple strategies to ensure positive audience reception. The rhetorical strategies considered to fall under the category of distancing mechanisms are commonly used in tandem with one another. There are three key rhetorical strategies that function to distance joke-tellers from bearing responsibility for the bigotry extolled in their jokes: (1) Third-person strategies that position comics as merely repeating what they heard rather than bearing those world views. (2) Modern-day minstrelsy or donning the affect of an Other for comedic purposes. (3) And, comics billing themselves as equal-opportunity offenders so no one can suggest that comics are targeting any group in particular. Comics invoking this strategy may also be referred to as shock comics. In the case of the first strategy, if someone else said it, the progenitor of the joke is not held accountable for any bigoted sentiment conveyed in the joke. Comics attribute such bigotry to family members, friends, and conversations overheard in a public setting, carefully positioning themselves as observers rather than producers of racism, sexism, or homophobia. Comics commonly cite their parents as purveyors of bigotry, as when Bill Dawes positioned his father as a racist Republican against interracial dating. This distancing mechanism negates criticism by emphasizing that jokes spring from the observable world; similarly, modern-day minstrelsy supposes that the comic is merely imitating real people.

Modern-day minstrelsy repackages stock characters within comedic discourse a la impersonation, as with Chris D'Elia's impersonation of a black gangster. In this example audience fear of this Other is mitigated by clothing incongruent (e.g., a t-shirt featuring Charlie Brown) with performances of hegemonic masculinity. Without donning visual signifiers used in 19th and 20th century blackface minstrelsy, like burnt cork or mock Chinese queues (a single braid extending from the back of the head), modern-day minstrelsy makes Others the target of humor by using accents, dialectical shifts, and body language. From Jewish folks to LGBTQ persons to black people to women, no marginalized group has escaped being impersonated for the sake of entertainment. I use the generic term minstrelsy, but this can be identified more specifically as: blackface, yellowface, brownface, Jewface, Arabface, or queerface (and more). Deploying modern-day minstrelsy functions to distance the jokester by imagining the impersonation as creative theatricality. Pérez observed that comedy coaches praised minstrelsy for invoking qualities of a savvy "dialectician" ("Learning" 493). Several of the jokes examined thus far included minstrelsy in concert with other rhetorical strategies: Malik imitating his gay brother, Dawes imitating a black and then Asian Eve, D'Elia imitating a black gangster. It is a crowd-pleaser but must be carefully contextualized and framed so as not to appear malicious or rooted in actual beliefs about Others' inferiority.

When it comes to the final distancing mechanism, fans easily let equal opportunity offenders off the hook for bigoted jokes because such a strategy invites the audience to laugh at everyone, not any group in particular. If comics target enough minorities, they need not apologize; rather, they can fall back on the comedic style of shock comedy as their modus operandi. Many comics position themselves as equal-opportunity offenders while negating any accusations of verisimilitude between their comic and off-stage personae.

This joking seems innocuous enough, especially when set in a context of playfulness, yet there are consequences to consuming comedy that denigrates Others. Donald Saucier, Conor O'Dea, and Megan Strain argue that humor disparaging Others results in the "devaluation of outgroups, often loosening norms that discourage expression of prejudice, and possibly producing negative attitude change toward the targeted social group" (77).

Another study concluded that participants observing someone else being ridiculed by a stand-up comic were more likely to exhibit higher rates of conformity and an increased fear of failure (Janes and Olson 2000). It is not surprising that the more someone fears failure the more likely he is to exercise caution when it comes to taking risks that might set them apart from their peers. In a comedy club this might mean audience members are performing their role as patron in ways that do not attract unwanted attention from the audience or comic. Another way of summarizing this data would be that they pull listeners into collusion with the values and ideologies being disseminated and reduces the likelihood of overtly challenging what appear to be shared bigoted beliefs. The greater concern is that beliefs about inferiority and an unwillingness to speak up when confronted with prejudice will transfer into the daily lives and activities of people consuming bigoted comedy.

Conclusion: Flipping the Script

Rhetorical strategies socialize audiences to laugh at the ensuing punchline. They help to situate the comic as having good intentions, offer context for sensitive topics, establish community consensus, and remind audiences that this is all in good fun. While I have attended exclusively to jokes that demean minorities, these strategies are recognizable enough that they can be used to set up socially just, charged jokes or to discuss issues around identity in conscientious and complex ways that dispel stereotypes and challenge ideologies that shore up bigotry. Comedy is as surprising as it is formulaic. Psychologist David Huron studies how the arts, music in particular, can generate positive emotions by appealing to anticipation. We move through the world with untold expectations: the sun will set, the car will start in the morning, students will skip class, and humor will entertain. Many expectations are primed through repetition because we are socialized to anticipate the pleasure or pain of an experience. Repetition is a key aspect of comedy—repetition of words, standard set-ups, and recycled punchlines; even comedy club interiors are designed to look alike, a comic stands in front of brick wall with a single microphone and possibly a wooden stool. Comics and laypeople alike learn what makes us laugh: wordplay, puns, silly incongruities, taboo content, self-deprecation, and so forth, and then rely on the comic frame and audience expectations to achieve comedic success. Huron points out that we reap additional psychological rewards when our expectations are accurate; in other words, "[w]hen the stimulus is expected, the emotional response is positively valenced" (13). Indeed, the reward for correctly anticipating something is strong enough that we often experience a pleasure response for accurate predictions despite an unpleasant outcome. As consumers of stand-up comedy, we expect to be entertained, and when recognizable strategies for delivering humor invoke a stereotype or convey a premise that flies in the face of our individual values, it is likely that we will still laugh.

Humor about marginalized identities does not have to harm. We only expect that it does so because it is woven into the fabric of what we think humor must entail. But, humor can reinvest value and meaning where that has been stripped—it can mend, soothe, challenge, and empower. Saucier et al. write that racial humor may be used "to cope with adversity and stigma," "allow minority groups to safely discuss their experience of prejudice," as well as "provide an educational or corrective function through which social lessons for appropriate social behavior, including how to respond to being discriminated against, may be taught" (79). In *All Joking Aside: American Humor and Its Discontents*, I write at length about the history and economy of charged humor, a type of humor that intentionally seeks to identify social injustices, foment cultural citizenship for marginalized communities, and offer solutions to redress the balance. Charged stand-up comics are intentional in crafting their humor, and they work hard to provide appropriate context so that listeners absorb their intended meanings. Fabiola Scarpetta and Anna Spagnolli identify this conscientious crafting and performance of jokes as building "interactional context" or the labor that shapes the "recognizability and acceptability" of the jokes performed (211). Utilizing staid coding mechanisms with appropriate context offers a way of framing jokes to achieve maximum audience enjoyment without disparaging marginalized communities. Director of London's 99 Club James Woroniecki argues that performing politically correct, smart comedy does not a dull comic make; rather, "A good comedian can track how an audience is feeling about a subject and make their jokes as clear and effective as possible" (quoted in Brown). Doing so helps mitigate ambiguity and controls interpretation of the joke. While beyond the scope of this project, one could chart the ways charged comics utilize the rhetorical strategies discussed throughout in ways that avoid disparaging or reductionist beliefs about Others. Skilled charged comics such as Hari Kondabolu, Aparna Nancherla, Maria Bamford, Patton Oswalt, Margaret Cho, W. Kamau Bell, and Chris Rock make a point to talk about identities in ways that confront bigotry and its consequences for marginalized communities. Rhetorical strategies for generating laughs are unlikely to change; however, we can demand that comics make ethical use of them.

WORKS CITED

Brown, Jessica. "Is the Snowflake Generation About to Kill Off Comedy?" *Independent*, 3 January 2018, www.independent.co.uk/news/long_reads/comedy-snowflakes-millennials-over-sensitive-jokes-political-correctness-pc-a8129756. Accessed July 9, 2018.

Dawes, Bill. "Bill Dawes—Interracial." *YouTube*, posted by Laugh Factory, 7 April 2010, www.youtube.com/watch?v=3DMo9mbufRo.

D'Elia, Chris. "Chris D'Elia: Gangster Style, Stand-up Comedy." *YouTube*, 2:39, posted by Laugh Factory, 12 February 2010, www.youtube.com/watch?v=7xgEJunCji4.

Dodds, Klaus, and Philip Kirby. "It's Not a Laughing Matter: Critical Geopolitics, Humour and Laughter." *Geopolitics*, vol. 18, 2013, pp. 45–59.

Eco, Umberto. "The Frames of Comic 'Freedom.'" *Carnival!*, Edited by Thomas A. Sebeok. Mouton Publishers, 1984, pp. 1–10.

Gilbert, Joanna. "Response: Stand-up and Identity, Laughing at Others." *Standing Up, Speaking Out: Stand-Up Comedy and the Rhetoric of Social Change*, Edited by Matthew Meier and Casey Schmitt. Taylor and Francis, 2017, pp. 57–67.

Huron, David. *Sweet Anticipation: Music and the Psychology of Expectation*. MIT Press, 2006.

Janes, Leslie and James Olson. "Jeer Pressure: The Behavioral Effects of Observing Ridicule of Others." *Personality and Social Psychology Bulletin*, vol. 26, no. 4, 2000, pp. 474–485.

Katow, Sierre. "Sierre Katow—Asian American Problems (Stand Up Comedy)." *YouTube*, posted by Laugh Factory, 17 September 2014, www.youtube.com/watch?v=yBWbc40JLRI.

Krefting, Rebecca. *All Joking Aside: American Humor and Its Discontents*. Johns Hopkins University Press, 2014.

Kuipers, Giselinde. *Good Humor, Bad Taste: Sociology of the Joke*. Mouton de Gruyter, 2006.

May, Ralphie. "Ralphie May: Too Big to Ignore—'Mexican Movers.'" *YouTube*, 9 July 2013, www.youtube.com/watch?v=34stHo3pSNc.

Pérez, Raúl. "Learning To Make Racism Funny in the 'Color-Blind' Era: Stand-up Comedy Students, Performance Strategies, and the (Re)Production of Racist Jokes in Public." *Discourse & Society*, vol. 24, no. 4, 2013, pp. 478–503.

_____. "Rhetoric of Racial Ridicule in an Era of Racial Protest: Don Rickles, the 'Equal Opportunity Offender' Strategy, and the Civil Rights Movement." *Standing Up, Speaking Out: Stand-Up Comedy and the Rhetoric of Social Change*, edited by Matthew Meier and Casey Schmitt. Taylor and Francis, 2017, pp. 71–91.

S, Malik. "Malik S.—Gay Brother (Stand Up Comedy)." *YouTube*, posted by Laugh Factory, March 10, 2014, www.youtube.com/watch?v=s0-Q7rm6acA.

Saucier, Donald A., Conor J. O'Dea and Megan L. Strain. "The Bad, the Good, the Misunderstood: The Social Effects of Racial Humor." *Translational Issues in Psychological Science*, vol. 2, no.1, 2016, pp. 75–85.

Scarpetta, Fabiola and Anna Spagnolli. "The Interactional Context of Humor in Stand-Up Comedy." *Research on Language and Social Interaction*, vol. 42, no. 3, 2009, pp. 210–230.

Tuan, Mia. *Forever Foreigners or Honorary whites: The Asian Ethnic Experience Today*. Rutgers University Press, 1998.

Weaver, Simon. *The Rhetoric of Racist Humor: US, UK, and Global Race Joking*. Ashgate Publishing, 2011.

That's Way Too Aggressive a Word

Aziz Ansari, Comedy of Incongruity and Affectively Charged Feminism

Steven A. Benko *and* Eleanor Jones

The most obvious approach to an ethics of comedy is content analysis: what does the joke say? After content analysis, the next logical step is to analyze whatever response the joke elicits: laughter, groans, applause, boos, etc. Both of these approaches to an ethics of comedy are asking about the moral appropriateness of what the joke gives rise to. To approach an ethics of comedy this way is to begin an ethical analysis after the fact. Therefore, if an ethics of comedy is about assessing the praiseworthiness or blameworthiness of what the joke gives rise to, one must also understand how the joke gives rise to the response (which could be laughter).

Most attempts to understand laughter focus on the event of laughter and less so on what comes before laughter. Theories of laughter, which include superiority theory, relief theory, and incongruity theory, emphasize the rational dimensions of laughter while downplaying or obscuring how the affectively charged space creates the conditions for laughter. More than the other theories of comedy, incongruity theory obscures the role of affect and the environment in creating the conditions for something like laughter in order to reserve for intellect the place where shifting conceptual schemas occur. However, those conceptual schemas will not shift if the audience is not affectively primed to shift their emotional and logical investment in an object, concept, term, or group of people.

Laughter from incongruity is found in all comedic formats; but to understand the relationship between affect and incongruity, stand-up comedy is perhaps the best site of analysis (see Thomas, *Working to Laugh*). If affect is the atmosphere that the comedian, venue, and audience co-create so that surprise, enjoyment, and laughter are possible, then how the affective charge of terms, concepts, and ideas are manipulated during the stand-up routine demonstrates that incongruity is not just playing with just concepts and schemas; comedy of incongruity also plays in affective and emotional spaces. The comedian is drawing from what is in the air emotionally (the affective changes in the space around those terms, concepts, and schemas) in order to create the incongruity that gives rise to laughter. While this analysis could focus on any number of comedians, this essay focuses on Aziz Ansari both because, like a lot of comedians, Ansari uses incongruity to generate laughter, but also because the controversy stemming from the publication of the *babe* article, "I Went on a Date with Aziz Ansari. It Turned into the Worst Night of My Life," revealed a potential incongruity about Ansari's persona that further demonstrates that incongruity only leads to laughter if the affective energies and emotional states present in the space cohere with, and then allow for, a shift in the audience's cognitive schemas.

Ansari's uses of incongruity are not different from other comedians: he uses standard comedic tropes (ironic word play, hyperbole, sarcasm, etc.) to make his audience laugh. Ansari is an effective comedian not just because of his skill with words but also because of the atmosphere he creates by playing in the space created by the different cultures he intersects with. Ansari is able to elicit laughter from his audience through the ironic juxtaposition created by the intersection of his biography (he is the son of immigrants, Indian, raised in South Carolina) and on-stage persona (he effects a hip stage persona by peppering his jokes with references to hip-hop and an ironic attitude that suggests he might be slightly too-cool-for-the-room, but he gives off a friendly and approachable energy). At the same time, Ansari is a comedian who understands how to use the affective charge attached to and around words to give his comedy (and by extension, himself) a politically progressive charge. Ansari deployed incongruity during stand-up and promotional appearances for more than just laughter (and to sell tickets), but he also elicits laughs by juxtaposing, then collapsing the difference between, feminism as equality with traditional family values. Doing so through irony and sarcasm, Ansari creates the incongruity of articulating an attachment to political ideologies and positions, in this case feminism, by being dismissive of misogyny and patriarchal structures that marginalize women.

Prior to the publication of the *babe* article, Ansari was able to present himself as a feminist who was selling a feminism (social and legal equality) that was safe for both women and men to embrace. After Ansari was #MeToo-ed, the atmosphere around him changed, and a further incongruity emerged:

the disconnect between the feminist persona he had crafted in his stand-up (as well his Netflix series *Masters of None* and his book *Modern Romance*) and the sexually aggressive predator depicted in the article. Charting these multiple and intersecting incongruities shows that affect is the precondition for comedy of incongruity. Incongruity does not occur in a vacuum. Comedy of incongruity is only possible because of the emotional attachment to words, concepts, and schemas are disrupted and shifted by the punchline. This attachment is more than emotional; it is also political because it shapes and contours how we understand ourselves and relate to others. The possibility of an ethics of comedy is understanding how affect works and how comedians use incongruity to play in and with affectively loaded terms and concepts. An ethics of comedy attempts to delineate when laughter is morally praise-worthy (because it changes the affective charges around terms and concepts so that the audience joins in solidarity with marginalized groups of people) from when it is morally blameworthy (marginalized groups of people remain at the fringes of society or are pushed further out).

Incongruity Theory, Charged Humor and Affectively Charged Humor

Incongruity theory, as articulated by John Morreall in his *Taking Laughter Seriously* (1983) and *Comic Relief* (2009), emphasizes the intellectual and rational dimensions of laughter. Laughing is an admission that the conceptual schema, or the way the laugher sees or experiences the world, described in the punchline is at least as possible as the conceptual schema in the set-up for the joke. Each punchline redescribes a conceptual schema that the audience member believes can be likely. This redescribed conceptual schema is inherently political because it reaffirms or reshapes the attitudes that draw the boundaries of ingroup/outgroup dynamics.

Humor, be it parody, satire, irony, etc., does political work when the ingroup/outgroup dynamic is reinscribed or upended. In her *No Laughing Matter* Rebecca Krefting identifies three interconnected ways that humor is political: cultural citizenship, cultural capital, and charged humor. First, Krefting distinguishes between legal and cultural citizenship. Where legal citizenship refers to the ability to own property and vote, cultural citizenship speaks to the ways that individuals and groups are represented in culture. Krefting writes that "we experience citizenship as both a legal arrangement and a cultural arrangement unique to our social coordinates" and these include race, gender, ethnicity, religion, nationality, sexuality, and age (Krefting 19). Cultural citizenship is a way to explain an individual's or group's place in society—their importance or lack thereof relative to cultural norms, attitudes, and values. With or without legal citizenship, an individual or group is a cultural citizen experiencing support, ostracism, inclusion, exclusion, admiration, or a lack of respect from others. This treatment is reinforced by the cultural norms they reinscribe. Humor can reinforce or undermine an individual's or group's cultural citizenship.

Charged humor "seeks to represent the underrepresented, to empower and affirm marginalized communities and identities, and to edify and mobilize their audiences" (Krefting 21). She calls it charged humor because the comedian attracts and repels the audience by charging them with being complicit in perpetuating social injustices at the same time that she suggests alternative ways of being. In using charged humor, the comedian "has designs on an outcome, specific or general—a change in attitudes or beliefs or action taken on behalf of social inequality" (Krefting 25). Charged humor invokes cultural citizenship by seeking "to remedy experiences of second-class citizenship by celebrating and developing cultural citizenship among minorities—be they sexual, racial, ethnic, corporeal, material, or otherwise—and their allies." Humor of this sort can be used to affirm identity, build community, utilized "as a coping mechanism for cultural exclusion and oppression, and to mock social conventions, particularly conventions excluding them or reifying bigoted beliefs" (Krefting 28, 71). Incongruous humor can be charged when there are changes in the laugher's attitude toward those who are denied equal cultural citizenship, but this is a conceptual change that is registered in linguistic description and redescription of the laugher's conceptual schema.

Krefting talks about how charged humor and the (sometimes uncomfortable) laughter it elicits being the occasion for changing the attitude toward those who are denied cultural citizenship. That attitude is shaped and contoured by the words used to describe those marginalized groups of people— this is the content of the humor that comedy of incongruity disrupts and alters. However, before the meaning of those words can change, there has to be a shift in the emotional investment in, and the intensity with, the way people relate to those words (which become attached to people). Charged humor is more than an indictment of the audience's attitudes toward marginalized groups of people. Humor charges when it alters the affective intensity attached to words or concepts. This affective intensity can further solidify the audience's emotional investment in that word (and by extension, the attitudes it shapes) by intensifying it, or the charge of humor can undermine or redirect that intensity of investment in words or concepts. Hyperbole, juxtaposition, irony, etc., produce the kinds of incongruities that shift or undermine affective intensities.

That Word Is So Weirdly Used in Our Culture

Ansari appeared on the October 6, 2014, *Late Show with David Letterman* to promote his appearance at Madison Square Garden. In an exchange about his girlfriend, Ansari pointed out that she was the occasion for him becoming a feminist. He asked the audience to applaud if they were feminists and used their response to begin a small routine about what feminism is. *Slate* writer Amanda Marcotte used Ansari's routine to comment on the current state of celebrity-feminist-bandwagon-joining. Criticizing Ansari for his initial Dictionary.com definition of feminism (men and women are equal; men and women have equal rights), she praises Ansari for moving the conversation beyond that to include specific, relatable examples of what equity would look like. Marcotte wrote:

> But, to Ansari's credit, he didn't stop at the bland declaration of a vague belief in equality. He gave a good example: "You're a feminist if you go to a Jay-Z and Beyoncé concert and you're not like, 'I feel like Beyoncé should get 23 percent less money than Jay-Z,'" he said. "Also, I don't think Beyoncé should have the right to vote and why is Beyoncé singing and dancing? Shouldn't she make Jay a steak?" [Slate.com on 2017-04-03].

Marcotte's commentary focuses on how Ansari used humor to make a logical argument about equality. She gives Ansari credit for "arguing" with people even though his give-and-take with the audience was nothing more than asking them to clap (or laugh) in agreement. The part of the exchange that Marcotte does not comment on occurs before the Beyoncé/Jay Z routine and focuses on how people feel about the word "feminist." Ansari said:

> But, I think the reason that people don't clap is because that word is so weirdly used in our culture. Now people think that word feminist means like "some woman is going to start yelling at em." Like Precious's mom is going to start throwing things at you. Like, that's why even some women don't clap, like, "I don't want that crazy bitch yelling at me! Like, no thank you."

As he says this, Ansari is leaning back in his chair, his hands up as if he is defending himself from a physical attack by feminism or feminists. Ansari is not talking about feminism as a series of arguments that can be made about equal rights for women. Ansari is talking about how the term feminism carries a negative affective charge that repels people. The negative energy attached to feminism can be used to prevent people from identifying as a feminist. It is impossible to hear feminism as an argument about the merits of equal pay for equal work, when the word connotes anger, uncontrolled emotion, and potentially violent actions.

Ansari's explanation and defense of feminism is an occasion to think about the affective dimensions of laughter. Broadly construed, affects are flows of energy that move between bodies and push in the direction for the emotions, feelings, and the thoughts that happen afterwards. Affect consists "of bodily capacities to affect *and* to be affected that emerge and develop in concert" because "a body is always imbricated in a set of relations that extend beyond it and constitute it" (Anderson 9). A useful metaphor for understanding affect is provided by Jonathan Haidt in *The Righteous Mind* (2012). In that work, Haidt evokes the image of an elephant and its rider to explain how affect and feeling are always ahead of, and are conditioning, thought. The elephant is the mind which is always processing and always thinking. But the mind does not think in a vacuum. The mind is immersed in and is responding to its environment. This environment pushes the mind in a direction, and there is then an emotional and intellectual response. Studies of affect treat affects and emotions as corporate and state individuals producing "regimes of feeling," or, affects are the flow of vital forces through bodies outside of, prior to, or underneath language, or affects are the way that the world prompts us to move before the interventions of language (Grossberg 192, Schaeffer 4, 9). Put another way, affect is the energy flow that nudges the elephant in a direction that the elephant then has feelings about. Affects are the a-signifying properties that objects and spaces can possess that set parameters for what can be signified. Thinking is not determined by the direction the elephant is heading, but the range of possible things to think is narrowed by how the mind is affectively primed by the space or environment. It is still possible to think otherwise than the way the mind has been primed or is leaning, but Haidt's experiments show that thinking otherwise takes longer and takes more effort. Similarly, once the elephant has been nudged and started moving in a direction, it is difficult to turn it back to its original path. If the mind has been primed to think negatively, then that negativity sticks to the next experience, and vice versa. Affects stick to words and concepts; they become the extra-linguistic meaning that words and concepts carry. The affects that stick to words gives them their social meaning by narrowing what words can mean.

The social dimension of affect is that individuals strive to match that affective intensity which allows them to map the physical and emotional spaces they inhabit. Shouse, quoting Grossberg, says that "affect identifies the strength of investment which anchors people in particular experiences, practices, identities, meanings, and pleasures" (Shouse 41). This makes affect an amplifier that adds a quantitative dimension to qualitative judgments that creates differences between experiences. As Shouse puts it, the sensations produced by affects "are enfolded by the body and combine to produce our level of intensity in a given situation" becoming "the body's way of preparing itself to act in a given circumstance by attempting to match the intensity of its context" (Shouse 35). Affect, then, is the energy that makes the individual possible by organizing them in their historical context; from Grossberg, "the organization of affect is a 'mattering map' that makes possible certain objects of investment (what we can care about) and certain modes of investment (how we can care about such things)" (in Supp-Montgomerie 339).

If affects are free radicals that can attach to any object and give that object an affective charge, then it is also the case that affects can attach to words and concepts. This opens up a political dimension to affect and comedy of incongruity. Thrift says as much when he justifies the turn toward affect in light of how, first, "systematic knowledges of the creation and mobilization of affect have become an integral part of the everyday urban landscape," and, second, because "these knowledges are also being deployed politically (mainly but not only by the rich and powerful) to political ends: what might have been painted as aesthetic is increasingly instrumental" (Thrift 58). Joking is not just about moving an audience to laugh; joking is about moving an audience to see things and people differently. Feminism is an affectively charged word with its own atmospheres that provoke a response. The word feminism can provoke an angry response if the group has a negative association with the term; that negativity is palpable and will contour the response of people in that space. In sensing the anger of the group, a person might become angry and be swept up into the group. Another person might feel shame that they are not angry when so many others are. Still another person might want to remain separate and alienated from the group and feel joy at their anger. Maybe another person feels that group's anger and feels unsafe. In another group, the word feminism might have a different affective charge and would therefore yield different affective states: happiness or joy for the feeling of solidarity or anger or shame for now feeling alienated from the group. Given the marginalized position of women in society, how does Ansari move someone who enjoys a position of power and status in society to invest in a feminist point of view (at least, how Ansari defines feminism)? What is in it for them to do so?

Ansari attempts to change the negative affective associations—change the affective charge attached to the word feminism—that people have toward feminism by using incongruity to redirect his audience away from its negative associations toward something more positive. Ansari does this by naming those associations and then attempting to change them by, first, invoking the negative charge, then exaggerating behaviors that would follow from that negative association, thereby making a feminist argument in a positively charged way. If the feeling that precedes the laughter is positive, has Ansari changed the affective atmosphere around the term "feminism?" If the idea of Beyoncé making less than Jay Z is so ludicrous that it can no longer be thought, then Ansari has changed how the audience thought they would experience a feminist argument based on how the negative emotional atmosphere that swirls around the word feminism because of its negative affective charge. Ansari does not meet the negative affect charges/atmosphere with its equally intensive opposite. To do so would produce conflict and stalemate. Instead, he meets those negative charges indirectly, incongruously, and he uses incongruity to show how incongruous anti-feminist thought is. More importantly: the joke as argument was pleasant to experience and the pleasant experience of the argument, which resulted in laughter, transfers to the concept "feminist" thereby altering the term's affective charge.

It can be argued that if laughter equals agreement, then when Ansari's audience laughs at a joke (and their laughter is a result of incongruity), their laughter is a sign that they have done the mental work of seeing where the joke was headed and being pleasantly surprised when the joke turned in an unexpected, but not impossible, direction. So if laughter is agreement, then Ansari's use of incongruity either reinforces his audience's attitudes or affects a change in their relationship to feminism as a social and political movement. Having arrived at this unexpected, but pleasant conclusion, they agree with its logic and possibility. The audience arrives at this point together because emotions are social. Individuals feel emotions together, and "emotions play a key role in the surfacing of individual and collective bodies" because emotions "align individuals with communities—or bodily space with social space—through the very intensity of their attachments" (Ahmed AE 117, 119). What Ahmed writes in "Affective Economies" that "together we hate, and this hate is what makes us together" is true of all affects and emotions: affects are a vital force that shape group identity and ingroup/outgroup dynamics. Ansari has reversed the negative charge that attached to the term feminism—a negative charge that attached negative feelings to feminism before feminism was even thought—and changed that charge to something positive such that to hear the word feminism is to now hear something positive. The happiness that people feel when they laugh can be the setting for surfacing a new collective identity. The possibilities for enhancing the status of a marginalized can then be said to rest with getting an audience to laugh at charged affective humor so that the positive affect can transfer to that community. That is not the only way to bring about social change or to build community, but in understanding the political work of affect, one can perform the political work of humor.

The Charge of Sexual Misconduct Allegations

The 2018 Golden Globe Awards occurred at the height of the #MeToo movement. Women had pledged to wear all black in a show of solidarity for the #TimesUp movement. As a continuation of his support for women and feminism, Ansari arrived at the awards ceremony in a black tuxedo and a #TimesUp pin. To some, the decision by men to show support for the #MeToo movement was suspicious because they wondered how long it would be before one of the "allies" would be accused of being a serial harasser like Harvey Weinstein (Cf. Framke 2018). Less than a week later *babe* published an article by Katie Way recounting a woman's ("Grace") date with Ansari in which she claimed Ansari, after returning to his apartment, pressured her into different sexual encounters before paying for an Uber to take her home. The article was controversial for a number of reasons, including the rushed publication, gaps in the story line, its labeling of Ansari as a sexual predator without establishing any corroborating facts or a pattern of behavior on his part, and editorial decisions that deviated from how publications like *The New Yorker* and *New York Times* had reported on other sexual assault allegations. Caroline Framke's "The Controversy Around *babe*'s Aziz Ansari Story, Explained" sums up the controversy around the *babe* article, but also explains why it was a controversy to begin with. More than just revealing the complexity of sexual behavior and politics in the #MeToo era, Framke explains what it meant for Ansari to be accused of being a sexual predator. After listing Ansari's feminist bonafides (referencing his TV show, his book, and examples of feminist jokes in his stand-up routine), Framke writes:

> I remember seeing Ansari practicing this months before, at a surprise set in a tiny Los Angeles bar. Part of me was frustrated at hearing truths that I and most any woman have known intimately our whole lives. But a bigger part was in awe that I was watching a male comedian say them, especially when so many others have used standup stages to play into countless sexist stereotypes. That set wasn't just refreshing—it was a relief [Framke 2018].

Ansari was supposed to be one of the "good guys"—someone that women could trust (and "Grace" says as much in the *babe* piece). Ansari, like Louis CK and other comedians who were accused of sexual transgressions/assault, went away for a while. The question of whether he could return and what jokes he could tell when he did return was answered in August 2018 when Ansari began workshopping new material for an upcoming comedy tour.

Ansari's return to stand-up comedy can be split into two distinct moments: in the first, Ansari was not overtly discussing the sexual assault allegation against him but was directly referencing the cultural norms and trends that led to it. These jokes were not well received. In the second, Ansari has course corrected by talking (not joking) about the allegations and how he hopes to have learned from them. Both moments are illustrative of how an affectively charged space can create an emotional atmosphere that creates the conditions for not only what can be said in a space but shape and limit the meaning of what is said.

When Ansari returned to stand-up, the elephant in the room was

108 Part Two: Laughter, Gender and Race

whether or not he would directly address the *babe* article. That anticipation—
would he deny it? Would he make light of it with a joke? Would he use the
stage to tell his side of the story?—was shaped by uncertainties over how
Ansari would balance whatever frustrations or regret he felt about that incident and how it was reported with his public feminism (Cf. Silman 2019).
Specifically, how would Ansari negotiate the claims that, in coming after him,
the #MeToo movement had gone too far and was undermining the credibility
of any future claims about sexual assault vs. his own history of supporting
women and using humor to shed light on what women endured? Put another
way, how could a guy who told this joke about "creepy dudes"—"You know
what I realized recently? Creepy dudes are everywhere. It really sucks 'cuz
women have to worry about creepy dudes all the time. And it's very unfair
because men NEVER worry about creepy women. That's not a thing."—either
still tell jokes about creepy dudes (totally ignoring the elephant in the room)
or, instead, tell jokes that try to steer the elephant in a direction that serves
him best (i.e., that he had been wronged, that he had seen the light and the
#MeToo movement was wrong, or, that based on his personal trials and reflec-
tion, he knew a better way forward). However, he wanted to steer the elephant;
the social nature of affect meant that he did not have complete control over
the environment he was in.

Where early recountings of Ansari's new material indicated that his first
approach was to try to steer the conversation away from any indictment of
him or his behavior and toward an indictment of cancel culture, by the time
that tour was filmed for Netflix, Ansari struck a more conciliatory note. Stories about the early performances on the tour reported that the climax of a
series of jokes about the extremes of wokeness culture and the nauseating
exhaustion caused by white liberals, who virtue signal by pontificating about
the last think piece they just read, was Ansari trying to convince his audience
about the controversy surrounding a pizzeria where the pepperoni had been
arranged in the shape of a swastika:

> He described rumors that the image of the toppings had been digitally altered, then
> admitted that he had made the whole story up. Hearing this, the crowd erupted in
> laughter at its own gullibility. "You people that are clapping," Ansari shouted. "You're
> the fucking problem" [Orbey 2018].

It was a made-up controversy but one that the audience readily believed.
Ansari played the victim and charged the audience with being lazy and believing anything they are told as if to say "don't believe everything you read on
the internet." These jokes were roundly criticized for their self-serving nature.
Writing in Vox, Anna North laments the early direction of Ansari's comeback:
"Before they were publicly accused, these men wrestled with thorny questions
of identity and power in ways that, while not always satisfying, were usually

thought-provoking. After the allegations, they began parroting tired complaints about political correctness" (North 2018).

These jokes failed to adequately respond to the moment and environment that Ansari found himself in. Ansari sold his feminism not just on the truth of the feminist claims he was making in his jokes (Beyoncé is more talented than Jay Z and, therefore, deserves to earn more money than him, ergo, all women deserve salary equity), but that he sincerely believed what he was saying. What made Ansari's feminism convincing and safe was that he meant it in a way that was not self serving. If the secondary accusation against Ansari in the *babe* piece was hypocrisy (the first was sexual assault), then what Ansari had to recognize was that the atmosphere around him had changed. The good feelings and trust that had attached to him because of the air of sincerity he generated by his feminism being both a critique of himself and culture had dissipated. He could not go from being a comedian who told sincere jokes that benefited women to being a comedian who told cynical jokes that served his own interest. It's not that those jokes could not be incongruous and funny, but given what was swirling in the atmosphere around him as he attempted his comeback, Ansari had to find a way to direct that energy in a way that it was already going.

Criticism from these jokes seemed to push Ansari in a different direction, ironically, away from jokes. Perhaps revealing the limits of sincerity and humor, or furthering the point that it is difficult to turn sexual assault into a joke, Ansari turned to concluding his stand-up routine with what is described as a genuine confession and genuine thank-you to the audience for giving him the opportunity to continue to perform:

> "If that has made not just me but other guys think about this, and just be more thoughtful and aware and willing to go that extra mile and make sure someone else is comfortable in that moment, that's a good thing," Ansari said.

He went on to express gratitude for the fact that people still show up to see him perform.

> "There was a moment where I was scared that I'd never be able to do this again," Ansari said. "You canceled whatever you were supposed to do tonight, and you came out in the cold, and you waited in line…. You did all this shit just to hear me talk for an hour and some change, and it means the world to me, so thank you so much" [Serotta 2019].

When the tour was filmed for the Netflix special *Right Now*, Ansari opened with the first quote and closed with the second, thus framing the entire performance as an apology and testimony to what he learned and how he changed. Sandwiched in between these statements, however, are jokes about the unfairness of judging one's past behavior in light of changing social mores, especially when those social mores change as fast as the attitudes toward sexual assault and violence with the #MeToo movement. Ansari jokes that if they were to reboot *The Office*, Jim would be fired for sexually harassing Pam and "in the series finale you find out that's what the documentary was: they were just gathering evidence against Jim" (Ansari). In a self-serving continuation of that thought, Ansari admits that some scenes from *Parks and Rec* have not aged well, and if he was given some of those scripts today, he would refuse to perform in those scenes. The double meaning of the title of the stand-up routine, *Right Now*, comes to the fore in these jokes: Ansari is commenting on/joking about what is going on right now, but his attitude toward those events (an attitude informed by his experiences of the last two years) is morally right, now.

For Ansari's apology to work, he has to recognize what affects and emotions had attached to him and the sexual assault allegations. The word "assault" has already steered the elephant toward anger, violence, and betrayal. A response or apology that intensifies these emotions would not be successful because they are the very intensities and emotions that apologies are supposed to de-escalate and assuage. For his apology to work, Ansari had to show that he was the same yet different. Ansari had to show that the positive affective energies that had attached to him were both still there and, because he had changed, that his audience could safely invest in them by trusting that they would continue to be there. This is why Ansari's apology works: first, it brings his sincerity to the fore. Second, by confessing his transgressions, saying that he learned something about himself, and then promising to be better, Ansari intensifies the air of sincerity around him and makes it safe for his audience to invest him in again.

Maps of Meaning and Incongruity as Critique

Comedy can be said to be ethical, and laughter morally praiseworthy, when existing social norms are subverted and ingroup/outgroup boundaries are redrawn to be more inclusive of those who had been denied equitable cultural citizenship. The boundaries that deny people equitable cultural citizenship are not just unreasonable, they are not solely based in reason. Therefore, to understand their constitution and flow is to understand how affects pull people together and push people apart by intensifying attitudes and beliefs. Affects act as an intensifier or inhibitor by opening up and closing off alternative ways of inhabiting a space, thinking about a concept, and relating to other people. Through incongruity, charged affective humor implicates the audience in the marginalization of groups with less social capital or cultural citizenship by showing how the energy flows and emotional atmospheres that constitute and perpetuate that inequity can be thought otherwise. The justification for arguing that charged affective humor gets people to invest in perspectives that lack cultural capital is that it can be pleasant and, in the resolution of the punchline, logical to think different from the social norm. The political work of affect, then, is to create maps of meaning that people use to navigate culture. Comedy of incongruity points to the fact that the laugher has other ways—unspoken, unthought of ways, but possible ways—of mapping the space. The political work of comedy of incongruity is to redraw those maps. The affective element of these maps are spaces of more or less intensity that influence how people arrange and navigate those maps. Already affected, the encounter with affects redraws the map by changing our affective investments with the people, groups, objects, concepts, or spaces that constitute that map. These ways of being in the space are potential maps that have not yet come to fruition, so there is not yet an intense investment in seeing people, groups, objects, or spaces that particular way. The political and ethical work of comedy is to shift those intensities so that other things come to matter. The comedic work of Aziz Ansari on feminism attempts to shift the tone and tenor of the intensity around feminism so that it is not threatening, angry, or violent. Incongruity can be understood, then, as a form of critique that is also an intervention that is meant to "create turning points in the here and now" (Anderson 15). Sarah Ahmed would call these interventions "good encounters" that is, encounters that give more to life or open up potentialities that have not yet been thought.

Works Cited

Ahmed, Sara. "Affective Economies," *Social Text*, 79 (Volume 22, Number 2), Summer 2004, pp. 117–139.

Anderson, Ben. *Encountering Affect: Capacities, Apparatuses, Conditions*, Ashgate Publishing, 2014.

Ansari, Aziz. *Aziz Ansari: RIGHT NOW*. Netflix, 2019.

Caplan-Bricker, Nora. "New Research Suggests Millennials Want More Traditional Relationships Than Teens Did in the 1990s." *Slate*, 31 March 2017, https://slate.com/human-interest/2017/03/millennials-want-more-traditional-gender-roles-per-council-on-contemporary-families-symposium.html.

Fernandez, Maria Elena. "Netflix is Happy to Make Another Season of *Master of None* 'Whenever Aziz Is Ready.'" *Vulture*, 29 July 2018, https://www.vulture.com/2018/07/netflix-master-of-none-season-three-plans.html.

Framke, Caroline. "The Controversy Around *Babe. net's* Aziz Ansari Story, Explained." *Vox*, 18 January 2018, https://www.vox.com/culture/2018/1/17/16897440/aziz-ansari-allega-tions-babe-me-too.

Grossberg, Lawrence. *Cultural Studies in the Future Tense*. Duke University Press, 2010.

Haidt, Jonathan. *The Righteous Mind: Why Good People Are Divided By Politics and Religion*, Vintage, 2013.

Krefting, Rebecca. *All Joking Aside: American Humor and Its Discontents*, Johns Hopkins University Press, 2014.

Morreall, John. *Taking Laughter Seriously*, SUNY Press, 1983.

_____. *Comic Relief*, Wiley Blackwell, 2009.

North, Anna. "Louis C.K. and Aziz Ansari Have An Opportunity for Redemption. They're

Squandering It." *Vox*, 9 January 2019, https://www.vox.com/2019/1/9/18172273/louis-ck-comeback-parkland-aziz-ansari-meto.

Oreby, Eren. "Aziz Ansari's New Standup Tour Is a Cry Against Extreme Wokeness." *The New Yorker*, 4 October 2018, https://www.newyorker.com/culture/culture-desk/aziz-ansaris-new-standup-tour-is-a-cry-against-extreme-wokeness.

Romano, Aja. "Aziz Ansari Says He Hopes He's 'Become a Better Person' Since Being Accused of Sexual Misconduct." *Vox,* 12 February 2019, https://www.vox.com/culture/2019/2/12/18222390/aziz-ansari-responds-sexual-misconduct-village-underground-comedy-set.

Schaeffer, Donovan, *Religious Affects: Religion, Animality, and Power*, Duke University Press, 2015.

Serota, Maggie. "Aziz Ansari Addresses Sexual Misconduct Allegations in Standup Set." *SPIN,* 12 February 2019, https://www.spin.com/2019/02/aziz-ansari-addresses-sexual-misconduct-standup-nyc/.

Shouse, Eric, "The Role of Affect in the Performance of Stand-Up Comedy: Theorizing the Mind-Body Connection in Humor Studies," *Journal of the Northwest Communication Association*, vol. 36, Spring 2007, pp. 34–49.

Silman, Anna. "Aziz Ansari's Comeback Show Was a Lot to Process." *The Cut*, 8 February 2019, https://www.thecut.com/2019/02/aziz-ansari-road-to-nowhere-show-review.html.

Supp-Montgomerie, Jenna, "Affect and the Study of Religion," *Religion Compass* 9/10, 2015, pp. 335–345.

Thrift, Nigel, "Intensities of Feeling: Towards a Spatial Politics of Affect," Geografiska Annaler 86 B, no. 1, pp. 57–78.

The *Boondocks* and the Ethics of Black Comic Rage

CHRISTOPHE D. RINGER

The "Trial of R. Kelly" may be one of the most memorable episodes of *The Boondocks*. Its scathing critique of R. Kelly, as well as what many experience as the counter-intuitive support of Kelly, established the episode as noteworthy. However, the episode misses an important opportunity to transform aspects of culture that adversely affect young black girls. I will argue this missed opportunity is rooted in an inadequate and incorrect explanation of the support of R. Kelly. More specifically, the satirical treatment of R. Kelly's support fails to account for the differences in collective identification based upon gender within the black public sphere. I'll pursue this task by first outlining the relationship between satire, society and social ethics. Second, I'll engage in a critique of *The Boondocks* through Russell Brown's theory of "black protectionism." And third, I'll argue that the recent scholarship of the role of affect in public life serves as a critical intervention for understanding the limits and possibilities of black protectionism as well as the satirical tradition of black comic rage.

Satire, Society and Social Ethics

The relationship of an animated television show and social ethics may not be immediately apparent; establishing a basic framework for understanding the relevance of the two is necessary. The ethical analysis of society presupposes culture, where culture is understood as interdependent of human activities such as economics, politics, morality, religion, and art that satisfy human goods. These goods can be necessary for sustaining existence (e.g. life, safety, leisure, or knowledge) or they can be subjective goods that ward

113

off alienation and provide peace of mind (Anderson 26–27). Satire, as a form of cultural criticism, can disclose the ideological distortions that contribute to human suffering and deprivation of human goods. Satire has served as a perennial form of cultural criticism. Within these interdependent spheres I want to define the relationship between cultural politics and political culture as well as the black public sphere.

There is a reciprocal relationship between political culture, the formal public institutions that organize our common life and cultural politics, and the various forms through which the members of a social group negotiate, contest, and make sense of themselves. Scholars have, as one might suspect, taken up different sides of the value of highlighting this relationship. Some have emphasized the importance of cultural politics for African Americans given our persistent exclusion from formal politics (Iton 4–5). Others are concerned that the effectiveness of political mobilization is threatened when focusing on popular culture which can confuse politics with "posing" (Reed 267). Still others see black cultural institutions as a rich source to make sense of the complexities of political ideology (Harris-Perry 1–35). I want to argue for a relationship closer to George Lipsitz who argues that cultural politics create "conditions of possibility, they expand the present by informing it with memories of the past and hopes for the future," and that "culture and politics maintain a paradoxical relationship in which only effective political action can win breathing room for a new culture, but only a revolution in culture can make people capable of political action" (Gray 5). Moreover, he argues that culture is not a substitute for politics but it can be a way to examine beliefs and values that are forbidden in social life but possible in art (Gray). Thus, in addition to critiquing and disclosing ideological distortions, satire as a cultural form also contains the possibility offering new normative visions of what could be. Although it is still the case that African American satire faces unique challenges.

Terrence T. Tucker has argued persuasively that we live in an age where comedy is a primary weapon to expose "the absurdity of ideological dogmas, hypocrisy and pop cultural/media failures" (22). In addition, he argues that hit shows such as *The Daily Show* and *The Colbert Report* express a deep anger and frustration with the state of our society. However, there is a distinct marginalization of voices of black rage that stand in a tradition of black humor that critique American racism. Tucker's argument has continued relevance given the short life of Larry Wilmore's *The Nightly Show* and Robin Thede's *The Rundown*. For Tucker, Aaron McGruder's *The Boondocks* is an example of comic rage that uses militancy and humor to "highlight the presence of white supremacist hegemony in the rhetoric of post-racial" society that obscures and discourages frank discussions about race (23–24). Moreover, I find Tucker's claim that *The Boondocks* resists both stereotypical representations of blacks as well as essentialized counter-representations to be accurate. When it comes to cultural critique, no social group is off limits in *The Boondocks*. In addition to its comic irreverence, *The Boondocks* takes advantage of a reconfigured black public sphere.

The idea of a black public sphere owes a debt to the idea of a public sphere articulated most forcefully by Jürgen Habermas in *The Structural Transformation of the Public Sphere*. Many of the assumptions in this work were critiqued for its idealized conception of European history that glosses over its exclusions and subordinations (Calhoun 109). The debates regarding the emergence of and contemporary existence of a black public sphere crystalized in the volume *The Black Public Sphere* produced by The Black Public Sphere Collective. Political scientist Michael Dawson argues that if by black public sphere we mean a "set of institutions, communication networks and practices which facilitate debate of causes and remedies" of the profound challenges our political economy presents to a vast swath of the Black community, then it has not existed since the 1970s (Black Public Sphere Collective 201). Others want to emphasize the presence of counterpublics where those who are excluded from dominant discourses can create and circulate alternative interpretations of their situation, identity, and interests (Black Public 157). Animating all these accounts is an ambiguity of discerning the contours of Black collective life in a post–Civil Rights era. Richard Iton goes as far as to argue for the presence of a "black superpublic" that marks a heightened visibility of blacks in American public life in the mid–1980s occurring simultaneously with a retreat from progressive politics in what he terms the "post-post–Civil Rights Era" (104). The trouble with Iton's account of a black superpublic is that it confuses questions of publicity, visibility, and market saturation within public life with our public sphere itself. I define the black public sphere as a range of interdependent and contiguous overlapping black mediating institutions and the various media technologies through which blacks negotiate the meaning of who they have been, are, and can potentially become in America life. *The Boondocks* is a prime example of the black public sphere as it began life as a syndicated comic strip prior to becoming a series on Adult Swim (Cartoon Network) and subsequently released on DVD. Thus, the series may be consumed and circulated in a variety of venues.

The Boondocks, R. Kelly and the Politics of the Black Public Sphere

At the center of *The Boondocks* are ten-year-old Huey Freeman and his eight-year-old brother Riley. Huey is the archetypal conscious-knowledge-dropping revolutionary whose youth frustrates his ability to carry out his freedom dreams. Riley is the face of an unexamined racial authenticity defined by thug life dedicated to "keepin' it real." Their suburban existence and the cast of characters provide an opportunity for McGruder to examine the deep complexities of race. Whether it is Jazmine's identification with white mainstream ideologies, the self-loathing of Uncle Ruckus, or Huey's embrace of conspiracy theories, McGruder examines the ideological complexities that come with race as co-present with gender, class and generational shifts. Huey and Riley's perspectives are brought into sharp relief in the episode "The Trial of R. Kelly."

The second episode of the first season finds the R&B artist on trial for child molestation and child pornography. An episode directly addressing conflicts with the black public sphere around the infamous video made by Kelly where he urinates on an underage girl. Tucker's interpretation of the episode rightly notes that when Kelly arrives at the courthouse there are two groups present. Riley proudly associates with the group of "unnamed African Americans barbequing and listening to R&B who staunchly support Kelly" (Maus and Donahue 29). Huey stands with a group of older civil rights activists and academics "who critique Kelly for the problematic images of race, gender and sexuality he promotes" (Maus and Donahue 29). The group of older civil rights leaders and activists are only three in number and include the unmistakable likeness of Cornel West. Such a small number implicitly questions the legitimacy, possible paternalism, and cultural exceptionalism of black scholars and activists in relationship to the broader community. In a similar vein, the other group is not simply featured barbequing. Rather, a large black woman eating a chicken leg while lickin' her fingers represents this group. Her support of R. Kelly is based on his musical talents. When confronted with the accusations against him by the opposing activists, she states "all they talk about is reading and eatin' right. If I want to get high blood pressure, that's my business!" ("Trial of R. Kelly" 5:39–5:50). This representation of opposing views on R. Kelly within the black public sphere is preceded by Huey explaining the black community's support of R. Kelly: "I think you underestimate the extent to which n-slur love R. Kelly" ("Trial of R. Kelly" 8:29). This binary representation of Huey's peoples, blacks who embrace truth, and Riley's people who deny truth in favor of bodily and aesthetic satisfaction, is the key to the trial. It is also important to recognize the historical backdrop of this representation.

Explorations of intra-class tensions within black comedy are not new. However, as Richard Iton has noted, during Jim Crow transgressive aspects of black comedy were articulated in such a way as to not register with white audiences (Iton 29). However, in post-civil rights era, such transgressive aspects of black comedy are now on full display for white audiences as well. Noting that many black comics position themselves in different ways as it relates to intra racial class politics, Iton notes an important difference between how

Richard Pryor uses the word "n-slur" and Chris Rocks' usage. Pryor used the term interchangeably with "black" as a sign of affection and solidarity highlighting issues of commonality within the black community (Iton 178). However, in 1996, Rock sent shockwaves throughout the black public sphere with a routine that drew a stark contrast between "black people" and "n-slur." Rock uses it as a source of contrast with "black" signaling his dis-identification with those whom he thinks the term applies (Iton 178). This is an important point as McGruder chooses to reiterate Rock's usage in the "Trial of R. Kelly." There is a slight difference in that Huey still feels like the "[n-slur] who love R. Kelly" are his people, although, there is a clear message that they are the problem. Another relevant point for analysis is the audience reception and identification with Rock's routine in the context of satire as it relates to *The Boondocks*.

In *Satire: A Critical Reintroduction* Dustin Griffin re-engages the thorny and perennial question of why we take pleasure in satire. More specifically, why does the satirist and those consuming satire take pleasure in what one critic has called rhetorical violence (Griffin 162)? The Freudian account emphasizes that satire allows for the expression of views and hostility that are prohibited by a given culture (Griffin 162). Another explanation is that when criticism is directed toward ourselves, such as Rock's war between "black people and niggas" and *The Boondocks* depiction of R. Kelly's supporters, we can receive it better with some comedy attached (Griffin 164). Other scholars have suggested that comedy that traffics in forms of self-hatred is a consequence of the dynamics of inclusion into the mainstream (Kessel and Merziger 166). Instead the role of satire in distinguishing between black people and n-slur in the context of Rock's standup and "The Trial of R. Kelly" is rooted in the complex intertwining of shame and linked fate within the black public sphere. This is a coupling which ultimately contributes to the inadequacies of McGruder's account of R. Kelly's support.

Scholars have found that through the experience of the social world, blacks largely believe their individual life chances are linked to the fate of the race as a whole (Dawson 11). Political scientist Melissa V. Harris-Perry rightly argues that linked fate can serve as a source of pride for an individual as well as source of shame (103). Guilt is associated with an individual act whereas shame is associated with the individuals themselves. As a political emotion, Harris-Perry argues that shame can be used to enforce the rules of a given community or to stigmatize that which renders one an outcast from a community (Harris-Perry 103). Together, linked fate and shame are critical to understanding the role of satire in "The Trial of R. Kelly."

The use of satire serves two critical purposes in the representation of blacks who support R. Kelly in *The Boondocks*. The first is the way that satire shames those who have failed to uphold a particular moral virtue. The other is a more complex representation of identification and disidentification. What distinguishes Rock's use of "nigga" from *The Boondocks'* is the former assumes a civil war within the black public sphere, whereas the latter is rooted in linked fate. Huey's revolutionary ideology and love for black people does not allow for a complete disavowal of those who support R. Kelly. The mode of satire that allows Huey to express hostility toward those whose support R. Kelly are both transgressing moral standards and holding back the race. As such, those who take pleasure in this representation may indicate that *The Boondocks* has tapped into a significant sentiment within the black public sphere missed by Chris Rock. The heart of this sentiment is expressed in the culminating scenes of "The Trial of R. Kelly."

During the trial, Tom DuBois, Huey and Riley's straight laced, black neighbor presents photos, eyewitness accounts, DNA evidence, and a video with R. Kelly facing the camera and taking a phone call where he gives out his social security number. In spite of all the arguments by both sides, the penultimate moment is when Kelly's attorney says, "this is the only thing that matters!" while placing a boom box on the table to play Kelly's music. At that point both judge and jury begin to move and sway to the music eviscerating what appeared to be a slam-dunk case. Huey intervenes by turning off the music and launching into the following speech:

> Hey! What the hell is wrong with you people? Every famous nigga that gets arrested is not Nelson Mandela! Yes, the government conspires to put a lot of black men in jail on fallacious charges! But R. Kelly is not one of those men! We all know the nigga can sing! But what happened to standards? What happened to bare minimums? You a fan of R. Kelly? You wanna help R. Kelly? Then get some counseling for R. Kelly! Introduce him to some older women! Hide his camcorder! But don't pretend like the man is a hero! And stop the damn dancing, act like you got some got damn sense people! ["Trial of R. Kelly" 16:07–16:45].

Huey's speech fails to carry the day. The music cuts back on and R. Kelly walks. As Huey reflects upon his failure to convince the jury and those assembled, he says somberly, "I did battle with ignorance today, and ignorance won. I admit that I'm often vexed at the behavior of my own people. Yeah, vexed is a good word" ("Trial of R. Kelly" 17:05–17:14).

Tucker's interpretation of this episode emphasizes McGruder's probing of the ways in which our ideas of authentic blackness can be manipulated by those in and outside of the African American community to "benefit certain individuals and behaviors, while excluding others based on arbitrary and often unstable criteria" (Maus and Donahue 29). Although this is true, this fails to account for the way McGruder chooses to present Huey's voice as the summary statement. *The Boondocks* here offers what we may refer to metaphorically as a split screen critique. The trenchant critique of the embrace of R. Kelly is explained as a failure of knowledge. Unlike Huey, the people are not as culturally and politically "woke" enough to understand the error of their ways. And moreover, the prosecution's central failure harkens back to Huey's opening salvo: the inability to appreciate how much "n-slur love R. Kelly." Ignorance and wrongly ordered love account for the response of black people to the trial of R. Kelly. Huey's speech also treads familiar ground in that this failure is rooted in a loss of community. A well-known account of this theme of a community lost appears in Cornel West's *Race Matters* where he describes the loss of "cultural structures of meaning and feeling that created and sustained communities; this armor constituted ways of life and struggle that embodied values of service and sacrifice, love and care, discipline and excellence" (West 15). One can hear this critique in Huey's lament and angry query as to what happened to "standards" and "bare minimums." Huey's vexation is not unique. Many in the black public sphere have looked with puzzlement at the visible public support of R. Kelly, a point explored in Katheryn Russell-Brown's *Protecting Our Own: Race, Crime and African Americans*.

Towards a Critical Black Protectionism

Russell-Brown's work attempts to navigate the curious territory within the black public sphere between interests and identification. More specifically, she examines why there are blacks willing to defend high profile figures accused of crimes regardless of their actual commitment to the black community. Russell-Brown defines black protectionism as "the response by large numbers of the Black community to allegations that a famous person has engaged in a criminal act or ethical violation. The response is protective in that it denies, excuses, or minimizes the charges" (87). To be sure, protectionism exists among all social groups. However, Russell-Brown effectively argues that black protectionism is specifically rooted in our historical response to racial injustice. Through an analysis of 34 cases from 1994 to 2004, four aspects make up the contours of black protectionism: (1) it is most often mobilized to protect black men; (2) its use is predicated on how famous blacks are treated by the media; (3) it is applied to blacks from a wide variety of political orientations; and (4) protectionism can be invoked for minor as well as serious offenses (Russell-Brown 34–44). Russell-Brown documents specific protectionist "trigger" questions that blacks invoke in response to the charge "Did he commit the offense?" First, "Even if he did, was he set up?" Second, "would he risk everything he has to commit an offense?" Or, "Is he the only person who has committed the offense?" And finally, "Is the accusation part of a plot to destroy the Black race?" By contrast, when faced with a famous black person being accused of a crime, whites only asked "Did he commit the offense?" (Russell-Brown 34–44). In contrast to pure ignorance or disordered affections, when placed in larger view of the history of blacks with the American criminal justice system, black protectionism is a complex and dynamic social phenomenon; a phenomenon not without its problems.

Russell-Brown acknowledges the benefits and drawbacks of black protectionism as currently practiced. The benefits are its ability to foster group solidarity that can resist society's stereotypes often depicted in the mainstream media (Russell-Brown 87). In addition, it provides a form of collective discernment weighing and balancing a person's moral or criminal lapses within the broader context of their life (Russell-Brown 88). Finally, black protectionism serves as a vehicle to challenge the legitimacy of the law and to articulate the persistent patterns of racial injustice rooted in American history (Russell-Brown 88). The major drawback of black protectionism is that it is rarely applied to black women in similar circumstances. In addition, an outgrowth of the practice being rooted in the history of false charges against black men is that it fails to distinguish between those who have engaged in misconduct and those who have not (Russell-Brown 90). Further, there is no concerted effort to require those who have received the benefits of black protectionism to feel obligated toward the black community (e.g., community service, etc.). Finally, black protectionism is often only offered to the famous as opposed to those whose social status offers little protection. Brown's full proposal for a renewed black protectionism is compelling and many aspects are being realized within the #BlackLivesMatter movement as well as in the case the #MeToo and #MuteRKelly movements (Russell-Brown 367). However, I want to focus on its value for sociological explanation and its relevance for comic rage as a practice of cultural criticism.

"The Trial of R. Kelly" is admirable and a courageous piece of cultural criticism. A key motivation is the abuse of young African American girls at the hands of a beloved singer. The episode serves as a critique of important aspects of critical black protectionism: the moral culpability of R. Kelly is foregrounded at the same time that there is a rigorous questioning of the criteria for who should receive the benefits of black protectionism. The failure of the episode is that it fundamentally misrepresents black protectionism as a social phenomenon: it represents black protectionism as solely constituted by the unreflective pursuit of bodily pleasure that trumps moral considerations and racial solidarity without political warrant. Moreover, the episode reproduces a stark moral contrast between the black masses and the black elite. It would seem that justice for the young girls rests solely in the hands of the black scholars and activists. Thus, the representation of the black masses in the episode literally represents the massification of the actual ideological diversity of the black public sphere. As such, the episode forecloses the possibility to represent a critical black protectionism even as Huey laments its absence.

I want to acknowledge that a particular challenge to McGruder's critique in "The Trial of R. Kelly" is the broader post-modern context through which a post-soul satire must articulate itself. The comic rage of *The Boondocks,* like traditional satire, holds up issues of human vice, folly, and injustice and critiques destructive practices throughout our culture. However, as Lisa Colletta has argued, "satire's efficacy relies on the ability of the audience to recognize the irony that is at the heart of its humor," and if "the irony is missed, or the better moral standard is also ironically presented as just another construction, then satire is no longer an effective social critique and may even be misunderstood as an example of the very thing it sets out to critique" (860). The challenge of post-modern satire is that it attempts to hold up a mirror to a society profoundly influenced by spectacle itself. The very responses to R. Kelly in the black public sphere are themselves spectacles. Thus, McGruder's critique in *The Boondocks* does not sufficiently account for the mediated representational economy through which its representational critique must intervene. The complexity of the historical experiences of injustices suffered by blacks within the criminal justice system circulates through media outlets that constitute the public sphere. The importance of Russell-Brown's work is to ascertain the motivations behind representational acts that McGruder seeks to satirize. This leaves us to another interesting question: given this new information, what would it take for the episode to engage in cultural criticism that might rectify some of the problems with black protectionism as currently practiced? One area that must be addressed is the issue of affect.

A critical aspect of the workings of black protectionism unexamined in Russell-Brown's account is the role of affect. In particular, the explanatory aspect of "The Trial of R. Kelly," is the underestimation of how much "n-slur love R. Kelly" fails to take into consideration the broader affective economy of black protectionism. Paula Ioanide's account of affective economies is worth quoting at length:

> Emotions shape the ways that people experience their worlds and interactions. They give people's psychic realities and ideological convictions (however fictional or unfounded) their sense of realness. Emotions cinch or unravel people's sense of individual group identity. They help motivate actions and inactions, often in unconscious or preconscious reflexive ways. Although they may seem fleeting and incalculable, emotions attached to race and sexuality have their own unique logics of gain and loss. Thus emotions function much like economies; they have mechanisms of circulation, accumulation, expression, and exchange that give them social currency, cultural legibility and political power [2].

In particular, affective economies of fear, anxiety, danger, desires, and pleasure can impact our ability to assimilate knowledge and participate in communicative acts (Ioanide 3). For Ioanide, hegemonic affective economies are those that reproduce structures of racism, nativism, and imperialism in the face of facts and evidence. Moreover, challenging the emotional investments includes cultural practices that can reorganize the way the public signs of race are invested with meaning. As such, black protectionism is also an affective intervention predicated on the history of racism within the criminal justice system deeply influenced by stereotypes of blacks as criminals. Engaging the issue of affect also allows us to grapple with the issue of gender that concerns both Russell-Brown and Aaron McGruder.

Challenging Colletive Identifications Through Black Comic Rage

The support of R. Kelly at the expense of the protection of young girls in the responses of the black public sphere is rooted in the precarious representations of black men in America. In *Rituals of Blood: Consequences of Slavery in Two American Centuries*, Orland Patterson reflects upon the relationship of two famous black men and their relationship to America: O.J. Simpson and Michael Jordan. Patterson rightly notes that Jordan was, to his own embarrassment, routinely thought of as a god. After scoring 63 points in a playoff game against the Boston Celtics, Larry Bird famously remarked "It's just God disguised as Michael Jordan" (Ryan). O.J. Simpson would become an American obsession and pariah as he embodied America's worst fears of black men as embodying unrestrained sexual and violent drives. Together they represent for Patterson the way blackness serves as the ultimate other in American history thus opening a cultural space for black men to be both demonized and deified, an "American Dionysus." Patterson's wide ranging use of classical, philosophical, and anthropological sources provides a compelling portrait of the ways black male bodies have simultaneously been the object of subversive pleasure and ritual brutality. The simultaneity of these representations that attach to black men in American society provides one-half of the questions regarding the gender disparity in black protectionism. In drawing on a more classical sociological figure, I want to argue that this same representational history occasions black men as having a totemic relationship with the black public sphere.

In the wake of the killing of Trayvon Martin by George Zimmerman in February of 2012, the lack of an arrest by the Sanford Police Department sparked widespread outrage. In addition to the 1.3 million signatures on a Change.org petition, rallies and protests were held across the country to voice anger over the inaction. Two objects emerged as symbols of Trayvon's death throughout the nation: a hoodie and a bag of skittles (Severson). While many Americans participated in these rallies and protest, within the black public sphere, black people in particular wore hoodies in solidarity. Elected officials including Congressmen Bobby Rush wore a hoodie during sessions, as did athletes and members of congregations. Through the symbol of the hoodie, Trayvon Martin also represented the precarious nature of black life in general and ongoing injustices in our justice system in particular. In a similar vein, one witnessed signs, t-shirts, and posters that read "I Am Troy Davis" in response to the execution of Troy Davis for killing a police officer in the state of Georgia (Marlowe)—a case where seven of the nine eyewitnesses recanted their statements and drew the support of human rights groups such as Amnesty International and figures such as President Jimmy Carter and Pope Benedict XVI. The slogan "I Am Troy Davis" speaks directly to the chances of a black person in particular being accused of a crime they did not commit. In both cases, the death of a black man represents the precarious nature of life and death for black people in America: black men have served in both life and death a totemic role in the black public sphere. The somewhat archaic term "totemic" is useful in these cases as it signals both a representational and affective economy as theorized by Emile Durkheim.

The aspect of Durkheim's account of the relationship between totems and collective life worth retrieving, absent reductive notions of the primitive and civilized, is that totems express the morality of a society. More specifically, totems mediate between collective consciousness and the consciousness of individuals, so much so that a representation or totem central to society's identity can operate without consideration of its ongoing usefulness or potential harm (Bellah 170). In addition, a society may also reject representations that challenge a totem's meaning as well as sanction actions that uphold it (Bellah 171). The salient point is that the inability for black women to have a totemic representational role in the black public sphere occasions an affective disparity within black protectionism. More pointedly, the same totemic relationship that allows the black public sphere to collectively identify with Trayvon Martin and Troy Davis occasions a collective identification with R. Kelly at the expense of the flourishing of young girls.

In order to realize Russell-Brown's call for a critical black protectionism, there must also be an affective intervention within the black public sphere. Here *The Boondocks* and the role of satire may be a cultural vehicle for that work. It would require however an affective shift within the episode. Huey, the primary narrative voice, would have to articulate both disagreement and *understanding* to challenge those supporting R. Kelly. Instead of Huey asking, "what happened to standards and bare minimums?" he would have to enter into the cultural logic of black protectionism to mine its possibilities and challenge its inconsistencies. For example, the episode could represent those supporting R. Kelly as asking the trigger questions or even a more robust debate within the black public sphere. The episode references that R. Kelly was nominated for an NAACP image award while under indictment. What is not referenced however is the significant outrage that prompted the NAACP to reconsider the honor as well as include a morals clause they stipulated for future nominations. In addition, the episode must establish an emotional connection to the young girl in the video as a representational strategy of black protectionism. Here is an updated version of the penultimate speech by Huey Freeman:

> Hey! I get the government conspires to put a lot of black men in jail on fallacious charges! I know we need to rally the troops to make sure our people get a fair trial. And maybe everyone doesn't deserve the full red-carpet treatment. Facts matter people! It's time to rally around the young girl in the video. Remember Rodney King? Let's let the world know that video evidence matters! What about Marian Jones, where were crowds at the press conference? Where were the claims of a conspiracy to strip her of her medals? None. Its time to step up our game! Now we all know the [n-slur] can sing! You a fan of R. Kelly? You Wanna help R. Kelly? Then get some counseling for R. Kelly! Introduce him to some older women! Hide his camcorder! But don't pretend like the man is a hero!

Now, I am no cartoonist or professional satirist. However, the desired effect of such a speech would be to render the social support for R. Kelly intelligible in order for it to be challenged. Leaving the social phenomena of black protectionism in the realm of ignorance closes the door to establishing a more accurate mirroring necessary for satire to do its work. And such work is sorely needed.

Postscript

The essay was completed before the airing of the harrowing "*Surviving R. Kelly*." The six-hour docuseries was expertly produced by filmmaker and music critic Dream Hampton. The series airing from January 3rd through the 5th of 2019 affirms two aspects of what I have argued in this essay. The first is that series demonstrates the tenacity of journalists and activists—largely Black women—to have the stories of young Black girls heard and their lives protected. As such, their efforts are eclipsed by *The Boondocks* binary representation of the Black masses and the Black elite. The second issue is the challenge of making an affective representational intervention in a society profoundly shaped by spectacle in general. In addition, to the heartbreaking testimony of survivors, "*Surviving R. Kelly*" documentary style reconfigures the familiar video footage of R. Kelly with eyewitness testimonies to reveal patterns that have been hiding in plain site. Citing the Lifetime series Cook County State's Attorney Kim Foxx called upon any accusers to come forward after her office was inundated with calls. (Peau) Foxx filed formal charges against R. Kelly on February 22nd of 2019. (Sedensky) It is a stunning example of what I have argued is the reciprocal relationship of cultural politics and political culture, or the formal public institutions that guide public life.

WORKS CITED

Anderson, Victor. *Beyond Ontological Blackness: An Essay on African American Religious and Cultural Criticism.* First Trade Paperback, Continuum Intl Pub Group, 1999.

Calhoun, Craig, editor. *Habermas and the Public Sphere.* The MIT Press, 1993.

Colletta, Lisa. "Political Satire and Postmodern Irony in the Age of Stephen Colbert and Jon Stewart." *The Journal of Popular Culture,* vol. 42, no. 5, October 2009, pp. 856–74. *Wiley Online Library,* doi:10.1111/j.1540–5931.2009.00711.x.

Columnist, Bob Ryan_____. "The Show Is Michael Jordan's, but Celtics Win in 2 OTs—*The Boston Globe.*" BostonGlobewww, https://www.bostonglobe.com/sports/1986/04/21/the-show-michael-jordan-but-celtics-win-ots/TbCPmZItluCnFzzIqP8PHM/story.html. Accessed 24 August 2018.

Crepeau, Megan. "State's Attorney Kim Foxx call on any R. Kelly accusers to come forward." 9. Jan. 2019. Chicago Tribune. https://www.chicagotribune.com/news/breaking/ct-met-r-kelly-kim-foxx-announcement-20190108-story.html

Dawson, Michael. *Black Visions: The Roots of Contemporary African American Political Ideologies.* University of Chicago Press, 2001.

Durkheim, Emile. *Emile Durkheim on Morality and Society.* Edited by Robert N. Bellah, University of Chicago Press, 1973.

Gray, Herman. *Watching Race: Television and the Struggle for Blackness.* University of Minnesota Press, 2004.

Griffin, Dustin. *Satire: A Critical Reintroduction.* University Press of Kentucky, 1994.

Harris-Perry, Melissa Victoria. *Barbershops, Bibles, and BET.* Princeton University Press, 2004.

Ioanide, Paula. *The Emotional Politics of Racism: How Feelings Trump Facts in an Era of Colorblindness.* Stanford University Press, 2015.

Iton, Richard. *In Search of the Black Fantastic: Politics and Popular Culture in the Post–Civil Rights Era.* Oxford University Press, 2010.

Kessel, Martina and Patrick Merziger. *The Politics of Humour: Laughter, Exclusion and Inclusion in the Twentieth Century.* University of Toronto Press, 2012.

Marlowe, Jen, et al. *I Am Troy Davis.* Haymarket Books, 2013.

Maus, Derek C., and James J. Donahue, editors. *Post-Soul Satire: Black Identity After Civil Rights.* University Press of Mississippi, 2014.

Reed, Adolph, Jr. *Class Notes: Posing As Politics and Other Thoughts on the American Scene.* The New Press, 2001.

Russell-Brown, Katheryn. "Critical Black Protectionism, Black Lives Matter, and Social Media: Building a Bridge to Social Justice." *UF Law Faculty Publications,* January 2017, https://scholarship.law.ufl.edu/facultypub/796.

_____. *Protecting Our Own.* Rowman & Littlefield, 2006.

Sedensky, Matt. "R. Kelly's Life mirrors that of Prosecutor who charged him." Associated Press. 23 Feb. 2019. https://apnews.com/69510c3852e24cbda7985232f15ac6b4

Severson, Kim. "Skittles Sales Up After Trayvon Martin Shooting." *The New York Times,* 28 March 2012, *New York Times,* http://www.nytimes.com/2012/03/29/us/skittles-sales-up-after-trayvon-martin-shooting.html.

Sister Citizen: Shame, Stereotypes, and Black Women in America. Yale University Press, 2011.

West, Cornel. *Race Matters.* Vintage Books, 1994.

Relief and Revelation

The Ethics of Comedy in the #MeToo Era
Through Dave Chappelle's The Bird Revelation

Olivia Moorer

During difficult cultural and political times, comedians across the board have taken up difficult topics to perform one of the main functions of comedy: to offer relief. Early philosophers questioned why we laugh and what function does humor perform for us. According to Freud's *der Witz*, the emotions which are most repressed are sexual desire and hostility, and so most jokes and witty remarks allow relief and articulate the cultural climate in ways that could allow us to face it with safety. This was not the case with Chappelle's controversial *The Bird Revelation*. Chappelle has performed as a relief comedian for years often engaging in topics of race, gender, sexuality, and politics throughout his other specials and through *Chappelle's Show*. His latest and final special, *The Bird Revelation,* does not follow his usual formula, resulting in great controversy and backlash. Chappelle's jokes about Louis C.K. and the #MeToo movement did not hold relief but rather brutal honesty through his raw opinions. This resulted in backlash assuming that Chappelle is not a support for women but rather one for a sexual assailant, and that he did not take the assault seriously. However, according to Chappelle, his comments are part of "the joys of being wrong. I didn't come here to be right, I just came here to fuck around," and that the cure for L.A. is in South Africa, where we must accept imperfect allies. Here, Chappelle decides to express controversial and difficult ideas that make the audience more uncomfortable with the current climate than relieved of it. This allows the audience to feel the same discomfort Chappelle does as a black man in the entertainment industry. In his final special, Chappelle ties his experiences of capitalism and racism to the current discomfort of the political and cultural climate, in a move to cause not relief through humor, but instead empathy and moral understanding from his audience, ultimately transcending relief theory.

Relief Theory in Action

Relief theory is a common understanding of the way humor works and what the job of the comedian is. First outlined in 1709 by theorist Lord Shaftesbury in which he believed "The natural free spirits of ingenious men, if imprisoned or controlled, will find out other ways of motion to relieve themselves in their constraint; and whether it be in burlesque, mimicry, or buffoonery, they will be glad at any rate to vent themselves, and be revenged upon their constrainers" (Shaftesbury). When John Dryden worked on his plays in the 1600s, he developed his own theories of comedy answering what we find funny and why we find those particular jokes funny. He distinguished between Comedy of Wit and Comedy of Humor. Comedy of Wit, for Dryden, was the highest form of comedy which reflected upon the joke's writer and those who enjoyed the joke, believing Comedy of Wit to require a higher thinking mind. Comedy of Humor, alternatively, required a lower thinking mind and little imagination (Gelber 266). In later comedy theory, Freud used this outline to write *Jokes and Their Relation to the Unconscious* where he outlines der Witz (jokes) and the purpose of laughter. He believed laughter is the by-product of superfluous energy the brain does not need to process nervous energy summoned by der Witz. Laughter is energy that would have kept emotions considered taboo repressed. According to Freud: "if there is a situation in which, according to our usual habits, we should be tempted to release a distressing affect and if motives then operate upon us which suppress that affect in statu nascendi [in the process of being born].... The pleasure of humor ... comes about ... at the cost of a release of affect that does not occur" (Freud, 293). More succinctly put, if the way a joke is told that can allow the audience to face a subject of life that should be distressing, but the motive allow the suppressors to relax, we experience laughter or relief. This is the aim of the comedian. The most popular comedians take something that should distress the audience and create the subject into something that rather is safe, allowing them relief. Moreover, Comedy of Wit and laughter from this type of comedy can perhaps earn less laughter if the audience does not have the capacity to imagine the joke, or if the writer does not execute the wit with tact. Therefore, often, comedians use Comedy of Humor to ensure the audience may understand and experience the laughter caused by distress and superfluous energy. This is the typical comedian's mode; and it is challenged in *The Bird Revelation*.

No Stranger to Controversy

Chappelle is a comedian who has always tackled issues of race, class, gender, and sexuality. On his first episode of the famed *Chappelle's Show*, he introduced one of his most famous characters: Clayton Bigsby, a blind, Southern, poor, racist, black man, showing the blindness in racism. Other sketches and characters from Chappelle include Black Bush, a version of Bush that only has black men working for him and says outrageous comments in public that juxtaposes President Bush as someone who acts in a lower American caste; "Black Jeopardy," where questions and answers are specific to the black community, bringing humor to facets of black culture that are considered lower in class in the American class system. He has never been afraid to, as he puts it in his latest special, "speak recklessly." Much of his comedy could be classified as Comedy of Wit aimed at a specific audience who have the imagination to understand why a Black Bush is funny. Chappelle has never shied away from controversy, nor has he ever shied away from discussing sexual misconduct specifically. Chappelle spent years making jokes aimed at R. Kelly about his alleged sexual acts including urination on his sexual partners, though it was not known at the time Chappelle was making these jokes that R. Kelly had been sexually assaulting women. Chappelle also made many jokes about Bill Cosby's assaults, as well as Michael Jackson and Ray Rice. Chappelle has a long history of joking about violence, especially sexual violence, toward women. However, in his latest special, *The Bird Revelation,* he earned great criticism for his comments on Louis C.K. and his sexual harassment toward women. I use the word "harassment" because there was no physical contact between C.K. and his victims, whereas if there were I would use the word "assault." This issue of wording is one I do not claim to be an expert of, and is something Chappelle explores in his special as well.

Speaking Recklessly

Critics of his special wrote headlines like "Dave Chappelle Calls Louis C.K. Accusers 'Weak' and 'Brittle' in New Special" (*Variety*), "Olivia Munn calls out Dave Chappelle for being 'tone deaf to the experiences of others' with his Louis C.K. jokes" (*Business Insider*), and "Dave Chappelle: Louis C.K. accuser has 'Brittle-ass Spirit'" (*Vulture*), to name a few. The New York Times gave a less scathing review of Chappelle in their article "Dave Chappelle Stumbles into the #MeToo Movement" but still calls his hour-long bit a "tired shtick" (Zinoman). A proven figure of tackling controversial subjects, Chappelle has seldom been the figure of controversy himself. It is no coincidence that in his last promised large-scale special be one of headlines about his jokes. Everything about the special noted different than the typical Chappelle, from the venue (a small club in L.A.,), to his appearance (Chappelle sat on a stool throughout the performance, fairly atypical for a stand-up). For those watching the special with intention, the entire set was atypical than Chappelle's typical routine. He offered little relief and instead challenged the audience with discomfort.

Chappelle begins his special with a disclaimer: "Sometimes the funniest thing to say is mean. You know what I mean? Tough position to be in. So I say a lot of mean things, but you guys gotta remember: I'm not saying it to be mean. I'm saying it because it's funny. And everything's funny 'till it happens to you" (Chappelle). He then opens up the true point of his special with the #MeToo movement and Harvey Weinstein scandal, showing his intention early on to be that of dealing with difficult topics to discuss, especially in the city where it is happening. He asks the audience "what is happening out here?" and references Weinstein, and Kevin Spacey as well as major predators for the city and acting community. After making jokes about Spacey's ability to "sniff [gay men] out," (Chappelle) and rape as the only way Weinstein could ever have sex, he reminds the audience of his position in the community as well. He is an actor and comic, and understands the cycle of abuse in the entertainment industry, being the reason he left it. After dealing with Spacey and Weinstein, he soon moves to Louis C.K., discussing his abuse toward women. In his special he says:

> One lady said, "Louis C.K. masturbated in front of me, ruined my comedy dreams." Word? Well then I dare say, madam, you may have never had a dream. Come on man, that's a brittle spirit. That is a brittle-ass spirit, that is too much, this grown-ass woman…. I know that sounds fucked up, I'm not supposed to say that, but one of these ladies was like, "Louis C.K. was masturbating while I was on the phone with him," Bitch, you don't know how to hang up a phone? How the fuck are you going to survive in show business if this is an actual obstacle to your dreams?

Chappelle is referring to writer Abby Schachner, a more public victim of C.K. After these jokes, he asks the audience if C.K.'s abuse is as bad as Spacey or Weinstein's, saying "it might be disproportionate, I can't tell." At this point in the special, the room is silent. There is no laughter, and a fog machine clearly begins surrounding Chappelle in mist. There is no relief for the audience in the same way there was with his jokes on Weinstein and Spacey. For those two, it is clear everyone in the room agreed on their monstrosity. For C.K., it is clear the room is tense. This is where Chappelle begins the point of his special, which is not to give answers to the audience on divisive and violent issues, but to rather incite some thought. Before, Chappelle was making the judgments for us. Here, he asks us how we as a society must address sexual assault and sexual harassment, and more specifically, do they deserve the same punishment? He finishes this segment with "I know Louis is wrong, ma'am, I'm just saying, I'm held to a higher standard of accountability than these women are" (Chappelle).

Relief and Reconciliation

Chappelle's theme of not answering questions for us is continued through the rest of the special, connecting the #MeToo movement to the Civil Rights movement and its legacies that extend to today, ultimately comparing racism and the black community's response with sexism and the current response of #MeToo. He reminds the audience who he is, a black man. He reminds the audience what he did, which was flee show-business and leave for South Africa, for a over decade, without any notice after three years of consecutive Primetime Emmy Award nominations and a $50 million contract with Viacom. He teases the audience while smoking alluding that he will finally break the silence on why he left Hollywood, a mystery up until this point. He then offers some wisdom to his audience, and greater #MeToo era activists at large: the cure for L.A. is in South Africa, specifically how the country handled apartheid. He says

> The end of apartheid should have been a fucking bloodbath by any metric in human history, and it wasn't. The only reason it wasn't is because Desmond Tutu and Mandela and all these guys figured out that if a system is corrupt, then the people who adhere to the system, and are incentivized by that system, are not criminals. They are victims. The system itself must be tried. But ... the only way we can figure out what the system is, is if everyone says what they did. Tell them how you participated.

This is his great piece of advice, a piece of the special his audience has been patiently waiting for, is the point of bringing this subject up. Chappelle clearly wants to challenge the #MeToo movement, but not in the way of judging what sexual assault is worse as critics aforementioned believed. Rather, he is urging for a movement like Dr. King's or Mr. Mandela's. He is urging those who listen to struggle to reconcile, rather than find momentary relief through comedy, or worse, judgment and excommunication. This type of cultural cancelling, as Chappelle finds, will eventually cancel the movement's potential allies as well. He argues "men want to help, they're just scared. Ben Affleck tried to help. 'What happened to these ladies is disgusting.'" "Oh, n-slur, you grabbed a titty in '95.' 'All right, fellas, I'm out. Fuck that, I ain't helping.'" What Chappelle points to, and one of the key moralities of his special, is that people like Ben Affleck who want to be an advocate should. The movement will not last if the enemy is not only those who oppose women's safety and freedom but also an "imperfect ally" as Chappelle names Ben Affleck. To him, the movement cannot be fueled by fear of mistake; we must be able to "speak recklessly," "fuck around," and understand that a mistake is not defining and a person must be taken at their entire context. "You can't make a lasting peace this way," Chappelle warns through his understanding as a black man who has both lived in both America and South Africa. "You got all the bad guys scared. And that's good, but the minute they're not scared anymore, it will get worse than it was before. Fear does not make lasting peace," although it allows temporary relief. What can make lasting peace is a revelation and a reconciliation.

The Cage

After a few sets of jokes, he finally tells the audience he will answer the big question of what happened to prompt his escape to Africa. But he doesn't. He makes an analogy. He tells the story of the Iceberg Slim, recounting from his biography *Pimp: The Story of My Life*. The story is of a sex worker reaching the end of her career. She begins asking for her freedom from Slim, to which he is hesitant, as she is his best worker. Slim sends her on one last job, which included the temporary drugging of the client. The sex worker drugs the client but soon notices his heart stops beating. She calls Slim, and he blames the death on her. Slim covers up the death, a hefty price, and tells the sex worker she must pay back her debt. Scared of what she has done, and scared of her debt, she stays with Slim. The catch of this story is that the client who died was an actor Slim hired. The men who took care of the body were movers down the street, all doing favors for Slim. At this reveal, Chappelle says this is why he left Hollywood. He says "That's the game. That's the motherfucking capitalist manifesto" This is not an answer to what happened that lead him to fly to South Africa and escape Viacom. This does not answer why he felt the need to walk away at the top of his own game. He offers us no relief, once again. That is not his goal. He wants us to answer why he left Hollywood, and make a judgment on the type of endurance he must have needed to survive, and endurance that, like the sex worker, was tried and manipulated. As Chappelle's fame and success grew, he recognized the white-washing that was being done to his show and lack of creative control he had by his retirement. Unlike the sex-worker, Chappelle eventually saw through the ruse, and, before he could be tricked by the game, he escaped.

Critics of Chappelle's special believe his joke on C.K. is simply a comedic mistake; a sexist joke that fell flat, and even perhaps indicative of Chappelle's sexist nature. These critics have not recognized the structure of this special, which points to Chappelle's connections between Hollywood's oppression of people of color and Hollywood's assault against women, nor have they recognized that Chappelle is often not joking at all when he makes his larger points of the special. He introduces his topic with perhaps the most serial rapist in Hollywood, Weinstein, to ingratiate his subject to the audience with a case that most people agree on the punishment for. He moves to Spacey, who, like Weinstein, most agree on the punishment for his case. Then he moves to C.K., a case that is more nuanced than Weinstein's or Spacey's. There was no rape, no molestation, and C.K. often would ask his victims for consent. His crime is that he abused his position of power. After offering advice to women entering a battle for power in Hollywood, and offering wisdom to #MeToo activists based on the history he has witnessed, he then enters his own nuanced case. The flow of this special begins with black and white subjects, and then moves to gray ones so he may introduce subjects that deserve a conversation in our society. The structure of his show implies an urge for understanding; if he was simply telling insensitive jokes to gain attention, there would be no reason for the venue, the staging, nor the structure of his special. He would not use Weinstein or Spacey to introduce his C.K., nor would he respond to C.K.'s abuse of power to introduce his own story. Using Comedy of Wit, Chappelle urges his audience to use their imagination to understand his underlying moral message. Rather than using Comedy of Humor, the inferior yet more applicable humor that *Chappelle's Show* producers urged, Chappelle demands wit and patience; making a strict judgment at his C.K. joke and turning off his special will not allow the audience to intake and process a deeply important message. It is the structure of his special that points to a deeper reflection on abuse and resistance, and it offers a challenge to women of the #MeToo era to reflect on abuse and resistance as well so that #MeToo can perhaps become a hashtag of the past in the most positive of ways. Chappelle is challenging all who watch to listen to him entirely, rather than cancel him and brand him as a "bad guy" like Chappelle points to in his special. Perhaps a forgotten or misunderstood line toward the end of his special is his comment: "Paul Revere's ride was only one night, then 40 years of him being like: Remember that time when everyone was asleep and I was up, and the British was coming. Boy, good thing I was awake" (Chappelle). Through his experience of abuse, Chappelle is the original Paul Revere of Hollywood abuse. Everyone around him was asleep but him. Chappelle witnessed this early, and known for a single heroic act, chose his values over money. Chappelle did not do this special "to be right" as he admits, nor did he do it to give us any sense of relief. He made these jokes "to fuck around" in his words, or to get us to begin a conversation.

What's never mentioned or addressed in his special is the title of his show. *The Bird Revelation* is Chappelle and the women of the #MeToo moment. It is the understanding that the bird, talented and naturally free, is trapped in a cage. While the bird can fly, it cannot perform as it would without its trapping. Like Chappelle had over a decade ago, women of the #MeToo era are beginning to have their own bird revelation. Women in the entertainment industry are beginning to realize the extent of the abuse and ultimate caging they have endured over their careers. Their noose echoes much of what Chappelle experienced a decade ago and, ultimately, revealed in this special. His desire for a distinction between Weinstein and Spacey, and C.K. is not out of a desire to defend those who commit sexual harassment. It is a warning to women and people of color that the Hollywood system will take advantage of them. The industry is Slim, and these vulnerable artists are the sex workers. For him, Weinstein and Spacey committed violence against the body, a violence that could not be defended; but in the case of C.K., a star who abused his power by placing his co-workers in harmful and frightening positions, the victim will unfortunately have to defend themselves if they want to survive. He warns women of the #MeToo movement that if they want to be successful, they will have to fight the way those of the Civil Rights movement did: without giving up their dreams. If a woman of the #MeToo movement, or a budding artist in the entertainment industry, wants to be successful, for Chappelle, they will have to hang up the phone and continue on. And rather than telling the audience this directly, he forces them to come to these revelations themselves. The bird's owners will not tell her she is caged, and while they will keep the bird sustained, the bird will not thrive. Chappelle is not free, but he has had his bird revelation—one that he could not have known unless he left Hollywood. For those impacted by the #MeToo movement and major abuses by the entertainment industry, they must discover their bird revelation on their own. Alike civil rights activists in South Africa, L.A. and #MeToo have to reconcile the imperfect allies of this movement if they want to be successful and understand that even perhaps C.K. is a victim of the same system he benefits from. The cure for the cage is in South Africa. That is his Bird Revelation. Chappelle can no longer act as a typical comedian in this era; he knows if he does, he is in the game again and back in his cage.

Ethics and Reconciliation

This essay aims not to ask or answer what types of sexual assault are worse than others; moreover, critics of Chappelle wrongly assumed that his special aimed to answer how we judge sexual assault. Currently, there is a trend toward canceling those who commit #MeToo offenses, "47 percent indicated that they would be less likely to watch a movie or TV show starring an actor facing #MeToo allegations when asked about 20 specific actors accused of sexual misconduct, however, respondents only identified two— Kevin Spacey and Louis C.K.—whose work they would be less likely to watch" (Hillstrom). For Chappelle, this judgment and canceling needs to be nuanced, not black and white. Critics of his special fall into the same trap of judgment and excommunication, or cultural cancelling, that Chappelle is asking the ethics and practicality of, when they focus only on his joke about Abby Schachner. Unethically taking the joke out of the context of the rest of his special, critics attempt to culturally cancel the imperfect ally that Chappelle is. Throughout his work, Chappelle has a habit of enticing his audience with an insensitive punchline, and expanding on the joke with a moralistic, just explanation. It is his formula, and why his jokes cannot be taken out of context. One such prime example is his joke on transgender genitals in his other Netflix special, *Equanimity*, in which he addresses complaints that he is against the trans community because he said in a prior comedy set that seeing Caitlin Jenner's genitals in a magazine made him say "yuck." However, in full context, the real point to his bit is to express discontent about transgender folks like Caitlin Jenner being more readily received by society than black people, and a deep suspicion that Caitlin is more accepted because she used to be known as a white man. His formula of enticement, exploration, answer is typical in his sets, and often leads him to controversy; after *Equanimity* aired, he, like with *Bird*, received much backlash to his comments. Also like with *Bird*, many of the comments were about the enticing punchline, but left out the exploration. However, unlike *Equanimity*, *Bird* does not give an answer. He leaves it open for his audience to answer. Unfortunately, if the audience does not listen to the entire joke, they miss out on the exploration and, in cases like his trans jokes, the answer. Not only is this impractical but deeply unethical in an age of spin.

When audiences fail to listen to Chappelle's message on revelation and reconciliation, they create a birdcage for themselves. By expecting only relief and rejecting more difficult messages, they refuse the guide Chappelle offers to them not only to think about sexual assault, but a just society at large. His jokes do not ask audiences to consider what sexual assault is worse, but rather, what type of action should be expected of survivors. Chappelle is concerned with responsibility; rather than giving up his comedy dreams due to an unjust system, he returned to comedy to discuss the system that prompted his exit. He owed his community, and he owed himself to not allow others to take his dreams away from him. He utilizes one of the most famous dreamers in our history, Dr. King, to hyperbolize but also offer analogy for #MeToo survivors. For Chappelle, he isn't asking what assault is worse; however, he is asking what responsibility do survivors have to continue fighting their fight to advance the rights of others, and themselves.

The comedian is concerned with another question as well: how should individuals and communities respond to an assailant. He seems to have no qualms with the cancelling of Harvey Weinstein or Kevin Spacey; and he admits repeatedly that Louis C.K. was wrong. He also admits he found C.K.'s methods of abusing his power funny; that they were the only ones that "Kinda made me laugh," (Chappelle). This isn't to say that C.K.'s is less offensive, but it is to say that C.K. and Weinstein used different modes of abuse, and that C.K.'s harassment is atypical to the types of abuse usually nationally highlighted. The peculiarity of the offense is not the method Chappelle is using to judge sexual harassment or assault's gravity, but the peculiarity points to an important matter: not all offenses are the same, nor all offenders. An offender like Weinstein who used his power to rape and threaten women over decades is certainly different than one who asked to masturbate in front of women. Chappelle does not answer why he finds C.K.'s method of harassment funny, but through finding Weinstein so disgusting the only way he can have sex is through rape (Chappelle), and finding C.K. disgusting and hilarious, he shows that not all abusers and abuses should be judged equally. Under the United States Justice System, these abusers and abuses are not judged equally, especially given that C.K. asked for consent. While Chappelle does not address the ethic of power, he does address the ethic of the abuse through his finding of C.K.'s funny. As he admits, he should not find it funny. That is true. However, through providing a varied response to C.K. versus Spacey and Weinstein, he shows that perhaps the ethical response is not that which is rehearsed and to promote politically correct language, but that which is reckless and our truth. Furthermore, he explicitly states the movement must accept imperfect allies; while Weinstein will likely never be an imperfect ally, individuals who committed mistakes like Ben Affleck should not be culturally cancelled like serial rapists. That is unethical and will not make "lasting peace": Affleck is a victim of the society that perpetuates abuse of women, and through his desire to advocate for women of the #MeToo era, for Chappelle, he deserves forgiveness. The comedian provides new ways of thinking during an era that monitors language more closely than ever before; those being to speak your truth, speak recklessly, admittance, and forgiveness. None of which provide any sort of immediate relief, but can provide lasting restoration.

Perhaps the most important part of Chappelle's special, one that has been vastly overlooked by critics, is his digression into South Africa. His comments on apartheid and institutional victimization are his main moral source for his guide to individuals and communities responding to assault. The idea that "if a system is corrupt, then the people who adhere to the system, and are incentivized by that system, are not criminals. They are victims," (Chappelle) is not a new one. Theologian Reinhold Niebuhr explored these ideas through what he deemed Christian realism, relating his philosophies on power and institution to the Civil Rights Movement of the 1960s; these philosophies that would later greatly influence Dr. King, whom Chappelle cites as person who understood morality, resilience, and institution. Niebuhr understood the lack of morality of the group; that while the individual can be moral, the group they belong to does not. A group of moralistic individuals does not equate to a moralistic group, as the ego of the group and the lack of control of the moral individual over the group causes the immoral society. In his opening paragraphs of *Moral Man and the Immoral Society,* he argues "In every human group there is less reason to guide and to check impulse, less capacity for self-transcendence, less ability to comprehend the needs of others and therefore more unrestrained egoism than the individuals, who compose the group, reveal in their personal relationships" (Niebuhr 1). If the society is inherently immoral, so much that if an individual is a product of that group, such as C.K. as a product of the Hollywood patriarchy, then those who act immorally such as the group encourages are victims of the society. This is a deeply difficult concept to practice. Dr. King would consult his philosophies and tactics for the Civil Rights Movement with Niebuhr, as he too had a difficult time developing his practice of non-violence. In the practice of non-violence, Dr. King embraced Niebuhr's morality of justice, in that "[a]ny justice which is only justice soon degenerates into something less than justice. It must be saved by something which is more than justice" (Niebuhr 141). This is essential to Chappelle's moral guide through his special. Individuals and communities coming to a reckoning with sexual assault are wise to understand that justice, while deeply tempting, will certainly not yield results of a moral society. In bringing up C.K.'s assault, and asking if his punishment fits the crime, he is not asking if what C.K. did was wrong; but rather urging an understanding that simply culturally cancelling C.K. will not bring about a moral society free of assault. Rather, activists of the #MeToo era must understand that all are victim of the system that encourages sexual assault, and that liberation is interwoven between assailant and assaulted alike. Niebuhr's ultimate philosophy on justice and shared liberation is exemplified: "Where rights and interests are closely interwoven, it is impossible to engage in a shrewd and prudent calculation of comparative rights. Where lives are closely intertwined, happiness is destroyed if it is not shared. Justice by assertion and counter-assertion therefore becomes impossible" (Niebuhr 145). If the #MeToo era will ever be successful, including the success necessary by an ethical movement, the group must forgo its natural ego and pursue a justice that transcends typical notions of justice. Chappelle, a member of the Hollywood patriarchy and a person of color deeply harmed by the group he belonged to, is ultimately the messenger for #MeToo activists. Chappelle, a comedian that fits the stereotype of a damaged, cynical, observer of the group's interrelations, not only observed this in his own life and in others, but is a moral individual in an immoral society. Who better than him to express this deeply difficult truth to individuals already in pain?

WORKS CITED

Burford, Corinna. "Dave Chappelle Jokes That Louis C.K. Accuser Has 'Brittle-Ass Spirit.'" *Vulture*, Vulture, 1 Jan. 2018, www.vulture.com/2017/12/chappelle-pokes-fun-at-louis-c-k-accuser-in-new-special.html.
Chappelle, Dave. "Dave Chappelle: Equanimity & The Bird Revelation." *Netflix Official Site*, 31 Dec. 2017, www.netflix.com/title/80230402.
Chuba, Kirsten. "Dave Chappelle Calls Louis C.K. Accusers 'Weak' and 'Brittle' in New Special." *Variety*, 3 Jan. 2018, variety.com/2018/tv/news/dave-chappelle-louis-c-k-accusers-weak-brittle-1202650867/.
Collier Hillstrom, Laurie. "Impacts of the #MeToo Movement." *The #MeToo Movement*, ABC-CLIO, 2019, pp. 69–99. 21st Century Turning Points.
Gelber, Michael Werth. "Dryden's Theory of Comedy." *Eighteenth-Century Studies*, vol. 26, no. 2, 1992, pp. 261–283. JSTOR, www.jstor.org/stable/2739320.
Logan, Brian. "Dave Chappelle's 'Reckless' #MeToo and Trans Jokes Have Real After-Effects." *The Guardian*, Guardian News and Media, 4 Jan. 2018, www.theguardian.com/stage/2018/jan/04/dave-chappelle-comedy-standup-transgender-netflix.
Morreall, John, "Philosophy of Humor," *The Stanford Encyclopedia of Philosophy* (Winter 2016 Edition), Edward N. Zalta (ed.), URL = <https://plato.stanford.edu/archives/win2016/entries/humor/>.
Niebuhr, R. (1932). *Moral Man and Immoral Society: A Study in Ethics and Politics*. New York: Charles Scribner's Sons.
"Niebuhr, Reinhold." *The Martin Luther King, Jr., Research and Education Institute*, Stanford University, 5 June 2018, kinginstitute.stanford.edu/encyclopedia/niebuhr-reinhold.
Wittmer, Carrie. "Olivia Munn Calls Out Dave Chappelle for Being 'Tone Deaf to the Experiences of Others' with His Louis C.K. Jokes." *Business Insider*, Business Insider, 11 Jan. 2018, www.businessinsider.com/olivia-munn-says-dave-chappelles-louis-ck-jokes-are-tone-deaf-2018-1.
Zinoman, Jason. "Dave Chappelle Stumbles into the #MeToo Moment." *The New York Times*, The New York Times, 2 Jan. 2018, www.nytimes.com/2018/01/02/arts/television/dave-chappelle-netflix-special.html.

PART THREE

Laughter and Late Night

Blowing Off Steam

Freud, Smut and Samantha Bee's
Political Comedy

ERICA A. HOLBERG

In surveys of theories of humor, Freud is often cited as exemplifying relief or release theories of humor and also as an argument that this theory of humor should be rejected. This essay focuses upon Freud's account of tendentious jokes, which are jokes that aim to convey some truth and are the central concern of *Jokes and Their Relation to the Unconscious* (1905), to provide a nuanced interpretation of Freud's theory of joking as release. I then demonstrate the value of Freud's account of tendentious jokes by using it to explore the gender and power dynamics of the late night comedy show *Full Frontal with Samantha Bee*. Although Freud's account of the pleasure of humor has largely been rejected as reductive or implausible, many have found compelling the suggestion that, because comedic enjoyment provides a "safety-valve" for us to blow off steam in socially-sanctioned, playful violations of social taboos concerning sex and aggression, comedy functions to conserve existing social and political institutions. While relief theory helpfully illuminates the general nature of comedy as politically inert and performing a conservative social function, the example of *Full Frontal with Samantha Bee* reveals the power of comedy to advance non-conservative political ends, especially when utilized in innovative ways.

The Case Against Freud's Relief
Theory of Humor

Jokes and Their Relation to the Unconscious divides our experiences of the humorous into three categories: joking, which includes jokes but also puns, witty repartee, or any language play for comedic enjoyment; the comic, which centrally concerns humorous movement, but also funny visual images; and humor, which for Freud is occurs when an unpleasurable feeling moving toward expression is sublimated into pleasurable laughter or joking remarks. As the title indicates, the book is focused upon joking, with only one section on the comic and nine pages within that section on humor as Freud narrowly defines it. Within his broad category of joking, Freud distinguishes innocent jokes from tendentious jokes. Innocent jokes are word play done as an end in itself, for the enjoyment in the play. Tendentious jokes have the aim or purpose of expressing some truth in the joking. For Freud, the purpose served by tendentious jokes is hostile and/or obscene. On the standard reading, the hydraulic model of mind is Freud's theory of how jokes work: when an individual makes or hears a joke, the psychic energy that would have gone toward repressing the libidinous or aggressive urges expressed in the joke is instead released in laughter.

There is much to object to on this standard reading of Freud on jokes. Most importantly, the hydraulic model of mind this account relies upon is implausible. Why assume, for instance, that the psychic energy of repression is convertible to the kinetic energy of laughter, or that the depth of laughter at a joke tracks the pleasure provided by that joke? The linchpin of the account—that joking, the comic, and humor are all ways of saving psychic energy that then finds release in laughter—is unappealingly reductive. Furthermore, this schema of converted energy released in laughter seems overly general and not true to certain features of how humor works, as shown by two counter-examples from Morreall. The first concerns the professionalization of comedy: if joking is really about the pleasurable release found in the expression of unconscious urges that would otherwise have been repressed, it is not clear how persons could develop skill in the manipulation of the unconscious on demand (Morreall, *Comic Relief*, 20–1). The second concerns the correlation between humorous enjoyment and laughter and the repressive work within an individual: if the most pleasurable release in laughter is indeed equivalent to the most energy saved on repressive work, this would suggest that the most uptight, repressed, neurotic individuals would be the ones to most enjoy a dirty, bawdy joke, but often this type of person is not able to take a joke and more sexually open, coarser persons are the ones who find dirty jokes most humorous (Morreall, *Comic Relief*, 21).

The implausibility of the hydraulic model of mind as an account of the pleasure of humor, however, does not destroy the plausibility of a metaphorical interpretation of humor as releasing aggression and sexual tension. In "Funny, but Not Vulgar," Orwell writes,

A thing is funny when—in some way that is not actually offensive or frightening—it upsets the established order. Every joke is a tiny revolution.... Whatever destroys dignity, and brings down the mighty from their seats, preferably with a bump, is funny.... All this is not to say that humour is, of its nature, immoral or antisocial. A joke is at most a temporary rebellion against virtue... [Orwell 284–285].

Here we see echoes of many of the ideas in Freud: that joking is subversive; that joking is a hostile attack on established authority, especially through use of the obscene; and that joking, despite being the expression of a wish that things were otherwise, in fact, is not a serious threat to the status quo. One reason the power of humor to destabilize the status quo is constrained is indicated in the first sentence of the Orwell quote: any content that is too subversive, too offensive, or too aggressive is just not funny. The challenge to social norms, taboos, and authority structures that happens through humor always also needs to be playful. Freud's theory of comic relief provides an explanation of why comedy seems to conserve the established social order: in the pleasurable release of psychic tensions via the comedic lifting of inhibitions, either imposed externally or internally as demanded by society, the individual unburdens herself, and so finds a sort of peace with the status quo and its discontents. On this way of thinking about the pleasures of comedy, a belly full of laughter is just not the right starting point for the serious work of politics as bringing about a new, better social order.

A Better Take on Freud on Joking

Rather than construct our reading of Freud on humor as release around an implausibly reductive hydraulic model of mind, we should instead attend to what Freud himself is centrally concerned to argue: that the work of jokes is like the work of dreams. The first section of *Jokes and Their Relation to the Unconscious* is titled "The Technique of Jokes"; this section ends by stating that the techniques used in jokes are all involved in the formation of dreams. Freud asserts "so far-reaching an agreement between the methods of the joke-work and the dream-work can scarcely be a matter of chance" (105). In the next section, "The Purposes of Jokes," Freud claims that jokes "make possible the satisfaction of an instinct (whether lustful or hostile) in the face of an obstacle that stands in its way" (119). This obstacle is "the repressive activity of civilization" that has been internalized as the psychical process of repression (120). For Freud, the pleasurable satisfaction of lustful or hostile instincts that requires an overcoming of internalized repressive forces is the essential purpose of jokes, and his interest is in how jokes are able to achieve this. In a later section, "The Relation of Jokes to Dreams and to the Unconscious," Freud considers the similarities between how jokes work to *"open sources of pleasure that have become inaccessible"* in order to continue "pleasurable play" with this repressed content and "protect it from the criticism of reason," and how dreams work to transform and convert the dream-thoughts stemming from repressed wishes into the manifest content of the dream (123, 160). For Freud, dreams and jokes are crucial ways that unconscious, inhibited content is able to evade the repressive censor of reason, thereby freeing or releasing bound psychic energy. Dreams work by displacing the unconscious wish and making it not immediately recognizable in the manifest dream content, whereas jokes work by condensing, substituting, or making absurd the inhibited content so as to achieve the safety and pleasure of play.

Freud marks three crucial differences between dream-work and joke-work. The most important difference, Freud tells us, is that "a dream is a completely asocial mental product; it has nothing to communicate to anyone else," but "a joke, on the other hand, is the most social of all the mental functions that aim at a yield of pleasure" (222). Dreaming is what we do all by ourselves while sleeping. In contrast, the completion of a joke "requires the participation of someone else in the mental process it starts" because we joke together (222). For Freud, even if a joke occurs to an individual in isolation or some setting not conducive for joking, the pleasure of the joke only reaches fullness once the individual finds someone to tell the joke to (190). The second crucial difference follows from this first one: the transformation of content in dreaming is a compromise between the individual's inner psychic forces of the unconscious and the censorship of repression that does "not need to set any store by intelligibility, it must actually avoid being understood for otherwise it would be destroyed" (222). However, in joking the manipulation of repressed content must be able to "be set straight by the third person's [the hearer's] understanding," meaning "the condition of intelligibility is, therefore, binding on it" (222). Thirdly, a dream is a hallucination of a wish made unrecognizable, but "a joke is developed play" not from need but for pleasure. Joking is more voluntary and more under our control than dreaming. These three features explain how the professionalization of comedy is possible: although the source material for joking is socially repressed content, the manipulation of this content in telling a joke is conscious mental activity. Furthermore, many professional comedians swear the only way to improve at the developed play of comedy is by performing for a live audience to test, explore, and refine the joking; the need for a live audience supports Freud's characterization of joking as converting shared repressed content for safe, communal pleasure in the playful transgression of social taboos.

For Freud, joking has a triadic structure: joking is not only done with another, it is also done against a third person. Freud justifies this claim regarding the triadic structure of joking through an analogy to smut. As Freud describes it, smut is "the intentional bringing into prominence of sexual facts and relations by speech" done by a man, directed toward a woman as an attempt at seduction (115). If this act of sexual aggression is met with the "woman's inflexibility," the man develops hostility toward the woman and enlists a male onlooker as his ally (118). Instead of being a block to sexual action, the third (male) person now becomes the listener to whom the smut is addressed, providing defensive cover from sexual rejection. In turn, the third person receives the pleasurable, effortless satisfaction of his libido in listening to the exposure of the woman as object to the first person's hostile or sexual aggressiveness. Analogously, "a tendentious joke calls for three people: in addition to the one who makes the joke, there must be a second who is taken as the object of the hostile or sexual aggressiveness, and a third in whom the joke's aim of producing pleasure is fulfilled" (118). Jokes allow for the liberation of sexual or hostile impulses in play between the joke teller and the joke listener and against the object of the joke; the interpersonal play of joking enables what society would have otherwise required be repressed. In hostile jokes, we enjoy the overcoming of the second person [our enemy] by making him "small, inferior, despicable or comic" and the third person is turned into a "co-hater or co-despiser" (122, 163). In obscene jokes, we enjoy the shaming of the second person through her sexual exposure and the third person becomes an ally through the bribe of pleasure in witnessing her objectification and degradation. Importantly, being a co-hater or ally requires "sufficient psychical accord" between the joke teller and the joke listener, and at minimum, neutrality on the listener's part toward the person who is the object of the joke (184).

The similarities of joking to dreaming and to smut show Freud is not arguing for a release theory of humor via a reductive, mechanistic model of individual mindedness. Firstly, the sociality of jokes mean a mechanistic model of the individual as an independent system needing to release psychic energy cannot accurately capture why or how we joke. Jokes do release pent-up aggressive urges, but the purpose of jokes is to playfully convey some truth to another and so establish or solidify a relation of accord with the other. The different roles for the teller and the listener of the joke make manifest the different pleasures found in joking; Freud states the work of constructing the joke lessens the pleasure of the joke until the teller receives back the listener's pleasurable reaction to it (190–191). Secondly, that jokes involve work means that joking is more or less conscious and more or less voluntary. In some important sense, we choose to participate in joking as teller or as receptive listener. The element of choice in joking explains why more uptight individuals are typically least likely to enjoy a joke: the release of psychic energy in the play of joking is something the individual can choose to do, but this energy could stay bound, perhaps exacerbating neuroses, or it could find release in other ways, through dreaming, sublimation, etc.

Full Frontal *as Feminist Comedy*

To prove the value of Freud's analysis of joking, I will develop an example that may at first seem incongruent with Freud's account of the gendered nature of tendentious joke telling as done by men for other men. In fact *Full Frontal with Samantha Bee* reconstitutes Freud's gendered triadic structure of joking to achieve an explicitly feminist, political purpose. At the show's launch, Bee was the only female host of a late-night comedy show. That professional comedians are predominantly men, performing for a predominantly male audience suggests Freud's analogy to smut correctly characterizes joking as a way of relieving aggression with particular appeal to men. The very first segment of the show confronts the gendered nature of late night comedy, as evidenced in its hosts and its audiences, by joking that the only way Bee could have landed a comedy hosting gig is because she is a witch. In *Full Frontal*, the joke teller is a woman, and the listener is explicitly a feminist and implicitly female. This identification of the listener as feminist is evident in the "thought [that] seeks to wrap itself in a joke": Bee uses an aggressive, sexually explicit, hostile comedic voice to draw attention to hostility toward women in our political moment and also in the history of late-night comedy (162). The hostile and obscene aggression of the comedy is against Trump in particular, but also other men working to implement a sexist, anti-minorities agenda. As with hostile tendentious jokes, there is an overcoming of Trump through belittling him. And as with obscene tendentious jokes, the villainy, stupidity, and corporeality of Trump is held forward for exposure as shameful.

For Freud, "everything in jokes that is aimed at gaining pleasure is calculated with an eye to the third person" (190); while there are many pleasures on offer for the viewer of *Full Frontal*, three are especially worth noting. Most obviously, the jokes effect a symbolic revenge on Trump and other male targets for their actions harming some woman or women. In its hostile and obscene joking, Trump, who routinely objectifies women and is credibly accused of sexual assault, is objectified for the pleasure of the joke listener, achieving an imaginative emasculation of Trump. The appeal of the hostile overcoming is clear enough; here, though, the obscene shaming is done not because Trump is a potential desired sex object that threatens rejection, but to convey disgust at his grossness intellectually and physically, similar to the way ethnic jokes use physicality against their targets to convey prejudices. A second pleasure for the viewer is in the feeling of community with other viewers and with Bee. In explaining how a self-critical joke could be funny, as exemplified in "Jewish jokes which originate from Jews," Freud argues "a collective person" in whom the joke teller and listener has a share is formed (133). Similarly, Bee's audience gets the pleasure of identifying with her as powerful feminist joke teller and thereby being bonded with all other appreciative Bee-joke listeners. A third "pleasure by lifting suppressions and repressions" is found in "rebel[ing] against the demands of morality" (176, 131). Interestingly, the joking on *Full Frontal* is not simply a loosening of the external and internalized pressures of morality, but a direct challenge to certain social norms and moral expectations as "only a selfish regulation laid down by the few who are rich and powerful and who can satisfy their wishes at any time without any postponement" (131). Many of the segments and the jokes explicitly concern moral causes; examples include aiding Syrian refugees, Puerto Ricans still recovering from Hurricane Maria, rural women without adequate access to obstetric care; these are moral causes of intersectional feminism. The joking constitutes a frontal attack on patriarchal, oppressive aspects of traditional morality so as to supplant these "moral" justifications for bad behavior and bad institutional practices with a better, more just, more inclusive moral order.

Probably *Full Frontal* is most well-known for Bee's use of the show's platform to call Ivanka Trump a "feckless cunt" in arguing the moral abhorrence of the Trump administration's policy of separating migrant children from their parents (5.30.18 episode, segment now scrubbed from the internet). Coming on the heels of ABC's decision to cancel *Roseanne* after Roseanne Barr's racist insults on Twitter toward a former Obama adviser, conservatives seized on Bee's obscene insult as requiring some similar response. Many people on the left and the right condemned Bee's use of the word "cunt" as unnecessary and not funny. Rather than help adjudicate just how bad an idea this insult with this timing was, Freud's theory of joking explains why this insult could seem like a funny joke to make: (1) most obviously, the obscenity is an insult meant as a hostile attack on an authority figure that reduces the intelligence and agency of Ivanka Trump to a body part; (2) if there is anything clever in this insult, it is in the use of the word "feckless"; in great detail, Freud explores the pleasure of substitute-formation in wordplay, while the comedian's "rule of k" asserts that words with a "k" or hard "c" sound seem the most funny (not surprisingly, this sound shows up in many insults); (3) the misogyny of the insult "cunt" taps into the generally sexist structure of joking as described by Freud, but it also repurposes this misogyny into a moral criticism of Ivanka Trump as providing cover for the patriarchal Trump administration by presenting a feminine, softer face to its cruel, anti-minority, policy decisions; the complicity of spokeswomen for the Trump administration in enacting its anti-women, anti-minority agenda is frequently joked about. Moreover, Freud shows why criticism of the insult as unnecessary is somewhat misplaced. Of course calling Ivanka Trump "feckless cunt" was not necessary for Bee's message about the wrongness of "baby jails." But since joking is a sort of play, and in an important sense, none of it is necessary, joking is always excessive. Conveying political and moral messages is not why we joke, even if it is constitutive of how much joking works.

Bee's apology that opened *Full Frontal* the following week further evidences Freud's theory of the triadic structure of joking by making clear who her joking is for. She apologizes to women hurt by her use of "cunt" as an insult (arguably this includes all women, since use as an insult is not a valid way to reclaim a word), but explicitly refuses to apologize to men.

> I want this show to be challenging and I want it to be honest, but I never intended it to hurt anyone, except Ted Cruz. Many men were also offended by my use of the word. I do not care about that.

This clarification of the recipient of her apology both makes clear what she is apologizing for (using "cunt" as an insult) and who she takes her joke listener to be: first and foremost a woman, but through imaginative extension of the collective unity established in the joking, a feminist. She asserts, as a joke, that the show aims to hurt Ted Cruz. Then, contrary to the idea that conveying a moral message is not why we joke but congruent with the suggestion that moral purpose may be functioning differently in joking by a woman for women, she claims her primary concern is to help the kids harmed by Trump's juvenile immigration policy. The apology ends by making a distinction between civility and morality, and implies again that the purpose of the show is to push us all to be better morally:

> And look, if you are worried about the death of civility, don't sweat it. I'm a comedian. People who hone their voices in basement bars while yelling back at drunk hecklers are definitely not paragons of civility. I am, I'm really sorry that I said that word, but you know what? Civility is just nice words. Maybe we should all worry a little bit more about the niceness of our actions.

Bee here agrees with Freud that comedy is by its nature uncivil, because it uses hostile, obscene words and ideas to form a community of joke teller and joke listener against another. However, she is interested to argue the community formed in the pleasure found in speaking in uncivil ways against the status quo can also serve a moral purpose.

Political and Moral Purposes and Comedy

Freud's account of the pleasure and the actual physical laughter in joking as being the release of psychic energy that would have otherwise been used for the work of repression suggests the power of comedy to advance political ends is severely circumscribed. Even though the messages conveyed through joking will typically be attacks on the authority of persons or institutions, the upshot of these joke rebellions is to conserve the status quo by functioning as a release of aggression without translation into rebellious action (125, 129). The main explanation for the neutered political power of comedy is the circumstances surrounding the finding of comedic enjoyment: pleasurable release requires circumstances where play is allowable (213). "Imaginative or intellectual work that pursues serious aims interferes with the capacity of the cathexes for discharge" (272); likewise "the comic is greatly interfered with if the situation from which it ought to develop gives rise at the same time to a release of strong affect" (273). To go over well, a joke should not demand extreme effort in thinking or result in extreme feeling. Timing, including situational context, is everything. The serious grind of political action conflicts with the playful lightness necessary for comedic release.

The aggressive identification of the machinations and harms of patriarchy that orients the joking of *Full Frontal* pushes against this thought that joking cannot be politically actionable and political work cannot be funny. In at least three ways, the joking of *Full Frontal* seems to be doing political work. First, Bee's comedy makes explicit various power dynamics, pushing some audience members to take up her perspective, and helping sympathetic audience members to understand recent events. The feminism and the hostility work together to cement a shared sense of what is true and important. For Freud, all joking "will further bribe the hearer with its yield of pleasure into taking sides with us without any very close investigation" (123). The pleasure of symbolically shaming and/or dominating some person or outgroup, and doing this with others as some in-group, unreflectively communicates values and a perspective. Further, the playful mood of joking, with its lifting of inhibitions, makes possible the floating of certain ideas into the thoughts of joke teller and joke hearer that might seem too outlandish to justify in all seriousness (144). For example, Bee devotes the entire 5.23.2018 episode to arguing for abolishing ICE (Immigration and Customs Enforcement): when she first makes the proposal, "Let's shut [ICE] the fuck down," the audience laughs at this "joke" and Bee immediately counters, "I'm serious. It's awful." While all comedic joking has the potential to solidify a politically-localizable perspective through pleasure bribes and to put forward political ideas and arguments that are inimical to and hard to justify by lights of the status quo, the switched gender roles within the triadic structure of joking amplifies the political meaning of these potentialities. It matters that this is a woman talking to women and advancing a feminist perspective in the same way consciousness raising amongst women matters for realizing concrete feminist actions in resistance to particular manifestations of patriarchy. But Bee raises consciousness by joking. Seeing sexist oppression and thereby processing the world differently is not separate from moving through the world differently, even though the translation of recognition to action is not seamless nor painless. Knowing and feeling in solidarity with others is an important element for success in re-ordering one's own actions according to raised feminist consciousness.

Second, in belittling, e.g., Trump, Bee uses joking as a way to manage various affects that arise from lack of political power. The idea that because of its emotional resonances, joking advances political ends may seem to directly contravene the idea that by providing for the release of emotions, joking thwarts political action because there now is no need for practical outlet. Some jokes do function solely to relieve tension, as in cracking a joke before the start of an exam. However, I have argued that the hydraulic model of psychic energy is not the only, or even the best explanation Freud gives us concerning how jokes work. Holding to this idea that there are different descriptions possible of how jokes work or what jokes do means we can assert: (1) the emotional release provided by joking as depicted through the hydraulic model lessens the need for (political) action external to the joking, and also, (2) the emotions experienced in response to the content or messages of the joking can be the basis for political action. For how the experience of an emotion can both disarm rational assessment of it in the moment, but also make possible rational criticism of it afterwards and thereby allow for the incorporation of this changed stance toward one's own affects in one's actions, it is helpful to consider two other models of transformative release: catharsis through tragedy and more broadly, literature, and catharsis through therapy. On catharsis through tragedy, Lear writes:

> Freud talks of blowing off steam, but what is important is not this description of tragic catharsis but his characterization of the conditions in which it can occur. It is of the essence of Freud's account of the appeal of great literature that we can in some way, dimly, recognize ourselves in it. And yet, it is only because the spectator remains aware of the gulf that separates his own life from that of the dramatic hero that he can enjoy indulging in imaginative identification. It is in this fine balance of sympathy and distance that a catharsis can occur [Lear, *Love* 54].

On catharsis through therapy, Lear explains:

> In effect, Freud enables the hysteric to transform his emotional stance toward his own desires. Instead of being so threatened by them that he must repress them, he becomes able to accept his emotions and thus to allow them into consciousness. Emotional acceptance and conscious awareness are of a piece…. Freud's therapeutic practice consists in establishing a delicate balance of proximity and distance which makes it possible for the hysteric to experience a vivid, but nevertheless acceptable emotion response [*Love* 58–59].

The playspace of feminist joking on *Full Frontal* accomplishes a blending of the catharsis of tragedy and the catharsis of therapy: because it is play, there is a possibility for imagining thoughts about and interpretations of our political moment that are difficult to claim forthrightly, whereas the pleasurable context of joking counteracts and so facilitates the experience of emotions and consideration of topics that would otherwise be too painful. *Full Frontal* thus allows for the venting of affects definitive of our contemporary political moment that imperil political action: the feelings of anger and despair and the attitude of cynicism. Within the play of joking, through exaggeration, brevity, substitution, etc., these affects can reach expression since the right sort of distance is established. But if the joking is funny to us, the listener, the jokes with their affective resonances are understood to make something explicit and near that had been inchoate or unacknowledged: jokes are exercises in proximity and distance. Insofar as the pleasure enables us to think thoughts and feel feelings that would likely not be entertained from an attitude of serious self-possession, Freud's assertion that reason's critical function is confused or bribed by the pleasure found in the play of joking seems right. However, the pleasure found in the moment of joking does not foreclose the possibility for reason to critically return to the emotions and ideas expressed in the play to make a more sober judgment about whether and how to incorporate these thoughts into action (160–2). This return in thought seems all the more likely if some strong emotional response was experienced. Thus, certain kinds of joking allow for the release, but also the management of emotions. The management of emotions is empowering, and these more managed, directed emotions can be channeled into political aims.

Third, Bee uses the emotional community engendered by shared hostility to push the audience to take specific actions and thereby join a community of political agents. Admittedly, most of these requests take the form of buying merchandise of which some percentage of the proceeds go to good causes, although sometimes she prompts calls to one's elected representatives, such as in order to save the ACA from repeal. It's easy to sniff that politicized acts of consumerism will hardly light the world on fire. However, the corporate branding in wearing a t-shirt that says "Feminist," "Nasty Woman," etc., on the front and *Full Frontal with Samantha Bee* on the back, is also a branding of the self. Making explicit for oneself and to others one's desire to publicly embrace this political identity and its alliances provides the self-congratulatory pleasurable thrill of enlistment behind a worthy cause. But this imaginative identification, starting from one's couch, of oneself as a foot soldier for justice can lead to other actions to buttress this identification, and the public aspect of this self-branding can encourage others to enlist and normalize pride in this identification.

However, as Freud's analogy makes clear, comedy has only limited ability to bring about political action or to transform an audience member's political viewpoint. If an audience member feels herself implicated in that which is being attacked through comedy, she will explicitly turn against the comedian and her political purpose. Freud gives the example of "an excellent obscene joke if the exposure applies to a highly respected relative" to show that the audience "cannot be ready to laugh" is there is "opposition to the purpose the joke is trying to serve" (177). Importantly, "every joke calls for a public of its own and laughing at the same jokes is evidence of far-reaching psychical conformity" (185). Jokes can cement or clarify a viewpoint one is already favorably disposed toward, but they cannot transform the listener's view. Furthermore, as evidenced in the preceding examples of how comedy can push toward political action—by consolidating a political viewpoint and group, by allowing for the management of feelings that would otherwise cut against political activity, and by enjoining action in support of the political purpose and community undergirding the joking—the tension between political urgency and humorous enjoyment is not dissolved, but rather negotiated. When *Full Frontal* succeeds in producing political action *and* laughs, it does so not by marrying the two aims, but by dancing between them. Finally, Freud's repeated descriptions of the pleasures of joking working to bribe our powers of criticism lends weight to the worry that the contemporary blending of daily news and comedic entertainment in late night television encourages a passive consumption of the news in which the viewer is not minding the political events recounted in the way he should (e.g., 123, 162, 163). The sweet, pleasurable context of joking enables us to swallow wretched, alarming news without the political protest it should occasion. There is no easy answer regarding how to weight our psychic need to make the unbearable bearable against our practical need to reject as unbearable our political status quo. Certainly one aim of Bee's is to help her viewers get through the horror, pain, and powerlessness felt in response to contemporary news events, as seen in her many laments about the slowness of time under Trump's presidency with its barrage of awfulness. Even though there is a lessening of pain in the community found within the joking of *Full Frontal*, Bee still manages to do something quite radical. By inverting Freud's gendered triadic of joking and by situating all her jokes within a feminist political vision that aims to remake established political hierarchies, Bee's *Full Frontal* makes her viewers feel better by poking fun at the many social injustices surrounding us even as she challenges us to do something about them.

Works Cited

Bee, Samantha, creator. *Full Frontal with Samantha Bee*. TBS, 2016.

Freud, Sigmund. *Jokes and Their Relation to the Unconscious, The Standard Edition*. Translated and Edited by James Strachey, W. W. Norton & Company, 1960.

Lear, Jonathan. *Freud (The Routledge Philosophers)*. Routledge, 2005.

_____. *Love and Its Place in Nature: A Philosophical Interpretation of Freudian Psychoanalysis*. Farrar, Straus & Giroux, 1990.

Lippitt, John. "Humour and Release." *Cogito*, vol. 9, no. 2, 1995, pp. 169–176.

Morreall, J. *Comic Relief: A Comprehensive Philosophy of Humor.* John Wiley & Sons, 2009.
_____. "Philosophy of Humor." *The Stanford Encyclopedia of Philosophy.* Edited by Edward N. Zalta, Winter Edition 2016, https://plato.stanford.edu/entries/humor/.
Orwell, G. "Funny, but Not Vulgar." *The Collected Essays, Journalism and Letters of George Orwell.* Edited by Sonia Orwell and Ian Angus, vol. 3, Secker & Warburg, 1943–1945.

The Vices and Virtues
of David Letterman

CINDY MUENCHRATH SPADY

As a self-described super fan of David Letterman for twenty-five years, I initially thought he was funny in a gap-toothed, goofy way. But for me, his appeal was more than dropping a watermelon off a roof and ad libbing pithy comments on Stupid Pet Tricks. I laughed at his stunts and Top 10 Lists, but there always seemed to be something more purposeful to his comedy, even though it took time to emerge. Can comedy make us better humans and more purposeful, more virtuous? An exploration of the life and career of David Letterman will showcase how Letterman's persona was intertwined with his humor such that the evolution of his comedy is also the evolution of him as a person. The symbiotic relationship between his humor and his public persona (and private life, which he became more open about as time went on) allows one to conclude that as his behavior and outlook on life shifted, so did his humor. The question becomes at what stage of this journey, if ever, did Letterman achieve happiness or eudemonia?

Letterman, born in Indiana in 1947, knew early on that his purpose would be as a comedian. There was little doubt. He says, "The only thing I was ever good at was making people laugh" (Rader 4). After he graduated from Ball State University, where he used his comedic talents on the college radio station, he enjoyed a stint as a weatherman. He eventually journeyed to Los Angeles, where he started on the comedy club circuit. During this time, he honed his craft and was noticed by many as having a unique brand of humor. He eventually caught the eye of a talent scout for *The Tonight Show with Johnny Carson.* For a young comedian, this was a milestone only few could hope for. He was given his own morning talk show, but that only lasted four months; he had not yet found his niche. Letterman found that niche on *Late Night with David Letterman* (NBC), which he led from 1982 to 1992. He went on to finish his late-night career at CBS with *The Late Show* leaving in 2015.

In his later years with *The Late Show*, something in his comedy changed. Self-reflection became a mainstay. He was still irreverent, but his jokes became more purposeful. This is the Letterman that attracted me. He was funny, but I saw Letterman evolve as a comedian and human being right in front of my eyes. I laughed at his stunts, but I really admired how he could take the mundanity of human life and reflect on it not only with humor, but with insight. He also challenged the status quo, whether it be a politician or an actor; when he saw something askew he used his comedy to reflect on the matter. He also seemed different as a human. Somehow, he seemed happier, more satisfied, and more at ease.

I often wondered what changed in him. It is clear his comedy was informed by both his public and personal personas. There were life events that perhaps could explain it. There also were world events that he was in the midst of that perhaps could be part of his transformation. He was different in the ways he interacted with others: he was kinder, more witty, more honest, more self-reflective, and more humble. In short, Letterman was more virtuous.

Could it be that in practicing the virtues of wittiness, honesty, atonement, humility, and others, that Letterman began to fulfill at least in part what virtue ethics claims to be the human purpose: was the audience watching Letterman become happy right before their very eyes? I contend, and hope to show, that Letterman's evolution as a comic is also his evolution as a person. What follows is both an academic undertaking—one that shows the link between virtue theory and humor but also a personal narrative. In attempting to understand how Letterman evolved into a better comedian, and maybe more virtuous person, I hope to also understand my own appreciation for his humor and persona. Virtue ethics is the appropriate lens through which to view the intersection of Letterman's humor and persona because of how virtue ethics links the practice and performance of the self to a qualitative evaluation of the person as praiseworthy or blameworthy.

Virtue Ethics

For Aristotle, virtue starts with purpose (teleology) toward the ultimate goal of happiness. In Greek "telos" means goal or purpose. In his *Nicomachean Ethics,* he investigates the purpose of things. "Every art and every kind of inquiry, and likewise every act and purpose, seems to aim at some good, and so it has been well said that the good is that at which everything aims" (qtd. in Solomon 56). Humans reason, knives cut, and birds fly. Virtue is the difference between just doing something and doing something well. If something performs its purpose well, then it is virtuous; it is moral.

The question at the heart of virtue ethics is "who ought I to be?" It differs from the question of "what ought I to do?" in that virtue ethics focuses on the character of the person as a whole, not just what one might do in a particular situation. The primary tenet of virtue ethics is that life is a journey of building character and practicing virtues and avoiding vices. Here, virtue is defined as a trait that is morally good or desirable, while a vice is defined as the opposite of virtue—an immoral trait. The goal for one on this quest is to fulfill one's purpose, develop character, and live a life of happiness. For Aristotle, this is happiness, which in turn leads to the good life. Happiness is an activity that leads to human flourishing. Aristotle used the word "eudemonia." Even though the meaning of the translation is often debated, one way to understand eudemonia is the state of "being well and doing well in being well" (MacIntyre 148). Blessedness, happiness, and prosperity are other translations (MacIntyre 148). When one is full of eudemonia, one is living the good life, the virtuous life, the moral life. According to Aristotle, how does one become happy? One becomes happy through a process of growing and practicing one's virtues while minimizing one's vices (Pojman 294). Happiness is not in fleeting pleasures; happiness is a life's work.

Being virtuous makes a person happy. Happiness is an activity for the soul that produces a person of high character. For Aristotle there is a clear middle, also known as the Golden Mean, between the extremes of vices that would be called virtue (Pojman 301). The Golden Mean is Aristotle's litmus test of a person's virtue: a virtuous person knows the right amount of action (or attitude or disposition) relative to a situation. A person lacking in virtue demonstrates too much or too little of the relevant virtue. For example, the virtue of courage has the vices of foolhardiness (excess) and cowardice (deficiency). Anger also can be a virtue in the right amount, but also can turn into a vice. The mean is key in virtue ethics for Aristotle.

Aristotle is credited with naming thirteen moral virtues, though lists vary. These include courage, temperance, generosity, magnificence, pride, aspiration, gentleness, truthfulness, ready-wittiness, friendliness, modesty, good temper, and justice (Solomon 82). Exploring some of these as they relate to Letterman's comedy demonstrates that his practice of some of these virtues (and others) led to his transformation and journey to happiness.

Virtue Ethics in Comedy

If teleology were to be applied to the comedic purpose, what might that be? What would a virtuous comedian look like? Can comedy lead one to virtuous living? Does comedy have anything to do with virtue? These questions arise when we try to look beyond the purpose of comedy as simply "to make us laugh." These questions have been addressed by many thinkers both classical and modern. We will look at three: Henri Bergson, John Morreall, and Aristotle.

The French philosopher Henri Bergson looked at what humor did for/to people. Bergson understands the human condition as often inflexible and plagued with seriousness. Mundanity and tragedy are the mainstay of daily happenings. We live in a world where we are forced to face daily problems of our existence and hardships. This can render some to function outside the human purpose and lead to unvirtuous living. Bergson saw comedy and a type of corrective laughter as a solution to this problem: "the function of laughter, according to Bergson, is to humiliate the inflexible person into acting humanly once more" (Morreall 130). Through humiliation and humor a person can be led back to the human fold to pursue the ultimate goal of being happy. Here, humor and laughter can be a gateway to self-correcting behavior. For example, when a public figure commits misdeeds their behavior becomes fodder for comedians. According to Bergson, comedy's goal is "the correction of such negative behavior by the punishing humiliation of laughter which emancipates affected individuals from the bonds of rigidity into which they have fallen, so that they can respond with flexibility and grace that is inherent in their human nature and which is very much valued and needed by society" (Golden 284). A virtuous person does not hide from this humiliation. Instead, they recommit to practicing virtues that would improve their character. The laughter that comes from comedy can cause one to reflect on who they want to be and how they want to be perceived by others.

Bergson is not alone in his understanding that comedy can be used for a much greater purpose than just to make us laugh. For John Morreall, humor has the potential to be both morally negative and positive, relative to which virtues, attitudes, or dispositions are brought to the fore. Similar to Bergson, Morreall suggests that laughter is a gateway for evaluating a person's character and can be used to motivate people to turn away from vice and toward a virtuous life. In *Comic Relief*, Morreall focuses on three virtues that praiseworthy humor gives rise to: graciousness, humility, and perseverance. Praiseworthy humor encourages the virtue of patience, making "us more understanding of other people, what they think, and how they act" (Morreall 116). Similarly, praiseworthy humor encourages graciousness and kindness such that it allows "someone who is morally blameworthy to relax and not feel threatened" (Morreall 117). Practicing meeting someone with the right degree of kindness, instead of anger and aggression, encourages that person to correct their behavior. Two things happen as a result: the kind person is thought well of and, second, their habitual practice of kindness makes their life easier to live.

They are living well with others in their community and, at the same time, role-modeling how to live well. Finally, humility and perseverance also are fostered by humor. For Morreall, "if we see our failures and mistakes with a comic eye, we are less likely to be overcome by feelings of frustration" (118). We can persevere with humility through times of hardship and disappointment through the use of humor.

As Bergson suggests, Morreall too believes that comedy's and the comic's purpose is in part to let the subject see where they have been led astray and where their humanity has faltered. Humor and laughter, when used to correct vices and encourage people toward virtuous behavior, leads a person on the path toward virtuous living.

Bergson and Morreall both focus on the corrective power of humor and laughter, insisting that the right kind of joke, laughed at the right way, can encourage virtuous behavior. And while Aristotle had misgivings about humor and laughter (specifically, that they encouraged malice and, potentially, violence stemming from condescending laughter), it is still possible to use Aristotle, as others have done, to ask whether humor and laughter encourage virtuous behavior. The most relevant virtue for this question is "ready-wittedness."

Was Letterman Happy?

Aristotle defines ready-wittiness as "the tactful way of making and appreciating humor jests in everyday conversation or art itself" (McKinney 3). Like all Aristotelian virtues, ready-wittiness lies in between two extremes. The deficit (too little) is boorishness and the excess (too much) is buffoonery. Buffoonery is defined by Aristotle as vulgarity and carrying humor to the excess (McKinney 3). Widening the definition some, buffoonery can be defined as foolish or playful behavior or practice. Jesting just for the sake of a laugh, for no greater purpose, is an example of buffoonery. Buffoonery is a result of wanting a laugh and getting it, no matter the means. Humor at any cost is also inherent in Aristotle's explanation of this vice. On the other extreme, Aristotle defines the boor as "incapable of making or appreciating humor, someone is so overly serious and finds fault with everything that he is unable to have any comic sympathy with human foibles" (qtd. in McKinney 4). The boor does not see levity and looks at himself and the world with a negative view. Curmudgeonly character can be the root of the boor. One is not happy and sees no humor in life itself. The virtuous comedian would employ tact and self-control. The moral comedian would know how to limit the jokes to provide not only laughs but a greater purpose with the intent to live out virtue. The comedian who takes everyday occurrences and provides not only a laugh but reflects on the greater meaning of his jokes would be practicing ready-wittedness. In terms of the Golden Mean, ready-wittedness would be knowing when to remain silent, or, when humorous speech is appropriate, saying the right kind of light-hearted statement relative to the seriousness of the situation.

In the comedy of Letterman, both the vices and virtue of ready-wittiness are at play. Looking at the span of his comedic career, one can see an evolution from buffoonery (Stupid Pet Tricks) and boorishness (his open disdain for some of his guests) to ready-wittedness. Different periods of Letterman's life display defining moments that illustrate this trichotomy. But again, these virtues and vices accompanied others that helped focus his comedy to be more than just for laughs.

Buffoonery and Boorishness

Late Night with David Letterman on NBC was Letterman's incubator for his buffoonery and a stop on his journey to ready-wittedness. Whether it be wearing a suit of velcro, Alka-Seltzer, or sponges and throwing himself against a wall or being dipped into a vat of water, Letterman in his early career seemed to thrive on gags and stunts to get a laugh. Why would a grown man wearing a velcro suit and attaching himself to a wall be funny? Why would he choose to do such a gag? Letterman took the silliness of such a stunt and made light of himself as the buffoon who would do anything for a laugh. In doing so, he was puncturing the illusion that late night comedy was serious. If Carson had his visits from Joan Embry and Jim Fowler and mined comedy from his interactions with the animals, Letterman, ever the buffoon, was content to play the animal. If there is a vice in this behavior it is that he sinks too low beneath the level of human to be considered estimable. He made a mockery of himself, and everything around him seemed fair game for the sake of a laugh. He seems to prove Aristotle right that, "the buffoon, on the other hand, is the slave of his sense of humor, and spares neither himself nor others if he can raise a laugh and says things none of which a man of refinement would say, and to some of which he would not even listen" (Aristotle, bk. 4, ch. 8). However, the virtue might be that what had become rote and predictable with Carson's interactions with animals becomes, upon reflection, enlivened and liberating in Letterman's.

Another side of buffoonery is making light of others, sometimes to the extent of cruelty. For most comedians, making fun of others' mundanity or errors seems to be part of the purpose of comedy, and, as Bergson points out, this functions to correct and rehabilitate behavior. Letterman was no exception to this, especially in his early years. It seemed that everyone was fair game, especially celebrities. He took a stance that the business they chose to be in made them rightfully susceptible to his brand of humor (Lennon 94). Many performers would say that they were afraid to go on the Letterman show, knowing that they could be a target of his buffoonery. Some took it in stride; others admonished his mean-spiritedness. Some, especially some actresses, just stayed away from him and chose not to appear on his show even if it meant not being able to promote their next movie or television series (Zinoman 155). Many would argue that comedy is an art with the purpose of garnering laughs no matter the method, and this might lead one to think that laughter is proof of virtue, however, "so even buffoons are called ready-witted because they are found attractive; but that they differ from the ready-witted man, and to no small extent, is clear from what has been said" (Aristotle, bk. 4, ch. 8). Letterman's treatment of his guests would be an example of this attitude. However, it is not an example of ready-wittedness which requires the virtue of tact, which, at this stage of his career, Letterman was missing.

Where buffoonery is wit without tact, the other extreme of which ready-wittedness is the middle, is boorishness. The boor takes life seriously, does not delight in the humorous, and sees fault even where it doesn't lie. In Aristotle's words, "while those who can neither make a joke themselves nor put up with those who do are thought to be boorish and unpolished" (Aristotle, bk. 4, ch. 8). Aristotle observes that the boor does not enjoy the rewards of life but rather focuses of the negativity. Letterman was a famous and admitted hypochondriac, often labeled a curmudgeon, and had a reputation for never being satisfied with his craft. Although he was successful, had high ratings, and won awards, these achievements never seemed to be enough for Letterman. He would not relish them; he would rather focus on what was not perfect: "He never enjoyed the success and scrutinized every failure, musing darkly about the implications and pivoting from self-criticism to despair in a blink" (Zinoman 85). Letterman seemed to assume that being a boor, focusing on the potential problems, was the virtuous way to live. Again, this was overly evident in his early career. In 1982, he told an interviewer, "If you have any sense, you'll adopt the view of life that if the bucket of shit can explode, it will explode" and "if anything can go wrong it sure and the hell will" (Zinoman 86, Lennon 96). He didn't view it as a negative outlook. He thought of the stance as practicing the virtue of prudence. Boorishness of this sort is not a virtue because it is extreme and, therefore, not appropriate for every situation. All of these seem to fit under the vice of boor. It seemed like extreme behavior for someone with Letterman's gifts and talents.

Ready-wittiness and Courage

On the virtue of ready-wittiness, Aristotle notes that "there are, then, jokes he will not make; for the jest is a sort of abuse, and there are things that lawgivers forbid us to abuse; and they should, perhaps, have forbidden us even to make a jest of such" (Aristotle, bk. 4, ch. 8). For Aristotle, such a man will not use comedy for any laugh but will be discerning in doing so. As Aristotle points out, wit, like all virtues, is relative and varies with amount needed to be truly virtuous (McKinney 5). Knowing when to be funny and when to be stoic, many might say, is a mark of a truly balanced comedian. There are times for jokes, then there are times for a more serious disposition.

Over time, Letterman seemed to develop self-control and discernment, two of the marks of ready-wittiness. He became more reflective and wittier as time progressed. Over time there was a shift toward a more balanced perspective and response to what he would joke about and his relationships with his guests. Moving away from the buffoon persona, Letterman's response when asked why he did not make any jokes about the O.J. Simpson murder trial was that "double homicides just don't crack me up like they used to" (qtd. in Zinoman 253). Letterman chose not to use his comedy to shine light on a tragedy. This seemed like a comedic choice that might not have been made earlier in his career. Some might say it was courageous as other comedians and late night hosts were generating notoriety and ratings by playing the trial for laughs. Something stopped him from going back to buffoonery even when his ratings dropped. Nowhere in Letterman's career is this more evident than in his first appearance after 9/11. He was the first comedian to go back on air after the devastation. He admitted he did not want to go back. He wanted others to take the lead. In an interview with Regis Philbin, he said he did not know if the time was right. But when the mayor said that lives must go on and people should go back to work, Letterman knew he had to ("David"). Here it is evident that Letterman knew the significance of what it would mean if he went back to work. Sitting at his desk, he asked for indulgence as he talked about the utter tragedy. He went on to talk about the terrible sadness that had impaled the city and the nation. He talked about the heroes. He talked about his city, New York City. While he made small jabs at himself for the sake of humor, his seriousness and grief rang through his monologue. He went on for a while talking about the virtue of courage, especially as applied to the Mayor Giuliani: "There is one requirement for any of us and that is to be courageous. Because courage, as you might know, defines all other human behavior. And I believe, because I have done a little of this myself, pretending to be courageous, is just as good as the real thing" (qtd. in Giller). Letterman recognized courage in the men and women heroes of 9/11, but also a little in himself. Through his gateway virtue of ready-wittiness,

Letterman was able to employ other virtues, in this case courage. As he grew out of boorishness and buffoonery and displayed ready-wittedness more often, Letterman displayed a wider range of virtues than those only associated with tact and humor.

Patience, Humility, Perseverance, Gratitude

Most, including Letterman himself, thought that when Johnny Carson retired from *The Tonight Show* in 1992, he would inherit the NBC mainstay. He did not; instead, *The Tonight Show* desk was offered to Jay Leno. That was a blow to Letterman's ego and the little happiness he seemed to have at that point in his life waned. Through a bidding war he landed at CBS and had a successful 22-year run, but the lasting effects of being passed over for his dream job could be seen for many years after. Many believed that it added to his self-loathing and insecurity. Yet Letterman found a way to make light of the situation and developed his ready-wittedness even more (with some buffoonery creeping in). He poked fun on air at the executives, the network, and anybody who was involved in his not getting what he thought of as his dream job (Zinoman 223). He was not going to go quietly.

For a man who based his self-worth and purpose on his comedic career, the loss of *The Tonight Show* seemed like a monumental and defining event. Letterman demonstrated his growth as a person and comedian when opening up his comedy to include more of his life. Opening up his comedy to include his health problems and personal failings showed that Letterman was a more complete person: including aspects of his life that had been kept separate from his humor reflects Aristotle's claim that the pursuit of happiness or eudemonia is an activity of the whole person, not just parts of themselves. In 2000, Letterman underwent quintuple bypass surgery and this transformed his outlook on life and comedy. On the night he returned to the airways, tears formed as he spoke of his gratitude. He brought out the doctors and nurses that saved his life. He made some jokes, kissed the nurses, and showed his emotions. Letterman seemed utterly grateful for his life. This was new for someone whose buffoonery and pessimism could make one reasonably claim that he never seemed to really appreciate life and all he had.

The second life event that changed Letterman and points toward how his growth as a person led to his growth as a comedian was the birth of his son, Harry, at age 56. At the time, Letterman remarked that he "could never imagine being part of something this beautiful" (qtd. in Zinoman 279). Letterman is not unique in this regard. For him it was a major turning point, and his life would never be the same. He would not view the world with the same eyes. Everything now was filtered through the lens of how it would affect his son. He worried about the world Harry would inherit. He boasted about Harry often on *The Late Show* and talked about fatherhood in interviews. The once-private Letterman was happy and wanted the world to know. Where Letterman's previous worries about the world were rooted in his pessimism, specifically the solipsistic concern of how the world around him was going to come undone and harm him, Letterman's worries seemed to shift toward the world that would be left for his son (Marchese 37). The happiness that Letterman displayed on air and in interviews could be an example of Aristotle's virtuous person who has achieved eudemonia. At the same time, Letterman's subsequent lapses reveals a truth of virtue ethics: one is never done practicing the habits that contribute to the living of a virtuous life.

Contriteness and Honesty

On October 1, 2009, Letterman sat as his desk, as he did he did multiple nights a week, and started talking about what seemed like was just another story of some buffoonery or mundane happenings. He told a story about a package he found in his car and then went on to tell the audience that he soon realized he was being blackmailed about some "terrible things" he did. The audience, at this point, was laughing, still not knowing the seriousness of his actions. His history of buffoonery led them to believe there would be a joke emerging. He then explained that the "terrible things," the "creepy things," he did, was having sex with women who worked for him. Letterman, instead of giving in to the would-be blackmailer, admitted his wrong doing to thwart the attempt. Some lauded Letterman for his courage and honesty. Others admonished him for abusing his authority, pointing out (pre #MeToo) that he was able to "get by with it" because of his privilege and celebrity. Another interpretation would be that Letterman has never shed his buffoon persona. Because he did not take anything seriously, then no one should take anything he does seriously. The buffoon was not just a character he played, it was his character and the lens through which people viewed him and evaluated his behavior. For Jack Tuckner, writing on women's rights in the workplace, this attitude toward Letterman and his transgressions ultimately undermines women's authority in the workplace:

> At the crux of the issue are his responses and responsibilities as a media personality who has been accorded viewership.... Letterman has violated the workplace ethics by involving in sexual relationships—not just with one woman, but with several, while being an employer. He has also displayed disgusting attitudes towards women in understanding their limits and potential. And his making references to his "affairs" in jocular fashion only adds to his already established sexist image [Tuckner].

What is clear is that self-preservation was at work in Letterman's confession. Where he might have been displaying the virtue of tact in not naming the woman he slept with, he was not honest enough with his viewers about the wrongness of his behavior. A week later, he finally apologized to the women who worked for him and to his family, especially his wife. One might assume that after such revelations, Letterman would avoid sexual innuendos as jokes; but this was not the case (Zinoman 288). Years later, Letterman admitted in an interview with Oprah Winfrey that only he was to blame for the scandal, that he is still atoning for his actions, still trying to figure out why he did it, and that he grew from it in ways even he could not explain. Letterman also admitted something that had not been heard from him frequently: "My life is fun and full of joy I only pretended to have before" (qtd. in "Oprah"). We return to the main question of this essay: could it be that practicing the virtues of wittiness, honesty, atonement, humility, and others that Letterman did begin to fulfill at least in part what Aristotle claims to be the human purpose, to be happy?

Pride and Aspiration

Letterman has been labeled the king of late night, a comedic genius, a culture icon, and much more. In 2015, after 33 years on television, Letterman retired from *The Late Show*. In his retirement he was lavished with praise for what he did to change not only the culture of TV and the culture of comedy, but the American culture (Zinoman 148). He was thanked and admired for what he did. Letterman seemed to take it in stride. He accepted the compliments as best as he could, occasionally denying his impact on the landscape of American culture. A number of avenues were open to Letterman in his retirement: a private life out of the public eye, another show, comedy specials, etc. However, the choices Letterman did make for his public life after retirement allude to mending his previous wrongs in order to better the greater good. The first project he chose to do post-retirement was an episode of the show *Years of Living Dangerously* for The National Geographic Channel. He traveled to India to see how they are trying to lead the way in renewable energy to solve their energy crisis and diminish the effects of climate change. The environment was a pressing issue for Letterman (qtd. in Itzkoff). In this episode, Letterman demonstrates the kind of ready-wittedness that can only be accomplished if the individual understands what ready-wittedness is because they have practiced it before. Whether it was amazement when he saw many huts being warmed and lit by burning cow dung or when he was interviewing the Prime Minister of India, he used his wit to teeter between comedy and seriousness. Letterman used humor seriously so that the audience would be inspired to the right attitudes and dispositions.

At the same time, this might have only been the public performance of ready-wittedness: "Sydney Trattner, a senior producer who traveled with Mr. Letterman, said that he was dogged by self-doubt throughout the journey. 'He never thinks he's doing a good job,' Ms. Trattner said" (Itzkoff 2016). Other instances of Letterman lamenting, perhaps too much, his buffoonery include his lament to President Barack Obama that instead of marching for civil rights in 1965 ("Why wasn't I in Alabama? Why wasn't I aware?") he was on a cruise ship getting drunk with friends ("Obama"). He came across as ashamed not only his lack of action, but his lack of awareness. In another post retirement interview he lamented "I wish I would have retired 10 years earlier, so I could have done something useful for humans" ("Seinfeld"). For him, his life as a comedian seemed like a waste when compared to the ways that others live out their humanity. He didn't buy into the notion Bergson suggests that comedy can help society better itself. This self-reflection became a common occurrence for Letterman in his post retirement years. The boor creeps up again and again as Letterman continues to focus more on what he did not do than what he did accomplish or what he means to others.

Conclusion

We return to the purpose of comedy. "The function of laughter according to Bergson, is to humiliate the inflexible person into acting humanly once more" (Morreall 130). Letterman was the inflexible person. If Letterman became more virtuous because of the major life events that changed his outlook on life, then he demonstrated virtues of openness and reflection. If Letterman became more virtuous because his of his humiliations and regrets, which he now seems to own, Letterman demonstrates the virtues of growth and introspection. Letterman grew from being just a guy in a velcro suit by showing that there could be a symbiotic relationship between the right kind of humor—ready-wittedness—and the pursuit of happiness through a virtuous life. Additionally, Letterman helped his audience see that the seriousness of life can be cut with laughter and that laughter can bring others back into the human fold.

On many occasions Letterman would diagnosis himself with anhedonia, the inability to feel happiness (Gay 78). In the defining moments of his life, Letterman's eudemonia started to emerge. His heart surgery, 9/11, the birth of his son, and other events helped him become not only a wittier and virtuous comedian, but a more evolved human being. He considered himself blessed and defined prosperity differently than he did earlier in his life. Even though his vices appeared to wane, they never fully vanished. Aristotle asserts that this is the plight of the human condition, yet there is still hope toward eudemonia when we practice virtues. Through virtues, Letterman evolved in his comedy and in his life. This is no small feat.

Works Cited

Aristotle. *The Nicomachean Ethics*. Translated by William David Ross, 1908, *Internet Sacred Text Archive*, 2010, www.sacred-texts.com/cla/ari/nico/nico042.htm. Accessed 6 August 2018.

"David Letterman Remembers 9/11." *Youtube*. CNN, 23 May 2012, www.youtube.com/watch?v=Z0HYF60U_Q8. Accessed 12 June 2018.

Gay, Jason. "Dave at Peace." *Rolling Stone*, 18 September 2008, pp. 74–84.

Giller, Don. "Late Show, September 17, 2001." *YouTube*. 3 May 2017, www.youtube.com/watch?v=2DcdVqivjgk. Accessed 12 June 2018.

Golden, Leon. "Aristotle on Comedy." *Journal of Aesthetics and Art Criticism*, vol. 42, no. 3, 1 April 1984, pp. 283–90.

Itzkoff, Dave. "David Letterman (and His Beard) Shop at Target These Days." *New York Times*, 18 October 2016, www.nytimes.com/2016/10/23/arts/television/david-letterman-late-show-retirement.html. Accessed 12 July 2018.

Lennon, Rosemarie. *David Letterman: On Stage and Off*. Pinnacle Books, 1994.

MacIntyre, Alasdair. *After Virtue*. 3rd ed., University of Notre Dame Press, 2007.

Marchese, David. "David Letterman." *New York Magazine*, 6 March 2017, pp. 28–38.

McKinney, Ronald. "Aristotle and the Comic Hero: Uses of the Moral Imagination." *Philosophy Today*, vol. 42, no. 4, 1998, https://www.questia.com/library/journal/1P3-39189455/aristotle-and-the-comic-hero-uses-of-the-moral-imagination. Accessed 2 June 2018.

Morreall, John. *Comic Relief A Comprehensive Philosophy of Humor*. Wiley-Blackwell, 2009.

"Obama, Barack." *My Next Guest Needs No Introduction with David Letterman*, Season 1, Episode 1, Netflix, 2018. https://www.netflix.com/title/80209096/.

"Oprah and David Letterman." *Oprah's Next Chapter*, OWN, 7 January 2013. https://www.youtube.com/watch?v=g5FqqGpKzzA&t=89s&list=PLvLsjiS8OChzI5MxVUwM6-7rr_JrFLEqy&index=8. Accessed 5 July 2018.

Pojman, Louis, editor. "Aristotle's Nicomachean Ethics." *Classics of Philosophy*. 1998, pp. 289–320.

Rader, Dotson. "I Love Nothing More Than Being in Love." *Parade*, 26 May 1996, pp. 4–6.

"Seinfeld, Jerry." *My Next Guest Needs No Introduction with David Letterman,* Season 1, Episode 7, Netflix, 2018. https://www.netflix.com/title/80209096/

Solomon, Robert. *Morality & The Good Life*. McGraw-Hill, 1984.

Tuckner, Jack. "David Letterman: Privileges produce Consensus." *Tuckner, Sipser, Weinstock & Sipser: Women in the Workplace LLP*, 7 October 2009, womensrightsny.com/david-letterman-privileges-produce-consensus/. Accessed 6 Aug. 2018.

Zinoman, Jason. *Letterman: The Last Giant of Late Night*. HarperCollins, 2017.

The Complex Ethics
of Jimmy Kimmel
as Confidence Man
and Scientific Communicator

SHELLY A. GALLIAH

This essay addresses the complicated ethics of two segments from *Jimmy Kimmel Live*. In these videos—"A Message for the Anti-Vaccination Movement" (February 26, 2015) and "Scientists and Climate Change" (May 2, 2016)—Kimmel satirically deconstructs two persistent manufactured scientific controversies. According to Leah Ceccarelli, a "scientific controversy is 'manufactured' in the public sphere when an arguer announces that there is ongoing scientific debate in the technical sphere about a matter for which there is overwhelming scientific consensus" (196). These controversies are perpetuated in two main ways. The mass media, in its drive to present both sides of a story, puts uninformed naysayers and/or maverick scientists in debate with scientific experts, resulting in the flaw of balance as bias (Boykoff). This flaw encourages the misconception that the science is unsettled on particular issues such as climate change. These controversies are also perpetuated by certain "merchants of doubt," who, driven by ideology, profits, and/or politics, also reframe them as liberal concerns (Oreskes and Ceccarelli). Although Oreskes and Conway focus on those perpetuated by the right, manufactured scientific controversies have also emerged from the left, such as the resistance to water fluoridation, the fear of GMOs, and the vaccine/autism connection (Englehardt).

As a result of this public confusion, comedians concerned about, if not outraged by, these misinformation campaigns might feel obliged to intervene by critiquing these manufactured scientific controversies. In fact, the best

167

televised contemporary satire has been praised for turning a spotlight on topics ignored, misrepresented, or exaggerated by traditional journalism, such as foreign policy issues (Baek, Baumgartner, Gray, and Jones) or scientific controversies, such as climate change (Brewer, Feldman, and Feldman).

Regardless of his intentions in these two segments, Jimmy Kimmel's approaches are ethically problematic due to the method of satire itself. Satire is the "literary art of diminishing or derogating a subject by making it ridiculous and evoking toward it an attitude of amusement, contempt, scorn, or indignation" (Abrams 284). At its best, it "uses laughter as a weapon" to expose weaknesses, injustices, and corruption; to correct persons, ideas, institutions, and events; and to promote change, or, at least, serious contemplation of it (Abrams 284). Whereas the Horatian satirist invokes gentle laughter at humanity's failings, the Juvenalian satirist, believing humanity is ultimately unsalvageable, usually invokes scorn (Abrams). Satire, in general, is morally ambiguous: the ends—amending that person, institution, or practice—supposedly justify its means of criticism. However, when this criticism devolves into cruel laughter, *ad hominem* attacks, or invective, satire's goals become suspect. And the reasons *for* and politics *of* this mockery are also ethically gray. That is, satire appears principled when it challenges hegemony and speaks truth to power, but unfair when it recalls its conservative roots and censures transgressive behavior while rewarding normativity (Day, Hutcheon, Osborne-Good). In this latter guise, satire provides an innocuous release of anger that does not really challenge power as much as denigrate those who have strayed from the status quo, even if that status quo is a sensible acknowledgment of the current environmental crisis (Day 11). Satire's ambiguous goals and politics become more problematic when the person delivering it is a comedian with both substantial power and a questionable ethical past.

For the most part, Kimmel's complex ethics derive from the way that he, and the experts he recruits, balance their potent criticism with comedy in order to keep viewers watching, to win their trust, and to persuade them. Or to put it another way, both Kimmel and his experts must act as confidence men.

This idea of the comedian as a confidence man is derived from Will Kaufman, who argues that the comedian resides in an uncomfortable ironic state. The comedian at work must exist in the divided condition of saying one thing and meaning another, of constantly balancing the roles of funny man (or woman) at play and the social critic at warning. Kaufman elaborates that the comedian keeps up this "inscrutable game" through "maintaining a web of ironic tension between falsehood and earnestness, play and criticism, defense and attack" (12). The comedian must balance "his conflicting and simultaneous urges to be heeded and indulgently dismissed" (Kaufman 12). I add to this list by arguing that the comedian moves between the roles of philanthropist and misanthrope, between the competing desires of saving the world, tearing it down, or simply walking away from it, perhaps in disgust. Living with this self-division may result in what Kaufman refers to as "irony fatigue," the state in which comedians no longer hide behind their masks but move toward becoming straight-faced social critics, as Lenny Bruce eventually did.

When the comedian's method of choice is satire, the ethics, in terms of responsibility to both the subject matter (message) and the audience grow even more complex. Keeping the audience "in fun" while still targeting societal ills is difficult and tricky. That is, if the message is too brutal, the comedian becomes a hardened social critic, that mean-spirited satirist who pushes the audience out of "play" (Eastman). By doing so, she breaks the contract of "fun" with the audience and makes them feel both unhappy and unsafe. She becomes the Juvenalian satirist, who, like Swift, drops the mask out of disgust. On the other hand, if the target is ambiguous or the criticism weak, the comedian doesn't rise to the level of satirist who enlightens her audience and motivates change. This is the main criticism that Hart as well as Hart & Hartelius direct against Jon Stewart. They argue that Stewart is not an effective satirist because his critiques don't motivate political action, but merely complacent cynicism. Jon Stewart, they argue, has committed only political sins. Satire, which Hutcheon refers to as an irony with an assailing function, comes with an additional side-effect: aggregating those people who get the joke and alienating those who are its targets. Satire, in short, creates both insiders and outsiders (52).

Kimmel's confidence game, then, is a delicate one: he must target these manufactured scientific controversies while not distancing his audience— both those faithful and those newly accrued fans. He must also act as social critic while keeping open the option of retreating behind the comic mask or implying that he's "only joking" when the material gets too uncomfortable. To play this confidence game, Kimmel must first convince his audience that he is a trustworthy, non-partisan satirist as well as a concerned, if not awkward, social critic. First, he must trade on his reputation as a popular late-night host to convince his audience of his power, and perhaps his right, to assemble the best experts. He must also exploit his relationship with his audience; because they trust him, they transfer this trust to the doctors and authorities on climate change he has recruited. At the same time, Kimmel's admission of his own lack of scientific knowledge—he is just a comedian, after all—allows him to appear trustworthy and ethical. However, when he safely retreats behind the comic mask by admitting he is not qualified to speak for vaccination safety or climate change, he also protects himself by allowing his chosen experts to take the risks and close the satirical case. The scientists in these videos must also play their own confidence games by trading on their credentials, donning comic masks, and moving between critiquing the audience and remaining in fun.

In making this argument, I complicate Kaufman's idea of the comedian as confidence man by bringing in the classical conception of *ethos*. Of the three rhetorical appeals—logos, pathos, and ethos—ethos, argument by character, is underrated but extremely important in persuading audiences (Heinrichs and Longaker). To create a successful ethos, the speaker must use her personality, experience, and abilities to appear credible and win the audience's trust. Lastly, the speaker must build a bridge to the audience's values and appear unbiased and knowledgeable: she must appear to be representing the audience's interests. It should be noted that ethos is about the performance, rather than the actuality, of credibility.

Kimmel's Complex Ethos

Jimmy Kimmel's early comic roots complicate his credibility. Between 1999 and 2003, he and Adam Carolla were the main creators and hosts of the polarizing *The Man Show*, which had a platform primarily based on skits, pranks, childish humor, sexual innuendo, and misogyny. The show celebrated loutish, sexist, male behavior and perspectives, such as its infamous and awkwardly long ending of buxom girls on trampolines. Although the program was supposed to be ironic, critiquing these very same hyper-masculine perspectives, its satire was usually buried beneath its juvenile antics, if not unrecognizable altogether.

After leaving *The Man Show*, Kimmel began as the seemingly innocuous host of *Jimmy Kimmel Live!* (2003), which began with a fairly standard late-night format—monologue, skits, desk interviews, and musical performances. However, since about 2013 and, especially lately in responses to the Trump presidency, Kimmel has grown increasingly more political, such as in his impassioned May 1, 2017, thirteen-minute opening monologue detailing his son's congenital heart defect. Here, Kimmel relied on his own personal experience to build a bridge to his audience, asking them to trust him not as a celebrity but as a concerned father. He pleaded with his audience to put partisan politics aside and prevent the Republicans from repealing the Affordable Care Act: "If your baby is going to die and it doesn't have to, it shouldn't matter how much money you make…. I think that's something that whether you're a Republican or a Democrat or something else, we all agree on that, right?" However, when he relied on his knowledge of growing up in Las Vegas to champion gun-control legislation after the Mandalay Bay mass shooting of October 1, 2017, he drew backlash from both President Trump's supporters and gun rights advocates, who accused him of being blinded by liberal bias.

In other words, his personal experience gave him credibility on one issue and charges of bias on another.

These two incidents reveal an additional problem when Kimmel uses satire. Because he is on ABC, a major network previously known for staying out of politics (before the controversy over the program *Roseanne*), Kimmel must censor himself and temper his social criticism; he must also recognize those previous loyal fans of *The Man Show* while courting new ones. And he has mostly risen to the challenge. Of the late-show hosts, Kimmel is known for having a steady viewership and an audience with the largest proportion of conservatives (Hiebert).

Admittedly, Kimmel's previous lowbrow humor makes critics question his ethics and his trustworthiness; some suspect that his "new" politically awakened self is just another mask worn to earn him praise, ratings, and dollars. By becoming political, these detractors argue, Kimmel has hypocritically sold out his older fans in order to win liberal ones and charm the Hollywood elite. Accordingly, naysayers on the internet have been circulating Kimmel's black-faced and very offensive impersonation of Karl Malone as well as his uncomfortable track record of sexual-innuendo-filled comedy to make their points (Pignataro).

But I argue that it is this very offensive comic past—one that the comedian himself often guiltily recalls in his monologues—that establishes Kimmel's ethos, making him imperfectly believable and his confidence game more successful. That is, his role as an equal opportunity offender on *The Man Show*, which challenged both the limits of taste and free speech, has won him right-of-center fans. And he caters to these and other audiences in his usually moderate approach to politicized issues, which separates him from other late-night more partisan satirical pundits. Unlike the exasperation of John Oliver, the annoyance of Seth Meyers, or the vitriol of Bill Maher, who all attract mainly left-leaning fans, Kimmel's attitude toward his targets is often one of bemusement and stupefaction—regardless of whether they are current events, political leaders, or government policies. He appears, like the average American, to have stumbled across a troubling problem that he is concerned about but perhaps unqualified to discuss. Rather than Swift's angry Juvenalian speaker, Kimmel is the Horatian satirist more accepting of human foibles. Carter affirms that Kimmel is effective for a reason that is completely antithetical to the charges of Hollywood elitism that many on the right have hurled at him. Kimmel simply sounds like a regular guy making reasonable points—because he is a regular guy. Probably more than any other current late-night host, Kimmel projects solid working-class and family values. He seems to most viewers a guy who could share a beer and slice of pizza with anybody.

Kimmel appears believable, as not practicing a safe, mediagenic Hollywood activism, but a human activism (Carter). His trustworthiness also derives from his reluctance to wear the mantle of America's conscience. On his political stands, he confesses, "I want this to be a comedy show. I hate talking about stuff like this. I just want to give you something to laugh about at night" (qtd. in Carter). Although Kimmel seems an odd choice for polarized scientific topics, his checkered comic history, his non-partisan fanbase, and his folksy blend of comedy and criticism help build a bridge to his audiences and solidify his confidence game.

Kimmel Does Science Communication

In "A Message for the Anti-Vaccination Movement" (February 27, 2015), aired in the middle of a multi-state measles outbreak traced to a California amusement park, Kimmel targets the manufactured scientific controversy that vaccinations cause autism. In the second segment, "Scientists and Climate Change" (May 2, 2016), broadcast the same evening that the Mark Morano–produced and Sarah Palin–endorsed climate-change denying documentary *Climate Hustle* was debuting in theaters, he deconstructs the claim that anthropogenic global warming is a profit-generating liberal-created hoax. Both segments have this structure: Kimmel begins with a monologue contextualizing and critiquing the controversy (approximately three minutes and five minutes, respectively), and then he turns the segment over to the experts: first, a team of six medical doctors; and second, a team of six climate scientists. In doing so, Kimmel attempts to reframe these controversies as public health issues that, as a human activist, he cares about while recognizing the limits of his expertise. When it comes to the comedy, Kimmel has used a similar strategy before—setting up a video and playing it. However, rather than buttoning up the segments, he steps aside here and lets the real authorities get the final word.

In the two introductory monologues, Kimmel strengthens his credibility and appeal to his fan base by being both centrist while respectively targeting liberals and conservatives. In "A Message for the Anti-Vaccination Movement," he focuses on the liberal enclave of Los Angeles, which may house his own celebrity peers, and where there are "20% of kids who aren't vaccinated" because parents "are more afraid of gluten than they are of smallpox." He then reproaches people for forsaking doctors' advice and learning about vaccine dangers from both "your friend's Facebook page" and from the playmate Jenny McCarthy, whose authority derived from "wearing clothes that day." These attacks on celebrity culture and liberals are nods to both the center and to the right. In addition, by making a misogynist comment about McCarthy, he recalls his politically incorrect past and gestures to those *The*

Man Show fans, as if to deflate his own authority and remind viewers that he is, after all, but a dumb comedian and TV host. As a confidence man, he seems to argue "trust me," for I am not a real celebrity but a fallible, concerned human. He furthers this idea by stressing that viewers should definitely not listen to him, but to doctors who have learned certain "magical" skills, such as preventing "children from dying from horrible diseases by giving them little shots." A contrast between these innocuous little shots and those of Botox, "which contains botulism, you know" drives home the irony that wealthy Californians are regularly injecting themselves with dangerous substances while withholding harmless vaccines from their children. In deconstructing this controversy, Kimmel has several satirical targets: far-left liberals, a group not usually associated with science denial; Jenny McCarthy, the Hollywood celebrity who helped publicize the notorious Andrew Wakefield article; Hollywood elites in general; those receiving their scientific degrees from the University of Google; and comedians, like himself, who must intervene on this issue, which represents a serious science communication problem. Despite these jokes, Kimmel appears ethical and believable by maintaining the serious message that avoiding vaccinations will cause a public health crisis. He also implies that protection from virulent diseases is a non-partisan issue.

A similar approach drives the segment "Scientists and Climate Change," but Kimmel's monologue is longer, given his increased number of targets: Morano's film, the alternative right, Sarah Palin, the depiction of climate change as a left-wing conspiracy, Americans' disbelief in this environmental crisis, and the selective distrust of scientific consensus. Using several clips from an interview with ex-governor Sarah Palin, Kimmel initially *appears* to be fair by letting her speak before questioning her claims. Palin wants "people to feel empowered to ask questions about what is being fed [SIC] them by the science community," such as the "inconsistent data that is being produced … and fed to their children." However, after airing her comment, Kimmel disparages it for being "one sentence, one very long, dumb sentence," before asking the audience: "Why do we believe in scientists when it comes to molecules and the speed of light, but not this?" In this one question, Kimmel makes two moves to enforce his credibility and protect his non-partisanship. First, he raises the issue of accepting scientific evidence on one matter (the speed of light), but distrusting it on others. In doing so, he addresses the fallacy of confirmation bias that may afflict his viewers—that tendency to believe facts supporting their own beliefs and values. And when Kimmel stresses the pronoun "we," he aligns himself with his audience; he is just a comedian without scientific expertise who may have once believed unreasonable things himself. But rather than generate more skepticism, he ethically acts as a role model—a responsible citizen who recognizes scientific expertise and the consensus on climate science.

Kimmel more conscientiously appeals to viewers across the political spectrum in his climate change segment. He repeatedly stresses that climate change is not "a liberal vs. conservative thing," "but the people who profit from ignoring it want you to believe it is." He then reproaches *all those* who politicize anthropogenic global warming before listing some disturbing facts about the warmest years on record. Like a confidence man, he balances these startling truths with two dark, unsettling jokes: "you know climate change is happening when the warmest year is always the one you're in." And "Climate change is good for anyone who wants to get swallowed by the ocean. It is good for Aquaman; it is bad for us." Although climate change's effects are definitely tragic, American lack of acceptance of this crisis seems like a cruel joke. And by using the term *us*, he once again addresses ALL Americans; that is, climate change doesn't care about the viewers' politics or whether they "believe" in it. Similarly, Kimmel is careful not to pinpoint the Republican Party directly. Although Palin obviously gets the most condemnation because of her support for *Climate Hustle*, Kimmel avoids other direct *ad hominem* attacks against specific politicians, targeting the larger climate-change-denying power structure instead. He stresses that the climate change hoax is perpetuated by "members of Congress who we don't even like, by the way, because people who take money from companies who make pollution for a living told us not to worry about it." The more obvious target here are those conservative thinktanks (CTTs), such as The Heartland Institute, associated with the fossil fuel industry.

Letting the Real Experts Speak: The (Complicated) Right Thing to Do

A crucial part of Kimmel's confidence game is knowing when to step down and further win the audience's trust by letting the experts speak. Following these two monologues, Kimmel hands over the science and the punchlines to the doctors and the climate-change scientists. He reassures that these people are not liberal or conservative but just like us, albeit smarter versions. It is fitting that for both segments, Kimmel chooses a diverse group of doctors, which not only appeals to his audience but also indicates that these issues cross the typical boundaries of race, class, religion, and gender.

In these taped messages, the initial symbolics of the videos themselves operate as confidence games, making the viewers think they have temporarily left the realm of comedy and moved on to the serious and trustworthy worlds of medicine and climate change science. These well-produced videos resemble generic Public Service Announcements (PSAs). The vaccination controversy video opens with this huge headline: "THE FOLLOWING PEOPLE ARE NOT

ACTORS/THEY ARE MEDICAL DOCTORS," which is accompanied by the caduceus, the symbol of medical authority. Similarly, the climate change video begins with a familiar and almost clichéd shot of the sun on the earth's dark horizon and the warning words: "THESE PEOPLE ARE NOT ACTORS." Both videos feature calm background music, an initial slow pacing, and minimalist backgrounds before presenting authorities who assert their claims. In the vaccination video, several doctors seriously, if not blandly, affirm the safety and effectiveness of vaccines: "I am a doctor and I believe in vaccinations"; "the downsides are non-existent"; "the scientific community is in consensus"; and "there is absolutely no reason not to vaccinate." Perhaps because climate change is a more pressing, wicked problem, and one afflicted by the denial of expertise, Kimmel's professionals here identify themselves and stress their credentials: Aradhna Tripati, paleo climatologist and isotope geochemist; Alex Hall, climate scientist; Jeremy Pal, hydro climatologist; Nina Karnovsky, polar ecologist; Chuck Taylor, environmental analytical chemist; and finally, John Dorsey, marine environmental scientist. After these introductions, these experts deliver staid affirmations about climate change before shifting to its more serious consequences, which could be "extremely dire" (Alex Hall), "catastrophic" (John Dorsey), and "apocalyptic" (Karnovsky). These scientists from different research areas stress the consensus on the current environmental crisis.

And despite the fact that Kimmel appeals to Republicans in one segment and liberals in the other, the doctors and climate scientists themselves exclude politics from their messages. Both groups of experts stress that vaccination avoidance and climate change are public (health) crises. Not one of the doctors and scientists offers a specific conservative or liberal criticism, nor do they offer their own political affiliations (Interestingly, as the doctors introduce themselves, they occupy the right and then the left of the screen, as if appealing to viewers coming from both left and right of center.). Instead, their arguments are based on their own specific knowledge and training.

But this seemingly sober tone and attitude of fairness are actually elements in the confidence games the doctors and scientists are playing. After this opening, these authorities drop their serious masks to put on satiric ones, rejecting both the conventions of the PSA and the expected behavior of professionals. Whereas speakers in a traditional PSA would continue to present the evidence and arrive at a balanced conclusion, these frustrated doctors and scientists simply refuse to argue their cases further, acknowledging the absurdity of appearing in PSAs about scientific issues on which there already is a clear consensus. They swear ("I can't f—in' believe we have to make this PSA"); they whine about their schooling and its disrespect by vaccine skeptics ("I went to school for eight years! Eight years!" and "I'm pretty sure I know what I am talking about"); and they sarcastically recall the success rate of vaccination ("Remember that time you got polio? No, you don't, because your parents got you vaccinated!"). They also insult the source of the public's misinformation while affirming their own qualifications: one laments that he is wasting his time "because you listened to some moron who read a forwarded email." Towards the end, a frustrated doctor breaks the fourth wall, commanding, "Get your f—in children vaccinated!"

Similarly, the climate change experts become increasingly indecorous when affirming that climate change is neither a hoax nor a conspiracy. They repeatedly assert that they're not "screwing" with the public: if they really wanted to profit from Americans' fears, they would "probably tell you that a meteor was coming and then try to sell you a helmet" (Tripati). "This is not a prank," say Karnovsky and Taylor, with Dorsey chiming in that he "once locked one of his buddies in a Port-a-potty, which definitely qualified" as one. In this carnivalesque image, Dorsey admits that though he is indeed a regular guy with a sense of humor, he is *not* joking now. Using a serio-comic tone, the scientists rehearse the signs of global warming before stressing that they're not duping the public because they have nothing to gain from lying. The video concludes with a shot of Tripati with a young boy on her lap. At first, this image seems a clichéd emotional appeal to protect the world for future generations, but then the camera zooms in on the child who utters this startling threat: "You motherf—ers better not f—k this up." Both videos conclude by returning, momentarily, to the genre of the PSA by stressing their messages. The first video ends with the following: "DOCTORS AGREE/ VACCINATE YOUR KIDS. PAID FOR BY PROFESSIONALS WHO KNOW WHAT THEY'RE TALKING ABOUT." Similarly, the climate change video ends with "PAID FOR BY PEOPLE WHO KNOW MORE THAN WE DO" before providing a link to a website: www.globalchange.gov. In this latter single line and link, the video suggests that unlike the "research" in *Climate Hustle*, funded by the spokespeople of Big Oil and special interest groups, actual climate change research is conducted by this esteemed government organization composed of thirteen associated, well-respected agencies. By directing viewers to this external source, Kimmel and his experts are empowering viewers to research the consensus on climate change for themselves.

From the perspective of great entertainment, having professionals and then a child swear and make threats are shocking but effective moves which garner both the audience's attention and their laughter. These tactics also appeal to those loyal viewers who appreciate Kimmel's political incorrectness and lowbrow humor. Swearing children also keep the audience in fun and allow Kimmel to retreat behind his comic mask, reminding viewers that he is only joking.

From an ethical perspective, however, these tactics are more problematic. By taking the time to publicize this message, stressing their credentials, acknowledging the safety of vaccinations and the seriousness of climate change, and recommending a course of action, the doctors and climate change experts seem to be acting ethically in these satiric PSAs. The problems arise when they break the fourth wall and swear directly at the viewers. On the one hand, this behavior could be construed as morally appropriate from the utilitarian standpoint of the end justifying the means. That is, these doctors must curse and be brutally honest caregivers in order to enforce the Hippocratic oath and protect vulnerable children; these scientists must use abusive tactics to support the scientific community, climate change consensus, and, most crucially, the planet. In short, these doctors and scientists violate protocol in order to respond accurately to the current historical moment and stress that both vaccine refusal and climate change skepticism are serious public issues, despite the latter's often shoddy coverage in the mainstream news.

That is, according to the *TV News Archive*, the phrase "climate change is a hoax" has experienced a recent upsurge: of the 3022 mentions of "climate change hoax" since 2009, 2344 are from 2016 to 2018. Conservative powerhouse Fox has been particularly instrumental in perpetuating this hoax as well as misrepresenting climate-change coverage through such tactics as false balance, cherry-picking, and *ad hominem* claims against climate scientists (Huertas and Kriegsman). Further damage, of course, has been effected by various fake news outlets, such as Morano himself, who runs the CC skepticism site *Climate Depot*. This tainted media atmosphere arguably forces scientists and their supporters to use any means necessary—such as this video—to assert that climate change is neither a hoax nor a liberal conspiracy, but an environmental crisis concerning all Americans. "We're not f—ing with you," though hardly the discourse of scientific papers, seems the best way to address climate change deniers, particularly Kimmel's right-of-center viewers who might watch and then be convinced by Morano's film.

Alternatively, these same tactics might be construed as bullying, particularly when the doctors and climate scientists abuse their power by denigrating skeptics and exploiting children. The people targeted by this satire—those who disagree with mandatory vaccinations or with the reality of human-caused climate change—may feel as though Kimmel is acting both unethically and unfairly. For one of these videos, the YouTube comment board reveals this viewpoint. Presently, Kimmel's two-year-old vaccination controversy video, which has over 7.8 million views, still sparks animated discussions about vaccine safety, but the criticisms of Kimmel's rhetoric are somewhat tame. However, it seems that Kimmel's more conservative fan base, whose beliefs are challenged in the climate change video (now at over 920k views), do not appreciate his weighing in on *this* controversy.

Some of this negative feedback was immediately addressed in the following evening's segment—"Jimmy Kimmel Reads Negative Climate Change Comments" (429k viewers). Kimmel begins by nostalgically recalling how in the old days, disgruntled viewers had to mail a letter, but "now when they get upset, they can go online and torpedo that rage at [him] immediately." One viewer doesn't appreciate Kimmel's mocking of Sarah Palin; people don't need a degree to understand that climate scientists are "lying to [sic] their teeth to help the government to control our lives in the name of global warming." Others assert that there is no global warming because the North and South poles still seem "pretty cold to" them and there is way too much snow. Along with rehearsing stale arguments for climate change skepticism, many die-hard right-of-center fans criticize Kimmel for being a "social justice warrior." In other words, he should just drop the politics and the satire and simply stick to being funny; he should remain a comedian and not a political commentator or a science communicator.

Kimmel is obviously airing these garbled negative comments for laughs, but doing so could comprise another confidence game. On the one hand, he mocks those viewers for their repetition of popular misconceptions, such as the beliefs that climate change is a hoax and it is not happening. He also implies that their angry resistance and irrational comments validate his earlier segment and prove that climate change education, even if it comes from comedians, is increasingly important. At the same time, he gets the last word by reminding his audience that despite the reactions to his segment, he is only a frustrated comic making dark jokes: although initially frustrated by these comments, he now "is kind of okay with global warming wiping out the human race. Turns out we deserve it!" (2:43).

Conclusion: The Role of the Confidence Man in a Post-Truth Society

In short, the ethics of Kimmel's satire are complicated. He appears fair and trustworthy in recognizing the limits of his own knowledge; he has a basic understanding of the vaccination and climate change topics (particularly the concepts of herd immunity and weather trends), but he is humble enough to consult the real experts. He openly disparages his own credentials and regularly recalls his flawed past: "I know I'll keep being beaten over the head by every whacko website, and I know there'll be a lot of 'what the hell do you know? Go back to girls jumping on trampolines.' This is not about what I know; this is about what scientists know." Despite the subject matter, he keeps the humor absurd by bombarding his audience with threats and with versions of the f-word. But whether these are moves of honesty, deception, or both cannot be clearly ascertained. And whether the goal is serious science communication or mainly the appearance of it accompanied by laughter is also unclear.

What is clear, however, is that the scientific controversies of questionable vaccine safety and climate change have become so mediatized that people might ignore them and neglect their seriousness. That Americans are choosing not to vaccinate their kids, which is leading to disease and death, and that a sizeable proportion of the population disbelieves in the consensus about anthropogenic global warming are disturbing facts. Therefore, from this vantage point, it may be ethical for Jimmy Kimmel to play this confidence game in which he exploits his (then) mostly nonpartisan fan base, adopts the role of concerned science communicator, and encourages doctors and scientists to play with their professional masks. All of these tactics are necessary to intervene on these manufactured scientific controversies.

Still, it may be far too late for Kimmel to retreat and say "I'm only joking." It's clear that he has resigned to moving more steadily left of center. And perhaps beginning to suffer from irony fatigue himself, he has often dropped his comic mask for the social activist one, both on and off the stage. In a recent interview with CBS correspondent Tracy Smith, when he was asked whether he was bothered if his more conservative viewership had dropped, he replied: "I don't say I don't mind … I mean, I'd love for everyone—I want everyone with a television to watch the show" (qtd. in Chasmer). That is, he understands that combining politics and comedy is definitely risky but worthwhile. In response to not alienating his audience, he feels "that's the wrong way to approach comedy and being on television.… I'll leave that kind of thing to big corporations. If you pasteurize your show, you'll be the worse for it" (qtd. in Chasmer). He admits that late-night TV hosts have often been reluctant to show their political hands because of the constraints of network television. Rather than wait until the waning years of his program, he jumped into political comedy out of a "real serious concern for the future of this country."

And the future of this country is unfortunately one that involves an uncertain relationship with the truth. That is, McIntyre argues that Americans are currently living in a post-truth society, one in which "facts can always be shaded, selected, and presented within a political context that favors one interpretation of truth over another" (173). In particular, we are living through a time in which the Flat Earth Society holds conventions in major cities, a time in which facts supporting one's ideology are felt to be *truer*, such as the certainty that vaccines are unsafe and that anthropogenic global warming is an exaggerated liberal hoax. In this post-truth era, it seems ethical and reasonable for comedians like Jimmy Kimmel to use any means necessary to communicate the facts about the vaccine and environmental crises. That is, it may be both right and fair to play a confidence game if it means educating viewers and potentially saving lives.

Works Cited

Abrams, MH. *A Glossary of Literary Terms*. 8th edition. Thomson, 2005.

Baek, Young Min, and Magdalena E. Wojcieszak. "Don't Expect Too Much! Learning from Late-Night Comedy and Knowledge Item Difficulty." *Communication Research, Sage*, vol. 36, no. 6, 2009, pp. 783–80. doi:10.1177/0093650209346805.

Baumgartner, Jody C. "Stoned Slackers or Super Citizens? *The Daily Show* Viewing and Political Engagement of Young Adults." *The Stewart Colbert effect: Essays on the Real impact of Fake News*, Edited by A. Amarasingham, McFarland, 2011, pp. 63–78.

Boykoff, Maxwell T. and Jules M. Boykoff. "Balance as Bias: Global Warming and the US Prestige Press." *Global Environmental Change*, vol. 14, no. 2, 2004, pp. 125–136. *JSTOR*, https://doi.org/10.1016/j.gloenvcha.2003.10.001.

Brewer, Paul R., and Jessica McKnight, "Climate as Comedy: The Effects of Satirical Television News on Climate Change Perceptions." *Science Communication*, vol. 37, no. 5, 3 August 2015, pp. 635–657. *Sage Premier*, doi:10.1177/1075547015597911.

Carter, Bill. "How Jimmy Kimmel Became America's Conscience," *CNN Media*, 3 October 2017, https://money.cnn.com/2017/10/03/media/jimmy-kimmel-las-vegas-conscience/index.html. Accessed 14 April 2018.

Ceccarelli, Leah. "Manufactured Scientific Controversy: Science, Rhetoric, and Public Debate." *Rhetoric and Public Affairs*, vol. 14, no. 2, Summer 2011, pp. 195–228. *Project Muse*, doi:10.1353/rap.2010.0222.

Chasmer, Jessica. "Jimmy Kimmel Says 'Riddance' to Republican Viewers: Wouldn't Want 'A Conversation with Them Anyway.'" *The Washington Times*, 16 October 2017, https://www.washingtontimes.com/news/2017/oct/16/jimmy-kimmel-says-riddance-republican-viewers-woul/. Accessed 20 March 2018.

"Climate Change." *TV News Archive*, https://archive.org/details/tv?q=climate%20change. Accessed 4 April 2018.

Climate Hustle. Directed by Christopher Rogers, performances by Mark Morano, Claude Allegre, and Judith Curry, CDR Communications, 2017.

Cook, John, et al. "Quantifying the Consensus on Anthropogenic Global Warming in the Scientific Literature." *Environmental Research Letters*, vol. 8, no. 2, 15 May 2013. http://iopscience.iop.org/article/10.1088/1748-9326/8/2/024024/meta.

Day, Amber. *Satire + Dissent: Interventions in Contemporary Political Debate*. Indiana University Press, 2011.

Dearing, James W. "Newspaper Coverage of Maverick Science: Creating Controversy through Balancing." *Public Understanding of Science*, vol. 4, no. 4, 1996, pp. 341–361. *Sage*, https://doi.org/10.1088/0963–6625/4/4/002.

Eastman, Max. *Enjoyment of Laughter*, Introduction by William Fry, 1936. Routledge, 2017.

Englehardt, H. Tristam Jr., and Arthur L. Caplan. *Scientific Controversies: Case Studies in the Resolution and Closure of Disputes in Science and Technology*. Cambridge University Press, 1987.

Feldman, Lauren. "Cloudy with a Chance of Heat Balls: The Portrayal of Global Warming on *The Daily Show* and *The Colbert Report*." *International Journal of Communication*, vol. 7, 2013, pp. 430–451. *Proquest*, http://ijoc.org/index.php/ijoc/article/view/1940/861.

_____, Anthony Leiserowitz, and Edward Maibach. "The Science of Satire: *The Daily Show* and *The Colbert Report* as Sources of Public Attention to Science and the Environment." *The Stewart/Colbert Effect*. Edited by Amaranth Amarasingham, foreword by Robert W. McChesney, McFarland, 2011, pp. 25–46.

Flood, Brian. "Jimmy Kimmel Was a Vulgar Comic Long Before He Was 'America's Conscience.'" *Fox News Entertainment*, 12 October 2017, http://www.foxnews.com/entertainment/2017/10/12/jimmy-kimmel-was-vulgar-comic-long-before-was-americas-conscience.html. Accessed 12 March 2018.

Gray, Jonathan, et al. "The State of Satire, the Satire of the State." *Satire TV: Politics and Comedy in the Post-Network Era*. Edited by Jonathan Gray, Jeffrey P. Jones, and Ethan Thompson, NYU Press, 2009, pp. 3–36.

Hart, Roderick P. "The Rhetoric of Political Comedy: A Tragedy." *International Journal of Communications*, vol. 7, 2013, pp. 333–348, ijoc.org/index.php/ijoc/article/viewFile/1950/857. Accessed 20 June 2015.

Hart, Roderick P., and E. Johanna Hartelius. "The Political Sins of Jon Stewart." *Critical Studies in Media Communications*, vol. 24, no. 3, 2007, pp. 263–272. *Taylor and Francis Online*, doi:10.1080/07393180701520991.

Heinrichs, Jay. *Thank You for Arguing: What Aristotle, Lincoln, and Homer Simpson Can Teach Us About the Art of Persuasion.* Three Rivers Press, 2013.

Hiebert, Paul. "The Political Leanings of Late Nights Big Three." *Today,* 30 September 2016, https://today.yougov.com/news/2016/09/30/late-night-talk-shows-politics-audience/. Accessed 3 September. 2016.

Holnan, Angie Drobnic. "2016 Lie of the Year: Fake News." *Politifact,* 13 December 2016, http://www.politifact.com/truth-o-meter/article/2016/dec/13/2016-lie-year-fake-news/. Accessed 20 January 2017.

Huertas, Aaron and Rachel Kriegsman. "Assessing the Accuracy of Cable News Coverage of Climate Science." *Union of Concerned Scientists.* https://xpda.com/junkmail/junk230/Science-or-Spin-report.pdf.

Hutcheon, Linda. *Irony's Edge: The Theory and Politics of Irony.* Routledge, 1994.

Jones, Jeffrey and Geoffrey Baym. "A Dialogue on Satire News and the Crisis of Truth in Postmodern Political Television." *Journal of Communication Theory,* vol. 34, no. 3, 2010, pp. 278–294, https://doi.org/10.1177/0196859910373654.

Kaufman, Will. *The Comedian as Confidence Man: Studies in Irony Fatigue.* Wayne State University Press, 1997.

Kimmel, Jimmy. "A Message for the Anti-Vaccine Movement." *YouTube,* uploaded by *Jimmy Kimmel Live*, 26 February 2015, https://www.youtube.com/watch?v=QgpfNScEd3M&t=10s.

_____. "Jimmy Kimmel and Scientists and Climate Change." *YouTube,* uploaded by *Jimmy Kimmel Live*, 2 May 2016, https://www.youtube.com/watch?v=9UCdFbyL8y0&t=7s.

_____. "Jimmy Kimmel Reads Negative Comments about Climate Change." *YouTube,* uploaded by *Jimmy Kimmel Live*, 3 May 2016, https://www.youtube.com/watch?v=Vkr0BSVUSi8.

_____. "Jimmy Kimmel Reveals Details of His Son's Birth and Heart Disease." *YouTube,* uploaded by *Jimmy Kimmel Live*, 1 May 2017, https://www.youtube.com/watch?v=MmWWoMcGmo0.

Lange, Patricia G. "Living in YouTubia: Bordering on Civility." *Proceedings of the Southwestern Anthropological Association Conference* (SWAA2008), Southwestern Anthropological Association, 2008, pp. 98–106.

"Legal Mandate," *Global Change,* www.globalchange.gov/about. Accessed 23 March 2018.

McIntyre, Lee. *Post-Truth. The MIT Press Essential Knowledge series.* Kindle Edition. MIT Press, 2017.

Ogborn, Jane, and Peter Buckroyd. *Satire.* Cambridge University Press, 2011.

Oreskes, Naomi, and Erik M. Conway. *Merchants of Doubt: How a Handful of Scientists Obscured the Truth on Issues from Tobacco Smoke to Global Warming.* Bloomsbury Press, 2010.

Pignataro, Juliana Rose. "Video Resurfaces of Jimmy Kimmel in Blackface Mocking Black Athletes." *International Business Times,* 13 October 2017, http://www.ibtimes.com/video-resurfaces-jimmy-kimmel-blackface-mocking-black-athletes-2601281. Accessed 7 March 2018.

Thelwall, Mike. "Social Media Analytics for YouTube comments: Potential and Limitations." *International Journal of Research Methodology,* vol. 21, no. 3, pp. 303–316. https://doi.org/10.1080/13645579.2017.1381821.

PART FOUR

Laughter and Ridicule

Ethical Features of Derogatory Humor in Medical Settings

RALPH H. DIDLAKE *and*
CAROLINE E. COMPRETTA

Introduction

When an individual becomes a patient in a health care system, he is almost universally seeking or has already been given a label. That label is usually in the form of a diagnosis, which often carries powerful implications regarding that individual's treatment and prognosis. From the patient's perspective, a diagnostic label is an expectation. It represents a definitive statement regarding the nature or source of the illness for which one desires treatment as well as an answer to the question "what is wrong with me?" The patient's expectation of a diagnosis and its powerful social implications are discussed well by Annemarie Goldstein Jutel in her monograph *Diagnosis: Putting a Name to It*. She points out that assigning a diagnosis carries important implications not only regarding the patient's current and future health by identifying one or more disease states or pathologic conditions that may be attended by serious life changes, but also carries profound socio-cultural implications regarding identity, social relationships, and even how we frame and conceive of order and disorder. Further, Jutel discusses the authority society grants physicians to make diagnoses and attach these life-altering labels to people, noting, "[D]iagnoses and their classificatory systems are an important collective arrangement that defines and enables the influence of professional medicine" (Jutel). This exemplifies the fact that society grants certain professions monopoly-of-access to specialized information or actions under the scope of practice of that profession.

However, just as the clinician has authority and position to make and act on a diagnostic label as an act of beneficence in precise alignment with the cultural role of a physician, he or she also carries the power to label in ways that stigmatize, marginalize, or mal-define those under their purview. Often framed as humor, such stigmatizing labels follow ubiquitous cultural stereotypes that expand the medical encounter from diagnosis and treatment to the reproduction and maintenance of established sociopolitical and economic hierarchies found in the clinic and beyond. Consider the following vignettes:

> (1) A chief medical resident, a physician in his or her final year of specialty training, is on morning rounds in a teaching hospital and is in conversation with a new intern. "We re-admitted Mr. Jones last night with acute alcoholic pancreatitis. This is the third time. Every time we get him back on his feet, he goes on another bender and winds up in the ICU. His primary diagnosis should be 'dirtball.'"
>
> (2) A medical resident is having lunch with a third-year medical student who is rotating on her service. "The patient in 502 is going to be a problem. She has multiple acute and chronic problems and is massively obese, a real BBW." "BBW?" the student queried, thinking he had missed an important medical acronym. "Yeah" the resident responded "a beached baby whale."

These simple exchanges represent the everyday ways that pejorative humor and demeaning behaviors help shape the medical environment. The use of ostensibly humorous terms for certain types of patients, specific conditions, or particular patient characteristics is not at all uncommon. In fact, these scenarios demonstrate not only the derogatory nature of this type of humor, but also the ways in which language can frame the social dynamics surrounding care. It would be very easy for the casual observer to relegate the use of terms like "BBW" and "dirtball" to the domain of cynical slang or simply the harmless product a few immature doctors. However, the use, origins, and social meaning of pejorative and derogatory humor in medical care are much more complex.

This essay explores this sub-genre of medical humor, examines its troubling ethical features, and builds a case that this type of humor is, at least in part, the result of socio-political power dynamics within the traditional medical training hierarchy. Finally, we will posit that the drive to be accepted into the clinical environment perpetuates the existence of this sort of humor.

Medical Humor

Humor about illness, disease, infirmity, and medical care can be found in a wide variety of forms. The broad spectrum of humor, wit, jokes, and satire with medical themes ranges from the trenchant essays on illness and doctors written by Michael de Montaigne in the 19th century to the stunningly insightful *Farside* cartoons created by Gary Larson in the 1980s and 90s. Even earlier, Geoffrey Chaucer found humor in the actions of physicians, leading him to include the greedy physician—a "verray parfit praktisour"—among the travelers of *The Canterbury Tales* who had standing arrangements with his apothecaries to prescribe expensive medicine. Across many genres, writers as diverse as George Bernard Shaw, Mark Twain, Molière, William Wycherley, and Laurence Sterne have woven humor derived from the behavior of the ill and the absurdity of those who attempt to care for them into enduring literary works.

Medical humor is also well represented in film. The 1954 British comedy *Doctor in the House* was the most commercially successful movie in the history of the Rank Organization production company and stands among an extensive catalog of cinematic releases that reside in the medical comedy genre. From *A Day at the Races*, featuring Groucho Marx as Dr. Hugo Hackenbush, through *M.A.S.H.* and *Patch Adams*, to the more recent portrayal of Dr. Vladimir Bomgard by Daniel Radcliff in *A Young Doctor's Notebook*, the world of medicine, hospitals, and clinics has been a fertile ground for the medical comedy film genre. Medical humor has also been a feature of traditional television in popular shows such as *Northern Exposure, House, and Heart of Dixie*, which are either primarily comedies or have recurring medical characters who are strong comedic foils. Overall, the medical world lends itself well to narrative and plot because it is an environment filled with tension, paradox, incongruity, and irony, all of which are essential elements of humor and the well-wrought joke.

A particularly common trope within the medical humor genre is the physician training environment. Medical students, young medical or surgical residents, and their faculty or mentors are common characters in this type of comedy. The combination of young, hormonally charged characters and high-stakes situations in which inhibitions are already reduced by the unique characteristics of the medical work environment increases the opportunity for comedic narrative. This especially fertile ground has supported comedic genres in literature, film, and television, including the markedly successful *Scrubs* (Disney–ABC Television Group) and *House* (NBC Universal Television), both of which are set in the world of physicians-in-training and have large doses of humor and numerous comedic characters.

Although such characters are common in these genres, they provide little comment regarding the consequences of such humor. However, looking more deeply into the role of humor, specifically derogatory humor, in the medical environment, we see that it can be used as a tool to isolate and separate both senior from junior clinicians and clinicians from patients. As a result, hierarchies are practiced and upheld even as the laughter dies down.

Beyond humorous fiction, jokes, and comedic elements about doctors and nurses embedded into narrative, humor has a well-established and well-documented place in the real world of clinical medicine. In her 1977 book, *Humor and the Health Professions*, Vera Robinson described humor as having a number of legitimate roles within the medical environment. These roles include stress relief, both for patient and provider, an effective coping mechanism for difficult, emotionally fraught situations, and as a valid educational tool. The efficacy of these claimed roles is supported by a growing body of academic literature describing legitimate, perhaps even important, effects of humor in medical environments (McCreaddie). Structured research studies have demonstrated such value-added functions for humor in clinical care such as reassurance of patients, team building in interdisciplinary care units, improved communication, and a teaching tool (McCreaddie, Oczkowski, Beck, Ziegler).

Prevalence

The scholarly literature, however, also supports the existence of a darker side of clinical humor, specifically, the troubling prevalence of pejorative and derogatory humor directed toward patients. As witnessed in the above vignettes, this form of ostensibly comic or amusing observation has been referred to in the academic literature using a number of terms in addition to pejorative or derogatory humor; these include cynical slang, sarcasm, backstage joking, medical folkspeak, and derisive humor. A recent article by Angela Tung in the online magazine *Mental Floss* described medical speech that included pejorative humor and patient labeling as "secret slang." The common denominator in all of these forms of speech is use of negative or uncomplimentary labels often unique to the clinical setting.

The prevalence of pejorative and derogatory humor in medical training can be gauged by reviewing the growing body of academic literature published on the subject over the last three decades. The use of derogatory terms by medical staff to refer to patients was noted in the academic literature as early as 1978, when George and Dundes, writing in the *Journal of American Folklore*, examined this phenomenon and included it under the broader heading of "in-group hospital folk speech." These authors concluded that specific terms such as "gork" for a neurologically impaired patient and "crock" for an individual suspected of hypochondriacal complaints are the products of frustration, anger, or hostility arising from difficult-to-care-for or "repugnant or disgusting" patients. However, they also recognized the more macro sociopolitical nature of such labeling, concluding that "…American hospital folk speech provides an esoteric socially sanctioned outlet…" for the stresses and frustrations encountered by medical personnel and further that stereotyping patients via labels maintains the "in-group" versus "out-group" status relationships. This early analysis was followed by an interview study of hospital personnel by Davit P. Gordon, who concluded that "[H]ospital slang for patients serves a group interest in working in an atmosphere of rapport without becoming overly personal." He was somewhat forgiving, even rather generous, in his assessment, stating "medical personnel confront a great deal of human suffering and must carry out demanding activities, often under a great time pressure. Under such conditions one might well expect a hospital slang to develop that is rich in humorous, derogatory, or euphemistic terms" (Gordon 173). While Gordon did not posit that care was impacted through derogatory language, he did acknowledge that the use of humorous or derogatory slang terms for patients has distinct socio-political features, especially in the hierarchical setting of clinical care. He noted "such speech is most likely to be used by a superior to a subordinate: MD or nursing supervisor to nurse; professor to medical students" (Gordon 182–183).

These initial descriptions of humorous and derogatory slang in medicine were followed by the work of Coombs, who compiled an extensive catalogue of slang terms, not only those used for patients but also for hospital activities, processes, and even derogatory terms physicians used for medical and surgical specialties other than their own. He reinforced the notion that humorous slang serves a social and overtly political function, creating "...a sense of belonging in a select inside group" (Coombs). Further, Coombs established that ostensibly humorous slang establishes a unique group identity and provides a private in-group means of communication. This observation positions clinical humor in the domain of an argot or secret language that serves to exclude the understanding of outsiders. In this context, "outsiders" would be patients and their families with whom physicians and staff wish to communicate in a very controlled and specific manner. As medical practitioners use derogatory humor to pejoratively label patients, they create an exclusive lexicon that establishes and maintains both professional positions of power and broader socioeconomic and political hierarchies that are reflected in these positions. Similar to medical jargon, derogatory humor learned and employed in the clinic and directed toward patients creates a linguistic tool to control and shape the medical encounter. Yet even when patients participate in or master clinical language, they are still denied participation in derogatory humor, precisely because they are the target of the joke and the humor rests on their lack of participation. Unlike medical jargon that can be increasingly learned outside medical school (i.e., internet, books, etc.), humor becomes the final linguistic barrier over which patients cannot ascend, and hierarchies thus remain—specifically, sociopolitical hierarchies that privilege clinician perspectives over those of patients or subordinates. Linguistics scholars have shown that languages and linguistic sub-groups are judged and incorporated into extra-lingual forces such as social, economic, and political stratifications (Kottak). In fact, Gall posits that linguistic features and forms have "no power in themselves" but reflect the power of the groups who use them. Therefore, pejoratively labeling patients through humor maintains and perpetuates social, economic, educational, and political differentiation between clinicians and patients and senior/junior physicians.

Medical Training Environment

Even more distressing from an ethical perspective is that pejorative and derogatory humor appears to be most commonly found and most strongly expressed in the medical training environment. Even within the unique world of medicine and health care, the medical training environment is a singular cultural microcosm, with a specific social structure and complex social dynamics. In this unique learning environment, medical students and resident physicians attain the professional skills necessary to become practicing physicians but experience the process as learners. As such, knowledge, practices, attitudes, and behaviors are acquired and displayed in ways specific to that role. This phenomenon of medical acculturation has been recognized at least since the work of Becker and co-authors and the publication of their seminal work *Boys in White*. They found that medical students

> ...took the hints furnished by the faculty and the organization of the school and developed perspectives on the problem of where to put their effort in their apprentice-like activities around the concepts of clinical experience and medical responsibility. Although they used these concepts from medical culture, they neither used them as practicing physicians do nor did they mean the same things by them. They adapted the core meanings to apply to their immediate situation as students. The student perspectives built around the concepts of responsibility and experience are thus influenced by medical culture but take their shape from the pressures of the situation in which students find themselves [Becker].

In the 1980s, concern developed among medical educators regarding the increasing use of derogatory slang and cynical or humorous labeling of patients within the learning environment. This attention was almost certainly amplified by the 1978 publication and widespread success of Samuel Shem's novel *The House of God,* in which numerous cynical slang terms such as "gomer" and "turf" were popularized—even glorified. It is hard to overemphasize the influence of this satirical novel among medical trainees of the 1980s or to ignore the fact that it has remained in print continuously since its initial release. Importantly, it also remains the subject of serious commentary in the medical education literature (Brody).

Both the sustained prevalence of cynical humor among students, resident physicians, and their faculty, as well as the level of concern among medical training programs, is evident in a series of articles that appeared in the academic medical literature over the last two decades. Among the earliest to publish on this topic was Parsons, who with her co-authors, examined student's attitudes toward humor and slang as they entered the clinical training environment. These transitioning students reported dissonant attitudes regarding hospital humor and slang, yet they expressed an understanding of the resident physician's frustration with difficult patients, while noting the tacit acceptance of questionable labels for those patients. Importantly, two additional features of derogatory medical humor were identified in this study. The first was the observation that there were "rules of appropriate usage" regarding this type of humorous language (Parsons). It was almost always initiated by a superior within the group and almost never instigated by students. The second observation was that students almost universally recognize "the inclusionary nature of humor and jargon, which allows one to fit into the clinical team and the medical profession" (Parsons). The exclusionary function of derogatory humor is one of its most important features, because legitimate clinical language may be learned by those outside the profession through such means as patient education websites, wherein they may become active participants in the language of their care. However, derogatory humor is taught and learned in the training environment and passed from clinician to clinician at the expense and exclusion of the patient. Understood in this way, derogatory humor was used to legitimize and maintain established professional authority and preserve the hierarchical relationships upon which the profession was built [sb6].

It is important here to establish a clear distinction between the technical language that is used for diagnosis and treatment and therefore for the benefit of the patient's clinical care and the pejorative humor, which may contain technical features and promote social acceptance into the profession but may harm the patient through stigma or marginalization. Of great ethical concern in this regard is a young physician's choice to engage in pejorative humor and the obvious failure to properly evaluate the beneficence-non-maleficence equation that should be applied to every medical action in order to comply with the principal of "do no harm."

The dissonance between the espoused values of the Hippocratic tradition and those suggested by the use of pejorative humor in clinical training was further documented by Wear, who noted that derogatory comments toward others was a "common transgression" among attending faculty. These investigators referred to this behavior as a "ubiquitous phenomenon in medical education" (Wear). Again, the strongly sociological nature and cultural role of this type of humor was made clear as they pointed out that medical students "...are immersed in a culture of which they all aspire to become members, and here they look to their teachers—the fully sanctioned residents and attendings—to tell them how to *be*" (Wear). The findings of the Wear study were more recently replicated by Tariq, who found, using a *Learning Environment for Professionalism* survey, that "the most common unprofessional behaviors noted by our students are related to physicians making derogatory comments about other medical professionals and derogatory comments about patients."

Theoretical Framework

A theoretical model through which the use of pejorative and derogatory humor among medical personnel may be more deeply understood arises from the work of Irving Goffman. His theory of labeling is fundamentally about establishing and maintaining power differentials within social systems. Although his work, originally published in the mid–20th century, has undergone a number of re-evaluations, it still maps dependably onto the modern environment of clinical medicine and especially to the milieu and culture of medical training, in which the labeling of others is so prevalent. Specifically, Goffman's concept of the "total institution" describes quite accurately the hierarchy of clinical training in which medical students progress from didactic basic science instruction into real-world training under the tutelage of resident physicians who are in later stages of medical training and the overall supervision of faculty attending physicians. In his 1961 monograph *Asylums*, Goffman examined the social structure in which patients experience hospitalization in 20th century mental institutions. He characterized asylums and certain other facilities such as prisons, military units, and boarding schools as "total institutions" that organizationally and functionally have certain characteristics in common (Goffman). The fundamental characteristic of such institutions is a large group of people (patients, inmates, and soldiers, for instance) managed by a smaller supervisory group. The former is often disconnected or isolated from the world outside of the institution, while the latter remain socially integrated with the outside world. The way the groups interact, the power dynamics between the groups, and the experience of group membership are strongly influenced by the categorization or labels given to the individuals or to the groups. An assigned label such as "schizophrenic" may carry with it specific assumptions, create certain expectations, and place stigmas, all of which modulate the experience of the patient in the asylum, the military recruit in training, or the prisoner's incarceration.

Within the framework of Goffman's thesis, one might question whether or not a conventional hospital or other modern medical institution meets the criteria for, or has all of the attributes of, the total institution. However, it can be argued that the social dynamics of the hospital environment are even more complex in comparison to a traditional asylum. This case is even stronger in regard to the complex social structure of the teaching hospital, in which multi-layered power differentials create numerous opportunities for various groups to be labeled and individuals to be placed in the position that Goffman perceived for the inmate or mental patient. In this understanding, patients, stigmatized or not, as well as students, physicians in training, or other groups such as nurses can experience group labeling, stigmatization, marginalization, and loss of social control. Even if the clinical training environment does not precisely meet the threshold criteria of Goffman's total institution, it is at the very least a *forme fruste* of the asylum in which derogatory humor and ostensibly funny labeling play a role in establishing and maintaining loci of control among groups.

There is, however, a significant contrast between pejorative and humorous labeling in conventional medical settings and Goffman's construct in mental institutions. The patients he describes in *Asylum* have direct knowledge of their label and have the opportunity to "manage'" their categorization and its stigmatizing effect. This dynamic is quite different from pejorative humor directed toward a patient that is always hidden, allowing no opportunity for the patient to mitigate the marginalization or to have any power in the determination of their own status.

The fact that the humorous labeling of patients by medical staff occurs privately or covertly makes it even more ethically egregious. Goffman points out that control of personal identity through concealing stigma, what he refers to as "passing," is a powerful driver of human behavior. The "hidden stigmatization" of the clinical world is insidious because it offers the patient no opportunity to control his identity, thereby reinforcing the hierarchy and the power differentials operative in the medical encounter. If one evaluates this behavior in terms of the level of harm or the extent of an ethical breach, the private labeling of a patient would rank higher than a more public derogation of another individual in that the publicly stigmatized have opportunity to engage in mitigation.

While the application of Goffman's theories allows us to consider pejorative patient labels as linguistic tools that perpetuate hierarchical and authoritative relationships between different groups, humorous labeling and derogatory humor in the medical training environment can also be understood as a linguistic resource marking group identity and enabling access to the material benefits of group membership. Pierre Bourdieu argues that linguistic practices may be considered a form of capital, specifically social capital, within institutions. He posits that social capital is expressly linked to "membership in a group—which provides each of its members with the backing of the collectivity-owned capital" (Bourdieu). Here, social capital refers not just to financial resources but also the pervasive economy of language, symbols, and relationships associated with a group's power and prestige. Moreover, the reproduction of social capital relies on a "continuous series of exchanges in which recognition is endlessly affirmed and reaffirmed" (Bourdieu 241–258). Understood through the lens of social capital, the sustained use of derogatory humor in medical training environments becomes a tool by which trainees can prove they are worthy of group membership, literally that they are "in on the joke." Most troubling from an ethical perspective are the multiple power differentials in the medical training environment that drive students and trainees to be accepted into and advance within that environment, all of which create low thresholds for mimicking behavior and the use of inappropriate humor modeled by those in positions of power.

Bourdieu maintains that, even for those individuals who recognize the negative nature of such humor, the acceptance of a language's authority can be "unconsciously inculcated" by subordinate groups, ultimately working to legitimize the dominant system. Therefore, even those medical trainees who do not approve of derogatory humor may unwittingly go along so as to not upset their emerging position in the profession.

Pejorative humor in medical training may be used not only to solidify group identity—here physicians—but may also be used to access tangible material resources. Kottak argues that our speech habits help determine our access to employment and wealth, and that mastering group linguistic practices associated with power and status is a "strategic resource—and a path to wealth, prestige, and power." Given that physicians are consistently one of the highest paid professions, participating in pejorative humor can be understood as a "strategic resource" that helps trainees maintain their membership in a high-status and highly remunerated professional group (Strauss).

Taken together, Goffman and Bourdieu offer a theoretical lens through which to understand how derogatory humor is used to both propagate external boundaries between groups and internal group membership. Following Goffman, the pejorative labeling of patients by physicians and physicians in training functions to sustain the boundaries between both groups (medical professional and "other") and legitimize power differentials based on such factors as education, socioeconomic status, and privilege. Moreover, Bourdieu's concept of social capital elucidates how linguistic acts such as demeaning humor can solidify within-group membership and access to group-based material and social resources. Employing both approaches develops a comprehensive understanding of the strategic use of derogatory humor in the medical training environment.

Summary and Conclusions

Humor is an important feature of the human experience and has important roles in socialization, emotional release, self-reflection, and coping. However, humor framed as cynical slang, stigmatizing jokes, and pejorative labeling creates and perpetuates stereotypes and degrades the dignity of individuals and groups. When this form of humor is deployed in the clinical setting, it is, quite simply, anathema to the long-espoused values of the Western medical tradition (*Code*). Barriers to eliminating this type of speech from the clinical world are numerous and entrenched. Most broadly, the professional authority and traditional social status of physicians create relationships wherein people can be easily viewed as "other" or belonging to a particular group, creating a low threshold for applying a label. Humor that excludes and demeans makes it hard for clinicians to connect with their patients due to "othering" and results in cyclical exclusions whereby derogatory humor is learned in the training environment and promotes social distancing from patients, which in turn supports more derogatory humor and so on. Goffman has provided a means of understanding the power and persistence of this type of social structure and its profound influence on the members of complex institutional social systems. A further barrier to change is the powerful drive of medical trainees to be accepted into the medical culture. Bourdieu, Kottak, and others give us a basis for understanding the persistence of pejorative humor as a type of linguistic leverage that assists acculturation and acceptance of trainees.

From an ethical perspective, the intent of demeaning humor must be clearly understood, given that ethical, social, and cultural ambivalence of humor is often core to its humorousness. While the practice of assigning stigmatizing labels in secret in the medical encounter denies a patient the opportunity to control their identity within the social system, we must bring this practice into better light in order to understand the ethical implications of this type of humor on the medical profession. This is especially true as we learn more about the social determinants of health and the role of socioeconomic factors on health outcomes. The role of humor in upholding power differentials that negatively affect care may prove to be an important area of ethical research. As the punchline to a joke often turns expectations upside down, this research may be used, *must* be used, to expose the unethical behaviors, cloaked as humor, that perpetuate marginalization of vulnerable individuals who seek medical care.

WORKS CITED

Beck, Rainer S., et al. "Physician-Patient Communication in the Primary Care Office: A Systematic Review." *J Am Board Fam Med.* vol. 15, no. 1, 2002, pp. 25–38.

Becker, Howard S., et al. Strauss. *Boys In White.* University of Chicago Press, 1961.

196   Part Four: Laughter and Ridicule

Bourdieu, Pierre. "The Forms of Capital." *Handbook of Theory and Research for the Sociology of Education.* J. E. Richardson edition, Greenwood Press, 1986.

Brody, Howard. "The House of God: Is it Pertinent 30 Years Later?" *AMA Journal of Ethics* vol. 13, no. 7, 2011, pp. 499–502.

Buxman, Karyn. "Humor in the OR: A Stitch in Time?" *AORN J.* vol. 88 no. 1, 2008, pp. 67–77. Doi: 10.106/j.aorn.2008.01.004.

Chaucer, Geoffrey and Thomas Tyrwhitt. *The Canterbury Tales of Chaucer: With an Essay on His Language and Versification, an Introductory Discourse, Notes and a Glossary by Th. Turwhitt.* Pickering, 1930.

Code of Medical Ethics of the American Medical Association. American Medical Association, 2017.

Coombs Robert H., et al. "Medical Slang and Its Functions." *Soc Sci Med,* vol. 36, no. 8, 1930, pp. 987–997.

Gall, Susan. "Language and Political Economy." *Annual Review of Anthropology,* vol. 18, no. 1, 1989, pp. 345–367.

George, Victoria, and Alan Dundes. "The Gomer: A Figure of American Hospital Folk Speech." *J of American Folklore,* vol. 91, no. 359, 1978.

Goffman Erving. *Asylums-Essays on the Social Situation of Mental Patients and Other Inmates.* Anchor Books, Doubleday & Co. Inc., 1961.

Gordon Davit P. "Hospital Slang for Patients: Crocks, Gomers, Gorks and Others." *Language in Society,* vol. 12, no. 2, 1983, pp. 173–185.

Jutel, Annemarie G. *Putting a Name To It.* Johns Hopkins University Press, 2011.

Kottak, Conrad. *Anthropology: The Exploration of Human Diversity.* McGraw-Hill, 2016.

McCreaddie, May, and Sally Wiggins. "The Purpose and Function of Humour in Health, Health Care and Nursing: A Narrative Review." *J Adv Nurs* vol. 61, no. 6, 2008, pp. 584–595. Doi: 10.1111/j.1365-2648.2007.04548.x.

Oczkowski, Simon. "Virtuous Laughter: We Should Teach Medical Learners the Art of Humor." 11 May 2015, *Critical Care,* vol. 19, no. 222, 2015. https://doi.org/10.1186/s13054-01500927-4© Oczkowski; licensee BioMed Central. 2015.

Parsons, Genevieve, et al. "Between Two Worlds: Medical Student Perceptions of Humor in Slang in the Hospital Setting." *JGIM,* vol. 16, no. 8, 2001, pp. 544–549.

Robinson, Vera M. *Humor and the Health Professions.* C.B. Slack, 1977.

Shem, Samuel. *The House of God.* Penguin Publishing Group, 1978.

Strauss, Karsten. "The 20 Highest Paying Jobs in America in 2017." *Forbes,* 10 January 2017, Forbes.com. Accessed 16 August 2018.

Tariq, Sara, et al. "Crystal Clear or Tin Ear: How Do Medical Students Interpret Derogatory Comments About Patients and Other Professionals?" *Med Ed Online,* vol. 21, no. 1, 2016, pp. 1–5.

Tung, Angela. "17 Secret Slang Terms Your Doctor Might Be Using." *Mental Floss,* 2016. http://mentalfloss.com/article/77618/17-secret-slang-terms-your-doctor-might-be-using.

Wear, Delese, et al. "Derogatory and Cynical Humour Directed Towards Patients: Views of Residents and Attending Doctors."*Med Education* vol. 43, no. 1, 2009, pp. 34–41.

Ziegler, John B. "Use of Humour in Medical Teaching." *Medical Teacher* vol. 20, no. 4, 1998, pp. 341–348.

Laughter, Bodily Pain and Ethics in YouTube Fail Videos

JONATHAN PETER WRIGHT

Fail videos are collections of dangerous, extreme, and often humorous video clips sent in by viewers from around the globe. Fail videos are funny, yes, but that does not mean it is necessarily responsible to laugh at them. There is a gap between having the impulse to laugh and following that impulse, and not all laughter is ethically sound. Fail videos, like many areas of the internet and internet culture, have not yet been examined critically. It is right to be apprehensive of certain areas of these untried online territories. For instance, media scholar Carol Vernallis writes, "The YouTube clips that have remained with me are often tied to guilty pleasures. More often than not, the butt of the joke is on humans or animals who refuse to play their proper parts. I'm not sure I'm responding with empathy. Some of its pleasure come [sic] from embarrassment and fear" (152). Acts performed online through clicks are still acts performed by humans and should therefore be included in the realm of ethical inquiry. At present such inquiries are more needed than ever before, not only because of the prevalence of online activity in many people's everyday lives, but also because viewership and content creation are connected with economic processes and incentives.

This essay addresses the obvious question that fail videos raise: is it acceptable to laugh at these clips, which often involve the real pain of another person? There are numerous objections that could be raised against laughing at fail videos. I have condensed these down to two broad objections: the first is that laughing at these videos is detrimental to the subject of the video, and the second is that it is detrimental to the laughing viewer. Before I address these objections, I will introduce fail videos with their context, categorization,

197

and two examples of how they function. I will then review some literature on pain and viewing images of pain. Finally, I will respond to the two objections and attempt to show that there are possible conditions under which it is ethically responsible to laugh at fail videos.

Fail Videos

The origin of fail videos is in physical comedy, with its most direct precedent being the television series *America's Funniest Home Videos* (1989–present). *AFHV* compiles video clips sent in by viewers and provides an introduction and commentary on these videos. In-studio audiences vote on which are the funniest three videos, and the winners receive prizes. YouTube fail videos developed this form of video compilation by enlarging the field of eligible content (more violence is allowed on YouTube than on network television) and presenting the compilation with one clip immediately following another without commentary (except occasionally for added music). While *AFHV* prepares viewers to experience the videos they show through spoken commentary, fail video channels leave viewers little time to catch their breath until the compilation's end.

The most popular source of fail videos on YouTube to date is "FailArmy," a channel that produces compilations of fails released every few days. The channel has categories like "Fails of the Week," as well as themed videos like "Expensive Fails." Videos from the channel average approximately 1.5 million views in the first month. Other fail channels exist on YouTube, like "The Best Fails," and other theme-oriented channels exist like "News Be Funny" and "Funny Local News." Because of its popularity, I will be using "FailArmy" as my source for fail videos and analysis, unless otherwise noted.

The platform on which fail videos are presented is YouTube, the Google-owned portal to an ever-increasing web of online videos. Since its creation in 2005, YouTube has grown massively in terms of both its amount of content and its cultural influence. Beginning as a social video sharing service for anyone with a webcam, it is now supported principally by advertising and populated by professional and prosumer content targeting hundreds of demographic groups.

The changes in YouTube's business model have deeply affected the site's content and viewership. This can be seen in scholarship written in the late 2000s and early 2010s. One of the most prevalent themes in early scholarship of YouTube is the movement toward amateur news, entertainment, and spectacle as opposed to the corporate model of television. This was indeed true of these early years, where the most watched videos were amateur and published by individuals. The years since these studies have seen large changes in production models and aesthetics on YouTube, where currently communities still gather around certain genres and videos, but those that garner the most views are commercially produced (mostly music videos). The way scholars speak about community on YouTube must change as a result, since YouTube has been splintered into seemingly endless smaller communities that might no longer interact in a way that assumes personal familiarity. YouTube is being used more than ever, but it has been coopted by entertainment industries, and while amateur branches still exist, they have been pushed to the sidelines of the platform.

In fail videos, though, there is a mixture of the professional and the amateur. The video content itself is sourced from individuals, almost always shot on smartphones in casual, everyday situations. FailArmy, on the other hand, is owned and operated by Jukin Media, a Los Angeles entertainment company. The mix of crowd-sourced content and for-profit channel is indicative of YouTube's concoction of the personal and the professional.

What is the attraction of fail videos? I see three main sources of enjoyment: spectacle, humor, and possibility. The spectacle involved in many fail videos is easy to recognize: cars careening off roads, people jumping off roofs, ATVs rolling down hills. These all come in quick succession. Vernallis writes, "YouTube demands a raising of the stakes: one clip is never enough. The YouTube effect may be most powerful if the next clip is crasser, bigger, or more ridiculous than the previous" (129). Most fail videos are also humorous in one way or another. This humor is often immediate, although not always simple, as will be shown further down. The third element, possibility, comes from the wide variety of situations, gestures, places, and people found in fail videos. One clip might be on a rural farm, the next in a mall escalator. While FailArmy predominantly features English speakers, other channels have more multicultural collections. Purely through succession and diversity, a sense of the world's size and the scope of human experience is given.

Fail Video Form

The form of an individual fail varies, but there are noticeable patterns between them. The average length of fails is around eleven and a half seconds, with a range between less than six seconds and forty-four seconds. There is often little context given before the act of failure itself. The viewer is thrown into the stunt or mishap almost immediately. One to three seconds might precede the fail, often providing building action. This is still enough time to recognize the setting, including features of the landscape or interior, and the figures involved.

In order to give a sense of the scope that fail videos cover, here is a crude and incomplete list of general fail video categories: bike/skateboard mishaps, mountain bike crashes, car crashes, close calls, pet fails (cats jumping and falling, dogs misbehaving), small natural disasters, small child fails, kitchen and living room roughhousing, do it yourself fails, falling into bodies of water, firecracker fails, people scaring other people, and parkour fails. Some fails involve a single person while others involve dozens. Some fails involve much movement while others remain mostly still. However, there is a clear pattern of a subject moving in a strange, unexpected, or unsuccessful way. Timing is important for rhythmic comedy to emerge, but most of these videos focus upon spatial humor.

Not all fail videos participate in the same type of comedy, however, or even comedy at all. While many fails are straightforwardly about the human body failing to perform an action, some fails, like car and boat crashes, tend to induce fright or suspense rather than laughter. Other videos, such as those involving pets, are more cute than funny. The miniature natural disaster videos (such as lightning striking a tree which then falls on a house) are often pure spectacle. To speak of fail videos is not to speak of a singular kind of video. There is a large range both of setting and of action.

The common feature that I will be focusing on in this essay is one that appears in many fail videos but not all: human pain. Some sort of violence to the human body is on display in videos from nine out of the thirteen categories listed above. Bodies are bent, bruised, thrown, bonked, smashed, knocked, dragged, and otherwise misshapen. These are the bodies of young children all the way to the bodies of retirees, but the most common bodies found in these videos are young, strong bodies of people in their teens and twenties.

Instead of aligning myself with one of the traditional philosophical positions on humor (the three main positions being the superiority theory, the release theory, and the incongruity theory), I will refer to Arthur Asa Berger's approach, which does not attempt to define what humor is but divides humor up according to categories of techniques (Morreall 6). The four categories are "language (e.g., allusion, exaggeration, irony, puns), logic (e.g., absurdity, repetition, reversal, unmasking), identity (e.g., burlesque, caricature, exposure, parody), or action (e.g., slapstick and speed)" (Berger 233–234). Of these, fail videos strongly employ logic and action, as shown in the examples below. However, Berger also writes, "What this list of techniques suggests is that jokes should be seen as complex texts that have many different techniques of humor in them" (236). Like Berger, I find traditional theories of humor, such as the superiority theory and the incongruity theory, to be restrictive when treated as all-encompassing. Instead, I see humor as participating in a number of techniques to produce its effect. The complexity of humor adds difficulty to forming concrete analyses of humorous texts, since the number of active elements is such that one person might respond to one element, and another to a different one. The following short analyses therefore represent just a limited and subjective set of humorous factors.

Two examples will serve to introduce some of the dynamics of fail videos. In both of these examples, the comedy seems to spark largely from the inversion of expectations, and mostly expectations about movement. In "No Training Wheels," a young girl rides a bike along a suburban sidewalk, filmed, presumably, by her father, who provides a running commentary: "Hello Meredith … here you go fast … no training wheel … slow down!" At this point the cameraman, moving alongside Meredith to record, collides with a street sign, sending the camera, and probably himself, to the ground. This fail runs thirteen seconds, and within that span, a straightforward comedic structure unfolds. From the very beginning, the child riding the bike seems to be the one in danger. This assumption is confirmed by the dialogue. We learn that this is likely the girl's first ride without training wheels, and the father even gives a warning about her speed. Suddenly the tables turn, and to the viewer's surprise it is he who runs amok.

The surprise also factors on a visual level. The clip is a full shot of the girl and her bike in profile, a "tracking shot" of sorts, although we don't know what mode of transport the father is using to stay abreast with the biker. Because of the clarity of the shot, the complete figure of Meredith in frame, there is a temptation to imagine how a fall might happen. It is easy to imagine the girl simply tipping over onto the grass next to her, hinted at by the "no training wheels" line. It is also very possible that an obstacle would enter the frame and she run into it, since we do not have a view of the ground in front of her. In short, we expect a fall that is contained within the confines of the frame. The impact that takes place ends up being outside the frame and causes a dramatic reframing, the camera swinging and falling into the grass. The clip's audio supports the jolt of this switch as well. A constant rattle of wheels can be heard throughout the clip, but this is dramatically superseded by a metallic *bang* and an outburst of surprise from the father. In this fail, there is clearly a setting of expectations that are then upturned because of some outside element.

The second example, a pole vault gone wrong, is less directly comedic, but continues to have an element of visual surprise. When this six-second clip begins, there is the immediate setting of expectations, since the equipment of pole vaulting is notoriously difficult to manage and has been coopted by comedy in the past. The vaulter makes his approach toward the camera, vaults, but does not make it completely over the bar. Instead, he lands on it. The bar bends under his weight, until he falls off and the bar launches high into the air. The two side supports fall outward, creating a symmetrical and dramatic movement that resembles an explosion. One object goes up (the bar), one down (the athlete), and one to each side (the supports). The athlete is the butt of the joke, insofar as the humor pertains to the irony of his ability to get all the way up to the height of the bar, and then to land right on top. But there is also humor that lies outside of his action, in the simple movement of objects within the frame. These brief analyses are of course incomplete, but they give a sense of how fail videos rely upon Berger's technical categories of logic and action.

Ethics of Laughing at Pain

Elaine Scarry, Arne Johan Vetlesen, and Edmund Burke will help me form a platform from which I will respond to two objections to laughing at fail videos.

Elaine Scarry, in *The Body in Pain,* describes how torture and war work to discount human pain, the first by transforming it into political power, the second by using language and metaphors that offset the human individual's experience. These instances of willfully overlooking another's pain have massive ramifications for those involved. In pain, particularly extreme pain, there is an experience of losing one's access to the exterior world, since pain becomes the primary sensation. Scarry calls this the unmaking of the world (45). Scarry believes developing a more specific and expressive language used to describe bodily pain is what might work against such acts. Although her examples of torture and war are extreme, her claims can be applied to more ordinary instances of pain. While Scarry does not make many direct statements about the ethical position of pain within our lives, it is fair to imply from her arguments about expressing pain that to laugh at the pain of another would be a fundamental misrecognition of their condition or a malicious and perverse enjoyment of another's world collapsing to one degree or another. Vetlesen writes, "To see other people's pain, to hear about other people's pain is, according to Scarry, like a model of what we believe can be doubted" (16). One can easily make light of another's pain if she believes that what that other person is experiencing is not really pain, but something else. Humor is just one way that this doubt is manifested. In the case of another's pain, neither doubt nor malice are ethically responsible. Insofar as pain causes suffering and world unmaking, it calls us to subdue it when we find it in others. Laughter at another's pain rarely works toward alleviating it but instead transforms it or comprehends it in a way that the one in pain is currently unable to. This furthers the rift between the two people, rather than supporting the one in pain.

Not all thinkers, however, have judged pain and the viewing of pain, to be evil or reprehensible. Arne Johan Vetlesen claims in *A Philosophy of Pain* that "*pain belongs to human life*," and that it is culture's task to encourage people "to meet pain in life (that of others and one's own) without creating more of it, intensifying it, passing it on" (74, 125). By seeing pain as something that allows other areas of life, like pleasure, to be more deeply experienced, Vetlesen's position is not entirely negative toward pain. Instead of denouncing pain as something to be fought, it seeks to recognize pain as a culture and carve out a space for dealing with and processing pain.

In terms of viewing pain, Edmund Burke goes a step further. He opens his discussion of sympathy by writing, "I am convinced we have a degree of delight, and that no small one, in the real misfortunes and pains of others.... There is no spectacle we so eagerly pursue, as that of some uncommon and grievous calamity" (Burke 42). Burke goes on to claim that this delight is the seed of sympathy, as it draws us toward those in distress. The word "delight" seems strong when applied to someone's pain, but Burke writes, "This is not an unmixed delight, but blended with no small uneasiness" (43). Burke's idea is a type of schadenfreude, the German term for taking pleasure in the pain of another. As Giselinde Kuipers notes, "Schadenfreude—as commonly understood in German—does not have one single specific intent, and certainly not 'malice'" (262). What marks Burke's idea as unique is his claim that this natural function is a catalyst for action: "The delight we have in such things, hinders us from shunning scenes of misery; and the pain we feel, prompts us to relieve ourselves in relieving those who suffer; and all this antecedent to any reasoning, by an instinct that works us to its own purposes, without our concurrence" (Burke 43). The mixture of feelings provides a twofold process, the delight drawing us toward a situation of misery and the discomfort pushing us to step in and help.

Just how applicable Burke's ideas about tragedy are to fail videos is arguable, because of their status as unscripted, documentary footage. Even still, fail videos do not allow the second part of Burke's process to take place. Their mediated form only presents them, without allowing us to get close enough to act. If we take up Burke's account, then the question becomes whether the inability to perform any gesture of help condemns fail videos as not properly training us toward right action. Sontag writes, "Perhaps the only people with the right to look at images of suffering of this extreme order are those who could do something to alleviate it" (42). Yet Burke upholds tragedy as beautiful because it does just this. However, he takes pains to mark the qualitative difference that the art's representative form has as compared with real situations of pain.

Let us return to the central question of this essay: is it ever ethically responsible to laugh at the real and present pain of another person? From the argument brought forward above from Scarry, I believe that it is not, since pain is an experience that unmakes the world for the one in pain, an experience we should never wish upon another. Laughing at the present pain of another is not acceptable, since it is making light of another's unmade world, and failing to help them bear that suffering or relieve that suffering is an ethical failure. That is not necessarily what takes place when one laughs at a fail video, however. This is because of two factors: there is no possibility for action since the person in the video is not present to the viewer, and the viewer is most likely not laughing particularly at the pain of the person in the video, but rather at another aspect related to the situation. Therefore, another question is needed: is it ever ethically responsible to laugh at an event in which real pain was involved? This question repositions and broadens what we might be laughing at. Pain itself is not comical, but, as Henri Bergson argues, the body is comical when it acts rigidly, and sometimes, as in the case of falling down, this comical rigidity involves pain (9). Even in a single situation, a number of different elements could provoke laughter. If we fill out Bergson's example of a man falling on the street, we can see these different sources of laughter. One might laugh at the man's expression as he falls, a look of surprise aimed at the oncoming ground. One might laugh at the way his clothes react to the fall, how his coat is blown up around his head. One might laugh at the splash, if he lands in a puddle. With each of these, the one laughing is responding to the immediate comedic element rather than the body's pain itself. To what extent this is acceptable is complex; if one were to continue laughing instead of helping the man up, that would be cruel. So the question becomes: how closely can laughter and pain be in relation to one another while still respecting the personhood of the one in pain?

Two Objections to Laughing at Fail Videos

To answer this question with regards to fail videos, we must turn to the status of the video as mediation and the function of that mediation. Two main objections can be leveled at laughing at fail videos involving another's pain. In responding to these objections, I will develop the thesis that there are possible conditions under which it is viable to laugh at videos involving another's pain. I will use the thinkers introduced above to do this. The first objection is that laughing is harmful to the subject of the video, since it does not maintain his human dignity. The second is that it is harmful to the viewer, insofar as it encourages passivity in the face of a person in pain. Both of these objections can be addressed by considering the form of videos' mediation.

The first objection is founded upon the understanding that laughing at someone in pain is making light of a state that is difficult and to a degree an unmaking of that person's world. What this objection assumes is that the meaning of pain is static. However, pain is not necessarily an unchanging state; it is dynamic. Pain can grow and it can die away. Moreover, the relationship of a person and her pain is rarely consistent over time. It changes, as pain moves from present to past. The meaning attributed to pain changes as we move away from it temporally. For instance, I accidentally cut myself with a knife while preparing dinner. When it occurs, the pain is sharp, and I can think about little besides wanting it to stop. Scarry writes, "Physical pain does not simply resist language but actively destroys it, bringing about an immediate reversion to a state anterior to language, to the sounds and cries a human being makes before language is learned" (4). The day after the incident, my bandaged finger hurts far less, but I still shiver when I think about what happened. A week later, the bandage is off and the finger nearly healed. Now I can think about the event easily, without the piercing sensation I previously had. It becomes a more neutral memory, in the realm of other memories. A few months later, I find myself joking about the event with my friends. Now this is certainly not the case with all pains. Experiences of trauma, diseases, or major injuries, rarely simply subside into memory. But I believe this holds for some experiences of daily pains, and sometimes with more serious accidents. Not only does pain subside as time goes by, but we can place different meanings upon it (or find different meanings in it). This process of linguistic expression can even help to work against the negative effects of pain. Scarry writes that "when physical pain is transformed into an objectified state, it (or at least some of its aversiveness) is eliminated" (5–6). The knife wound at first was just the shock of pain, but by the time I crawled into bed that night it was a sort of lesson: don't hold your fingers too close to the blade when cutting vegetables. In a crude neurological sense, pain is a signal of something being wrong in the body. Mentally, we can take this signal a step further back to understand what might have gone wrong outside the body that caused pain inside the body. Even a simple series of exclamations like, "Ouch! My finger hurts! I cut it with the knife!" displays a progression of coming to understand the cause of pain and place pain in its context. For this response to become a lesson, it often takes time.

Vetlesen writes of pain's transformation as being opposed to its transportation. Transporting pain is a matter of blaming or passing along pain to another, either physically or mentally. Transforming it is different. Vetlesen writes,

> The key word is *reshaping,* and such reshaping of pain depends on what is called *symbolization,* i.e., the individual is given the chance of processing that which hurts, that generates pain and thus exerts pressure on the inner life of the individual—a pressure that seeks release. Such processing can only take place in a mature and non-destructive way if the individual can make use of various types of symbols from various media [88].

By picturing, expressing, imagining, and communicating pain, an individual can process not only the event that caused the pain but the pain itself as an object and as an experience. In attempting to apply this conception of pain to fail videos we run into a number of epistemological problems. Pain may be dynamic and change to have some positive meaning in certain situations, but this cannot be applied to others' pain unless there is clear evidence of change. In order for laughter at someone's real pain in a fail video to be permissible, then, the viewer would need evidence that the victim does indeed relate differently to his pain in the present. In the example of my relating the vegetable slicing incident to my friends, they are free to laugh because my own relating of the circumstances provides a level of assurance of a shift in what the event means to me.

While fail videos might be too literal a form of processing for Vetlesen to call them symbols, I see the re-presentation of pain in fail videos as a possible instance of symbolization when the choice of submitting the video is taken into consideration. The act of submitting a fail video to the "FailArmy's" YouTube channel is more than a hint of the subject's change in relation to previously felt pain. It is hard to believe someone in a large amount of pain would submit a video to be laughed at. Once the pain is no longer present to the body, and once the victim has seen other meanings in the painful event, it would seem to be much more possible to share the experience with others. The characterization of the event can change from a simple, searing message of pain to a linguistic statement like, "that's a good story." Other aspects of the event besides the pain are now brought into focus, whereas before this was not possible—a car running over my foot, for instance. When it occurs, I am shocked, more by the pain than by the situation. The following day, I tell a coworker the story, not to find sympathy for pain I no longer feel, but perhaps to impress them, or just to pass the time. By the time of sharing, the event has taken on a linguistic form. In the age of social media, the act of sharing a piece of media online is construed to be similar to the act of telling a story. Friendships have become virtualized to a large extent, and the acts that make up participation in online communities are difficult to pin down. For the subject of a fail video, uploading can be a way of sharing an experience about his life. The fail, from his viewpoint, is no longer about the pain that dominated the experience during the event. It is now a story that the person is telling. So, in this instance, laughter at this video would not be a disservice to the subject, but a way of receiving the story that the subject chooses to share.

The second objection to laughing at fail videos is that these videos are detrimental to the viewer, since the videos might encourage passivity and callousness toward the pain of others. This is the case because there is no helpful action that can be taken toward the subject of the video, nothing the viewer can do to relieve the pain they see. Sontag writes, "Images have been reproached for being a way of watching suffering at a distance, as if there were some other way of watching. But watching up close—without the mediation of an image—is still just watching" (117). The objection is directed toward the long-term implications of viewing, and is therefore difficult to evaluate. The act of viewing fail videos is, in some respects, similar to the act of viewing any humorous form that involves making light of serious subject matter. What is significant to responding to the objection is specifying what sort of approach viewers may have to fail videos, since nearly any sensation has the potential to either deaden or sensitize, depending on contextual factors. What I am attempting to prove is not that it is always and in every case ethically responsible to laugh at fail videos, only that it sometimes can be. I will respond, then, by outlining a possible situation in which fail videos benefit the viewer. The benefits are (a) an increase in the sense of human relatedness, or a recognition of shared experience, and (b) a template for dealing with one's own experiences of pain.

Fail videos run the gamut of situations, but a large number of them take place in mundane environments and involve everyday activities. Driving cars, playing sports, interacting with pets, working in warehouses, and so forth. Not all fails resonate with every viewer, but many are to some viewers. At the most basic level, the human body is a shared element between viewer and the subject of most fail videos. The human body, as stated earlier, is on display in a range of circumstances and states. Not only is the frailty of the body regularly on display, but its durability, elasticity, and resilience are also present. Pain is not depicted as the only end result of subjects' misadventures. People sometimes shout with pain, yes, but others leap up, laugh or celebrate avoiding a worse fate. Like a great deal of comedy, the humor of fail videos can lead to a sense of wonder at the particularity and range of human experience. It is not only the experience of others, though, but a connection between another's experience and one's own. It is not rare to recognize an event in a video as harkening back to a similar event in my own life. I have been there, perhaps avoiding the mishap, or perhaps falling into it. Either way, the recognition is strong, a sense of solidarity that ties my past to the pasts of others, and does so through humor.

The past might provide a basis for human solidarity, but the future can also be affected by fail videos. Viewing a fail is viewing a narrative, and when the fail involves pain, the video itself or its narrative involves a response to pain over time, what Scarry might call an objectification of pain, or Vetlesen the transformation of pain (Scarry 5–6, Vetlesen 88). This means that the pain has been or is being processed, contextualized and perhaps made meaningful by the one who felt it. Viewing a fail video can be taken as viewing evidence of this process. By viewing these responses in the humorous context of a fail video, it is possible to understand the experience of pain beyond its immediate impact, which destroys language and unmakes one's world. Bringing these narratives with her, the viewer might be able to respond better to her own pain in future. She can do this by seeing similarities between her current circumstance and the narrative of another's pain. In doing so, she might recognize what her pain might be but is not yet: a part of a story. In this way fail videos might be seen as having a pedagogical element: they teach the changing meaning of an event or feeling by showing it in an objectified, symbolized, narrativized format. Thus, fail videos can be beneficial to a viewer both in their ability to create a communal sense in their representations of the human body, and in their representations of objectified pain, which can then be harnessed to process one's own pain.

Conclusion

From these arguments we see that there are situations in which it is appropriate to laugh at fail videos involving pain, because there are situations in which laughing is detrimental neither to the subject of the video nor to the viewer. However, situations in which such conditions are met are rare and can be even more rarely proven. I cannot claim that laughing at fail videos is always responsible, nor that it is even sometimes responsible, since there are plenty of conditions under which the laughter is detrimental to the viewer, the subject, or both. It is only *possible* that laughing at fail videos involving pain is responsible, since the conditions in which laughter would not be detrimental to subject or viewer can exist. Further claims would require a more sociological approach in order to gain insights into the reasons uploaders have in making the decision to submit a video of their own pain, as well as the psychological states of people while viewing fail videos. Such research could build on the findings here as well as contribute to theories of YouTube viewing.

As with most comedy, the ethics of fail videos is highly contextual, and the variety of intentions with which viewers approach the videos range from altruistic to malicious. Since the monitoring or control of intention is impossible, the next best thing is to encourage responsible viewing and hope that these videos are being uploaded and viewed in a way that respects those involved and that the end result is a better understanding of human capacities and tendencies. As Sontag notes, "Photographs objectify: they turn an event or a person into something that can be possessed" (81). While Sontag's statement might have been meant as a warning, there are cases in which "owning" an event can be the mark of moving beyond its negativity. Fail videos might display this objectification of pain and encourage viewers to do likewise with theirs.

WORKS CITED

Berger, Arthur Asa. "Coda: Humor, Pedagogy, and Cultural Studies." *A Decade of Dark Humor: How Comedy, Irony, and Satire Shaped Post-9/11 America.* Edited by Ted Gounelos and Viveca S. Green, University Press of Mississippi, 2011, pp. 233–242.
Bergson, Henri. *Laughter.* Translated by Cloudesley Brereton and Fred Rothwell, Floating Press, 2008.
"Best Fails of the Week: No Training Wheels! (March 2018) | FailArmy." *YouTube*, 23 March 2018, www.youtube.com/watch?v=KtvwDCNXbZA.
"Best Fails of the Year 2017: Part 1 (December 2017) || FailArmy." *YouTube*, 15 December 2017, https://www.youtube.com/watch?v=xnCsZ6YaWew.
Buckley, F. H. "Schadenfreude and Laughter." *Schadenfreude: Understanding Pleasure at the Misfortune of Others.* Edited by Wilco W. van Dijk and Jaap W. Ouwerkerk, Cambridge University Press, 2014, pp. 219–227.
Burke, Edmund. *A Philosophical Enquiry into the Origin of our Ideas of the Sublime and Beautiful.* Oxford University Press, 1998.
Kuipers, Giseldinde. "Schadenfreude and Social Life: A Comparative Perspective on the Expression and Regulation of Mirth at the Expense of Others." *Schadenfreude: Understanding Pleasure at the Misfortune of Others.* Edited by Wilco W. van Dijk and Jaap W. Ouwerkerk, Cambridge University Press, 2014, pp. 259–275.
Manoussakis, John Panteleimon. *The Ethics of Time: A Phenomenology and Hermeneutics of Change.* Bloomsbury Academic, 2017.
Morreall, John. *Comic Relief: A Comprehensive Philosophy of Humor.* Wiley-Blackwell, 2009.
Scarry, Elaine. *The Body in Pain: The Making and Unmaking of the World.* Oxford University Press, 1987.
Sontag, Susan. *Regarding the Pain of Others.* Picador, 2003.
Strangelove, Michael. *Watching YouTube: Extraordinary Videos by Ordinary People.* University of Toronto Press, 2010.
Vernallis, Carol. *Unruly Media: YouTube, Music Video, and the New Digital Cinema.* Oxford University Press, 2013.
Vetlesen, Arne Johan. *A Philosophy of Pain.* Translated by John Irons, Reaktion Books, 2009.

Laughing with "Horrible" People

Reaffirming Ethical Boundaries Through Laughter

NICOLE GRAHAM

Introduction

There is a (fine) line between humor and offence. Most of us like to believe that we know the difference and understand where to draw the line in terms of what we laugh at. Yet we are often surprised to find that where we choose to draw the line differs from our friends, our family, our colleagues, and strangers. As there is no universal agreement, understanding what it is right or wrong to laugh at has long been—and continues to be—contested. Much of the difficulty in identifying the rights and wrongs of laughter stem from its ambiguity. Moreover, what is deemed appropriate to laugh at changes from one generation, nationality, gender, sexuality, religion, ethnicity and race to another. There is a subjectiveness to the acceptability—or morality—of laughter which shifts and changes, and it can be used to challenge social norms or embed them further in society.

Recognizing this, Francis Hutcheson, an 18th century Irish-Scottish philosopher, sought to develop not only a theory of laughter but a morality of laughter; a set of rules which could offer guidance on the rights and wrongs of laughter. In considering what we laugh at and who we laugh with, and whether or not *who* we laugh with changes *what* we laugh at, Hutcheson began addressing a number of key questions which continue to be considered today. In recognition of his contribution, this essay will identify and explore Hutcheson's understanding of the morality of laughter. Moreover, it puts

Hutcheson's morality of laughter to the test, by bringing his moral position(s) into conversation with the contemporary card game *Cards Against Humanity*. Whilst the complex juxtaposition between the 18th century text and the 21st century game is recognized; Hutcheson's questions and considerations regarding the morality of laughter remain relevant today, providing a useful lens with which to view the game. There are three key considerations which are found in Hutcheson's writings which can be explored to draw out the ethical and moral issues of laughter. These three concerns are: the *context* of laughter, the *intentions* of laughter, and the *consequences* of laughter. Each can be considered in relation to the game as they reveal key questions regarding the ambiguity of humor across time.

Francis Hutcheson

In 1725, under the pseudonym Philomeides, Francis Hutcheson wrote three papers on the subject of laughter for *The Dublin Journal*. These papers were later published in 1750 under the title *Reflections Upon Laughter*. The first two of these papers offer a general impression of Hutcheson's approach to laughter and, as such, are briefly covered in this section. The third paper explores his thoughts on the morality of laughter, and this will be considered in relation to *Cards Against Humanity* later in this essay.

Hutcheson's first paper sought to challenge Thomas Hobbes' considerations of laughter written almost a century earlier. For Hobbes, laughter occurs as the result of a feeling of superiority when we compare ourselves with others:

> Laughter is nothing else but sudden glory, arising from some sudden conception of some eminency in ourselves, by comparison with the infirmity of others, or with our own formerly: for men laugh at the follies of themselves past, when they come suddenly to remembrance, except they bring with them any present dishonour [qtd. in Hutcheson 6].

Hutcheson was concerned that Hobbesian laughter was motivated by self-love and a feeling of superiority and so levied two arguments against Hobbes. First, Hutcheson refutes Hobbes by using counter examples to show that not all laughter is provoked by a feeling of superiority; laughter at, for example, puns, literary allusions, and parodies. Second, a feeling of superiority does not always lead to laughter; it can lead to other feelings such as pity or disdain. Hutcheson appears to suggest that, for Hobbes, *all* laughter stems from a feeling of superiority (Jaffro 133). Notwithstanding the difficulty in attributing this all-encompassing theory of laughter to Hobbes' work, Hutcheson's opposition to it provides an early indication of his own attitude to laughter as being a positive element of our human nature.

Having established his critique of Hobbes' position, Hutcheson seeks to introduce his own theory of laughter. His first challenge was defining laughter: "that sensation, action, passion, or affection, I know not which of them a philosopher would call it" (Hutcheson 16). Hutcheson appears to position laughter as "all of the above" rather than offering a distinct focus on laughter as related to physiology or any other specific factor. Whilst Hutcheson did not dwell on the nature of laughter he did seek to distinguish between the terms laughter and ridicule, noting that previous authors had failed to do this (12–13). According to Hutcheson, ridicule is a *form* of laughter; it is "laughter at the follies of others" (13). Hutcheson recognizes that ridicule can involve feelings of superiority but, in distinguishing between laughter and ridicule, he maintains his position of opposition to Hobbes. Thus, Hutcheson acknowledges that Hobbes' theory can be considered the cause for some laughter but not all. This reveals how Hutcheson begins to distinguish his understanding of the rights and wrongs of laughter.

In his second paper, Hutcheson proceeds to develop his own beliefs about laughter and its cause, stating:

> That then which seems generally the cause of laughter is the bringing together of images which have contrary additional ideas, as well as some resemblance in the principle idea: this contrast between ideas of grandeur, dignity, sanctity, perfection, and ideas of meanness, baseness, profanity, seems to be the very spirit of burlesque; and the greatest part of our raillery and jest is founded upon [19].

For Hutcheson, it is the contrasting of grand ideas with base ideas that leads spectators to laugh. He notes that as children we begin to see and make associations between ideas and objects; these associations arise "partly from nature, partly from custom" (17). For example: "sanctity of our churches ... affection between oak and ivy ... a pleasant sensation of grandeur in the sky ... an ass is the common emblem of stupidity and sloth..." (17–18). It is when these associations are incongruous that we laugh. Though there is still a moral aspect of laughter founded in incongruity—the morality surrounds the *decision* to bring two ideas or statements together in order to make a joke—it is less problematic than laughter grounded in superiority, as incongruities often emerge by chance and are not always based in disparagement. As such, the foundation of laughter that Hutcheson introduces here corresponds with his more positive attitude toward laughter.

Ultimately, Hutcheson saw laughter as a positive and important part of humanity, but he recognized it could be abused, and sought to mitigate this possibility by encouraging laughter from positive intentions, ensuring laughter took place with appropriate company, and identifying topics which should not be the subject of laughter. Despite writing nearly 300 years ago, Hutcheson asked important questions about the morality of laughter: what is it acceptable to laugh at? Are there subjects which are unlaughable? What are the consequences of laughter? Who should we laugh with? Is the intention behind the laughter important? These questions remain pertinent today. Whilst Hutcheson may offer only a small glance into the morality of laughter, his contribution should not be ignored; it is worth adapting his thoughts in order to consider them in relation to more current examples. I will, therefore, apply it to the game *Cards Against Humanity* to work through the complicated link between laughter and morality.

Cards Against Humanity

Cards Against Humanity launched in 2011 and is, as the name suggests, a card game. It is normally played with four or more people. To start the game each player draws ten white cards but does not reveal them. One player then reads aloud a black card, which contains a question or a statement which needs to be completed. All of the remaining players select one of their white cards to either answer the question on the black card or fill in the blank. The person who read the black card then reads the various cards aloud before deciding which card was the funniest and awards an "awesome point." The game repeats with the next player acting as the card reader. The person with the most "awesome points" at the end of the game wins. As the game requires the blind drawing of a question and a hand of answer cards, the statements constructed are potentially random, and the humor occurs as a result of the incongruities and accidental convergences that can arise in each round.

Given the game's rules, it might be neatly understood as exemplifying Hutcheson's focus on incongruity as the foundation of laughter. However, the subjects addressed in the game could potentially challenge the notion that laughter is a positive element of our human nature. *Cards Against Humanity* is described by its own creators as "a party game for horrible people"; this cult game encourages laughter at things which it would not normally be acceptable to laugh at, such as racism, sexism, and suffering (Dillon). Examples of the black (question) cards include: "Why do I hurt all over?," "The class field trip was completely ruined by [BLANK]," and "What would grandma find disturbing, yet oddly charming?" These could be responded to by white (answer) cards such as: "Soup that is too hot," "The milk man," "Racism," "Women's suffrage," or "Homeless people."

It is a game which is dependent on surprise or shock value, as everyday subjects are brought together with "horrible" ideas. *Cards Against Humanity* challenges players and encourages them to laugh at things that would usually be considered taboo. Despite the apparent negativity which exists within the

214 Part Four: Laughter and Ridicule

game, by playing *Cards Against Humanity* and laughing together at "horrible" things a group identity is affirmed. There is, then, a positive aspect to this laughter, and Hutcheson certainly noted that laughter is important for creating friendships, which corresponds to his belief that we are disposed to being social (27). Through the unique framing of the game players are offered the opportunity to laugh together without consequence, the opportunity to be absolved of responsibility for the laughter.

This game provides an alternative frame for social interactions. The popularity of the game suggests that there is a desire to suspend judgment, to pause the ethical expectations of society, to transgress boundaries, and to have the opportunity to release in a safe space. The opportunity to laugh at taboos is being embraced. The above section has suggested that the alternative frame of the game, which amends what it is socially acceptable to laugh at, has the potential to affirm group identities which can be thought of as a positive. However, there is a moral complexity to the game which can be addressed with reference to Hutcheson's sense of laughter and morality. Furthermore, the complexity in Hutcheson's morality relating to laughter can be addressed in light of the game.

You Shouldn't Joke About That!

Questions about the morality of laughter relate to the idea that laughter involves judgment. Judgment of the person who causes the laughter, judgment of the people who laugh, and judgment of the object or subject of the laughter. All of these judgments can be positive or negative. Rather than focusing on those who laugh, Hutcheson places most of the moral responsibility on the person who provokes the laughter; as they choose how to provoke the laughter they become responsible for the moral appropriateness of the laughter which follows. As a result, the person who causes laughter can find themselves embraced or shunned by their "audience." Hutcheson notes that: "we are disposed by laughter to a good opinion of the person who raises it" and laughing at a person does not entail "the least abatement of their good opinion" (27, 22). However, any attempt to make a well-respected subject the object of laughter can "raise contempt of the ridiculer" (28). Thus, the chosen subject of laughter can change the opinion of the audience as to their perception of the person who provoked the laughter. *Cards Against Humanity* conflicts with Hutcheson's position regarding the moral responsibility of the person provoking the laughter. The game *actively* encourages and expects players to select cards that are not only incongruous, but often offensive, to provoke laughter, and if successful they will receive praise rather than feelings of contempt as Hutcheson suggests.

Hutcheson identifies some objects of laughter which we do not tend to find funny, perhaps the greatest is when we are the butt of the joke. The reason we often feel uncomfortable when we are laughed *at*, is because of the negative judgment we feel we are being faced with. Hutcheson extends this further to include disdain for jokes when our friends are the subject as we feel that they, too, are being faced with a negative judgment (27).

Beyond the injury of our (and our friends') pride, Hutcheson identifies certain topics which should not be the subject of laughter. For Hutcheson, references to crimes, calamities, warfare, and similar suffering *cannot* provoke laughter, rather it must lead the listener to feel pity, compassion or distress. Moreover, for Hutcheson, any attempt to make these issues the subject of laughter can lead listeners to turn against the person telling the joke, or to make a negative judgment on their character. Often, much to our dismay and even protest, the things we laugh at are deemed to be reflective of our wider moral character. Whilst in everyday life this suggestion may be true, *Cards Against Humanity* facilitates laughter at things which can cause offence. In the game no subject is too sacred or sensitive to be laughed at; it is in the offensive that the laughter is loudest. Perhaps the game's format, addressing the subjects of crimes, war, and suffering in relation to incompatible questions provides a buffer to the offence. Reconciling the positive consequences of the game, such as providing entertainment for friends and affirming social bonds, with Hutcheson's prohibition of certain topics, we might ask: would Hutcheson only proscribe laughing *directly* at taboo subjects, and does *Cards Against Humanity* involve laughing *directly* at taboo subjects, or laughing at how they intersect with other subjects? When considering the morality of laughter does this distinction matter?

In addition to suffering, Hutcheson suggests that, as a rule, we should not make fun of "truly great" things (27–29). Hutcheson does not define what he means by great and whilst he references God and Scripture as subjects which should be revered, it is not clear what other subjects he would perceive as great. The identification of greatness seems rather subjective. Hutcheson slightly deviates from this position by suggesting that a play on words—even for sublime topics—is acceptable as their ultimate greatness cannot be undermined by laughter. According to Hutcheson, laughing at Scripture, for example, does not undermine its innate greatness; it will not "diminish our high idea of the great sentiment" (28).

Much like the incongruity which Hutcheson notes provokes laughter, *Cards Against Humanity* rests on word play; it is the juxtaposition of phrases and words which are either unexpected or offensive that leads to laughter. The creators of the game describe it as "a work of satire" and nothing is seen as too sacred to become the butt of a joke (Dillon). Topics covered include religion, race, gender, sex, death, suffering, historic events and public figures. The positioning of the game's humor as satirical is significant because it suggests the game is seeking to challenge social norms and even bring about change. Although Hutcheson expressed opposition to laughter and ridicule being directed at these subjects (i.e., suffering, war, calamities), satire can offer the opportunity to laugh at subjects which are otherwise "untouchable." Satire is valuable because of its ability to critique, expose shortcomings, and, ultimately, strive for improvement or change within society. According to Hutcheson, one of the values of laughter is its ability to highlight character flaws and correct shortcomings; whilst the "satirical" humor of *Cards Against Humanity* may not be corrective, it can certainly highlight requirements for social change (31–32). Can Hutcheson's theory of laughter stretch to cover satire or is there a conflict between ridicule and ultimately good intentions?

There is no universal morality of humor; what it is acceptable to laugh at differs not only in different societies, but at different times, and for different individuals: "what is counted as ridiculous in one age or nation, may not be so in another" (Hutcheson 24). Thus, as acknowledged by Hutcheson in relation to the laughter of his time and others, in the context of *Cards Against Humanity*, what is acceptable to one player may be unacceptable to another. It is therefore important to consider who we play, and ultimately laugh, with and when.

Considering Context

This is where the importance of *context* comes into play. In *Cards Against Humanity*, the context is that of a game which offers a different way of framing social interactions. The acceptability, the normal boundaries, and limits of what makes something funny change within the context of this game as the rules of acceptability have changed. For example, in answer to the black card "Daddy, why is mummy crying?" the white card "The glass ceiling" could be played and laughed at. It is worth noting that not all players of the game will find some of these "jokes" funny and may indeed find the game "horrible" but the popularity of the game suggests that many find it not only acceptable but enjoyable. Because of this, a degree of ambiguity can be added to the way Hutcheson accounts for the need for laughter to stem from positivity. The notion of finding enjoyment in horrible or offensive jokes suggests it is difficult to address the positivity or negativity of a joke's foundations in such binary terms. Hutcheson himself develops a position which may be able to reconcile this ambiguity and it relates to the need to explore intentions.

Identifying Intentions

When considering the appropriateness of laughter, it is not just what we say it is *why* we say it; the intention or message behind what we say. For Hutcheson, the *intention* behind what we say is essential. Though his exploration of intent is focused on laughter which corrects character flaws, he notes that laughter should "flow from kindness" and "love" (31, 36). For Hutcheson, a consequence of laughter which harbors negative intentions is irritation or offence: "ridicule, with contempt or ill-nature, is indeed always irritating and offensive" (36). Whilst there has always existed a fine line between what is humorous and what is offensive, for Hutcheson it is the intention behind what we say which leads to a shift from the humorous to the offensive. Thus, for Hutcheson, negative intent leads to negative consequences. If a racist joke is told, or a racially sensitive card in *Cards Against Humanity* was played, by a member of a racist organization—the intent is clear; the joke/card is told/played maliciously and therefore loses its humor for those who do not share the same views. However, if the same joke/card is told/played by someone who claims to hold no racist views is the joke/card as morally reprehensible—if at all?

There is certainly scope in Hutcheson's approach to humor which could allow a distinction to be made between the negativity of supporting a racist intention, on the one hand, and the recognition of the incongruous transgression of this taboo by a non-racist on the other. In other words, it is possible and necessary to distinguish between *Cards Against Humanity* offering the opportunity for socially acceptable hostility and it offering a harmless opportunity to laugh at taboos and transgress social norms. Whilst there always remains the possibility that the (social) transgressions which are laughed at during the game will be repeated outside of the context of the game, as Laurence Goldstein noted: "there is all the difference in the world between a humorous suggestion not intended to be implemented and the actual implementing of it." Given the game is often played within close friendship groups—operating as a bonding exercise—and has satire and chance at its core, does the game satisfy the requirement that the laughter flows from love and kindness?

Caring About Consequences

Considering the *context* of the laughter, the *intention* behind the laughter, and the *consequences* of the laughter are necessary steps when attempting to address the morality of laughter. The frame of a game leads to the belief that there are no consequences outside of the game, and for many games this may be true, but can the same be said for *Cards Against Humanity*? Often morality is considered in relation to the consequences of something which is said or done. Ronald de Sousa notes that: "central to most moral systems is an interest in consequences, actual, probable, or merely possible" (231). As noted above, for Hutcheson, a potential consequence of laughter, particularly when related to ridicule, is offence. Indeed, Hutcheson was aware that laughter could be used negatively: "this engine of ridicule, no doubt, may be abused, and have a bad effect upon a weak mind; but with men of any reflection, there is little fear that it will ever be very pernicious" (34). Thus, when playing *Cards Against Humanity* it is important to be cautious and aware that some players may be negatively influenced by the content of the game, even if other players intend no malice. However, the game seeks to discourage offence and any failure to suspend this offence would lead to players being perceived as a spoil sport or lacking a sense of humor.

Notwithstanding this, given the variety of the content of the cards, offence is a very real possibility for most players, but it is worth considering who is playing the game. Samuel Director seeks to argue that statistically there is a high likelihood, when we play *Cards Against Humanity*, that we will be making jokes about the suffering of a category of people while in front of a person who fits this category, and as a result the game is morally wrong (39–50). Whilst it is worth considering whether we would play the same cards if we knew one or some of the players fits the "punchline," can it be suggested that the morality is based purely on the identity (i.e., gender/race/region) and life experiences of our fellow players? If we knew a player fit the "punchline" would this change our intent? Is the belief that people (who are not playing) won't find out what we laughed at the reason we feel safe laughing in the context of this game? These questions, along with the distinction Hutcheson makes between weak-mindedness and "men of reflection," suggests that the morality of laughter can be determined *both* on the basis of the intent behind the joke and the consequences it has on any specific group.

It's Just a Joke!

We often consider the appropriateness of a joke to be dependent on the company we are in; what we laugh at changes depending on who we laugh with. For Hutcheson, particularly when joking about great things, we should be cautious of the company we are in (35). Hutcheson appears to differentiate company by their intelligence and ability to reflect on the subject of laughter. In Hutcheson's words, "men of sense" are able to identify what should or should not be laughed at, by reflecting on the true intentions behind the (potential) laughter, whereas those with "weak minds" may laugh at inappropriate subjects or be wrongly influenced by the subject of the laughter (36). For Hutcheson, the person provoking laughter has a responsibility to consider how their audience will respond; will they reflect and respond appropriately or not? In addition, the audience has a responsibility to reflect on the laughter, though Hutcheson accepts not everyone will have the ability to do so effectively. It is worth considering, briefly, the extent to which we are *able* to reflect during laughter. Hutcheson acknowledges that laughter is contagious and at times when we see others laughing we can laugh without even knowing what they are laughing at (27). For Hutcheson, we must reflect on the context, the intentions, and the consequences of the laughter to establish its moral appropriateness. However, laughter is impulsive and when we are laughing with others it is often difficult to stop. Thus, whilst Hutcheson identifies a dual responsibility for laughter (from both the person provoking the laughter and the people who laugh), as highlighted above, Hutcheson places most of the moral responsibility for laughter on the person who provokes laughter as they have the time to consider the context, the intentions, the potential consequences, and ultimately decide whether they should or should not say something which may provoke laughter.

When engaging in a game such as *Cards Against Humanity*, there is a risk that players will hear jokes, which may have racist, sexist, or cruel undertones, be influenced by what they hear, and seek to continue or develop these viewpoints outside of the game. The game could be seen to normalize such views (see also Strmic-Pawl and Wilson). Dennis Howitt and Kwame Owsu-Bempah argue that joke telling—in relation to minority groups—reaffirms prejudices and embeds them further in society: "jokes do more than merely reflect prejudices. They are active in the process of the construction of the meaning of 'otherness' and inferiority of social groups." (Howitt 59). This assumption of malice is (expected to be) absent when playing cards during the game and they are thus positioned as incongruous statements/jokes rather than serious intentional statements; if players were to reflect and detect any malicious intent then the humor of the game would be lost. Therefore, it is important to remember, even in the context of a game, Hutcheson's warning that: "Ridicule, like any other edged tools, may do good in a wise man's hands, though fools may cut their fingers with it, or be injurious to an unwary bystander" (34–35).

Johan Huizinga's study of play(-ing games) identifies how play offers an alternative frame to that of real life: "play is not 'ordinary' or 'real' life. It is rather a stepping out of 'real' life into a temporary sphere of activity with a disposition of its own" (8). When we play we recognize that we are entering a space designated for play, and understand that the game and its rules, and goals, are temporary (Huizinga 9). This recognition echoes the importance of context when we laugh for Hutcheson, and it has been suggested, for players of the game *Cards Against Humanity*. It is in the recognition that when the players are "inside the circle of the game the laws and customs of ordinary life no longer count. [During the game] we are different and do things differently" (Huizinga 12). Players seek success until the game ends (Huizinga 10–11). Therefore, it seems possible to reconcile the behavior which is exhibited when playing *Cards Against Humanity* in an attempt to win the game and suggest that there is a recognition that the laughter is only appropriate within the frame of this game.

Thus, if the frame of the game is acknowledged and engaged with as "men of sense," it can encourage players to reflect not only on what they are laughing at but why they are laughing, and why it is—if it can even be agreed that it is—only acceptable within the confines of the game. Whilst the game enables the ethical boundaries of society to be transgressed through laughter, it does not stop players from reflecting during the game and even after. For players who are able to identify and understand the expectations of society, there is an appreciation that the content *Cards Against Humanity* should not be used outside of the context of the game. Indeed, the game can reinforce societal expectations regarding the expression of derogatory views of others rather than break them down. There is a distinction to be made between the game which through chance can lead to incongruous and offensive cards being played in the context of the game, on the one hand, and intentionally offensive statements being made outside of the game, on the other hand.

When playing *Cards Against Humanity*, the expectation is that you are playing with likeminded people—often friends or family—and it is accepted that the unlaughable will be laughed at and that players will enjoy doing it. There is also an underlying assumption, that the players do not harbor the "horrible" views they present during the game; that they would not choose to make these jokes themselves but rather the game has made them do it through the chance selection of cards. The game, ultimately, offers an opportunity for reflection on the humor it creates rather than inciting participants to act on it. Whereas for Hutcheson the appropriateness of the laughter is a reflection on the person who provokes it, *Cards Against Humanity* requires players to suspend this judgment, playing a card is not seen as a reflection of the player and their moral character. Failing to suspend this judgment would mean the game ceased.

Conclusion

Laughter is a powerful force and one that allows social boundaries to be transgressed. This transgression is not only possible but it seems it is actively sought, within the confines of a safe space, which can be seen in the popularity of the game *Cards Against Humanity*. This game intentionally challenges social etiquette, expectations, and norms and as such it has provided a useful opportunity for exploring the morality of laughter in practice. Whilst the game appears to offer a suspension of some moral expectations for the duration of the game, I suggest it does not lead to the breakdown of social norms, but the reinforcement of their existence outside of the game because it underlines the unacceptable.

It is worth ending with a reflection on an implicit thread throughout Hutcheson's work: the subjectiveness of laughter. The fact that so many years have passed and little to no agreement has been reached regarding a "morality" or "ethics" of laughter suggests that there are many contributing and influencing factors and the morality of laughter will remain a subjective endeavor. As acknowledged by Hutcheson, just because laughter can be used negatively does not mean that it is not without its benefits: "that ridicule may be abused, does not prove it useless, or unnecessary, more than a like possibility of abuse would prove all our senses and passions, impertinent or hurtful" (34). For Hutcheson, the benefits of laughter, and ultimately its goodness, outweigh the harm it can cause. This essay reveals that laughter is bound in a set of complex relationships of the context, the community, the situation, and the moral reflection sustaining the ideas and interactions. This is significant in a world where the frame of laughter is constantly being redefined.

WORKS CITED

Billig, Michael. *Laughter and Ridicule: Towards a Social Critique of Humour.* Sage Publications, 2005.
_____. "Violent Racist Jokes." *Beyond a Joke: The Limits of Humour.* Edited by Sharon Lockyer and Michael Pickering, Palgrave Macmillan, 2009, pp. 27–46.
Cards Against Humanity. www.cardsagainsthumanity.com. Accessed 1 June 2018.
de Sousa, Ronald, "When Is It Wrong to Laugh?" *The Philosophy of Laughter and Humor.* Edited by John Morreall, State University of New York Press, pp. 226–249.
Dillon, Josh, et al. *Cards Against Humanity.* UK Edition, 2013.
Director, Samuel. "The Inhumanity of Cards Against Humanity." *Think,* vol. 17, no. 48, 2018, pp. 39–50.
Goldstein, Laurence. "Only Joking?" *Philosophy Now,* issue 34, December 2001–January 2002, www.philosophynow.org/issues/34/Only_Joking. Accessed 13 August 2018.
Hamrick, Dave. "Cards Against Humanity: What We Can Learn from the Most Successful Private Label Product Ever." *Jungle Scout,* 12 February 2018, www.junglescout.com/blog/amazon-success-story/. Accessed 1 June 2018.
Hobbes, Thomas. *The Elements of Law, Natural and Politic.* London, 1640.
Howitt, Dennis and Kwame Owsu-Bempah. "Race and Ethnicity in Popular Humour." *Beyond a Joke: The Limits of Humour,* Edited by Sharon Lockyer and Michael Pickering, Palgrave Macmillan, 2009, pp. 47–64.
Hutcheson, Francis. *Reflections Upon Laughter and Remarks Upon The Fable of the Bees.* Glasgow, 1750.
Huizinga, Johan. *Homo Ludens: A Study of the Play-Element in Culture.* Routledge, 1944.
Jaffro, Laurent. "The Passions and Actions of laughter in Shaftesbury and Hutcheson." *Thinking about the Emotions: A Philosophical History.* Edited by Alix Cohen and Robert Stern, Oxford University Press, 2017, pp. 130–149.

Kimball, Diana. "Case Study: Cards Against Humanity." *Kickstarter*, 26 July 2012, www.kick
    starter.com/blog/case-study-cards-against-humanity. Accessed 13 August 2018.
Morreall, John. *Taking Laughter Seriously*. State University of New York Press, 1983.
Strmic-Pawl, Hephzibah V., and Rai-ya Wilson. "Equal Opportunity Racism? Review of Cards
    Against Humanity, created by Josh Dillon, Daniel Dranove, Eli Halpern, Ben Hantoot,
    David Munk, David Pinsof, Max Temkin, and Eliot Weinstein, distributed by Cards
    Against Humanity LLC." *Humanity & Society*, vol. 40, no. 3., 2016, pp. 361–364.

The Caring Practical Joke

DAVID K. MCGRAW

A classic example of a practical joke was purportedly carried out by American painter Waldo Peirce (1884–1970) (as described by American playwright Charles MacArthur [1895–1956]). During the 1920s, while Waldo was living in Paris, he gave a small turtle as a gift to a woman who was the concierge of his building. Later, he surreptitiously replaced the turtle with a larger one, a process he repeated over the coming weeks. The concierge was amazed at the rapid growth of the turtle, and showed it off to the neighborhood. Then, Waldo reversed the operation, secretly replacing the turtle with smaller versions, to the puzzlement of the concierge.

Literature provides many examples of practical jokes. In Shakespeare's *Twelfth Night,* Sir Toby Belch and his friends produce a false letter to the character Malvolio to "make a contemplative idiot of him," persuading him that Olivia loves him and wishes him to wear a particularly hideous outfit of clothing involving yellow stockings. In Charlotte Brontë's *Jane Eyre,* Mr. Rochester dressed as a "gypsy woman" to tell the fortunes of his houseguests. In Alcott's *Little Women,* the character Theodore "Laurie" Laurence plays a prank on friend Meg by sending her a supposed "love letter" causing friction between Meg and her sisters. In the American novel *To Kill a Mockingbird,* the narrator Scout Finch tells of a Halloween prank in which some "wicked children" snuck into the house of two elderly deaf women and moved all their furniture into the cellar.

Practical jokes or pranks are a common part of American culture. They are prevalent in many workplaces, they abound on April Fool's Day, and have been fodder for television programs such as *Candid Camera* and *Punked.* They range from the simple and hastily-planned "kick me" post-it note to elaborate plans with props and the involvement of numerous supporting players.

The purpose of this essay is to explore the ethics of the practical joke.

223

Practical jokes are certainly morally dubious in that they often involve an action performed on a nonconsenting victim who might experience confusion, ridicule, or discomfort. On the other hand, practical jokes provide a variety of benefits, ranging from amusement to a psychological sense of bonding among a group. To be sure, in many cases the burdens and benefits do not accrue equally to all participants in the practical joke, as the subjective experiences of the actor and subject of the practical joke are likely to differ.

A utilitarian analysis of the practical joke would suggest that a practical joke may be described as morally "good" or "bad" in the sense that, in a given situation, it might produce more positive results than negative, or, conversely more net harm than benefit. A deontological analysis would seek to understand whether wrongful acts were perpetuated in the course of the execution of the joke, by coercing an individual's participation in an action without full knowledge and consent, or, alternatively, by using an individual as a means to the end of providing entertainment to others.

This essay will suggest that a more productive way to explore the ethics of the practical joke is to assess whether it is a caring or an uncaring act given the relationships between the parties. Empathy is the most important skill that must be employed to evaluate the morality of the practical joke. There are few objective factors that can differentiate the morality of the practical joke, because the difference lies not in the action itself, but in the relationship between the individuals. Empirical evidence and reason alone are incapable of determining the morality of a practical joke, because the benefits or harms of the practical joke are highly contextual, and, in particular, are dependent on the relationship between the individuals involved. An act performed between friends might further deepen the friendship, whereas the same act performed between strangers might be interpreted as hostile. However, the broad categories "friend" and "stranger" are too coarse for the extremely nuanced interpersonal relationship dynamics at play. There is often a fine line between whether the victim feels more included or more excluded as a result of the practical joke.

The competence used in assessing the morality of a practical joke is the skill of caring, based on how caring is described by Nel Noddings in *Caring: A Feminine Approach to Ethics and Moral Education* (1984). As explained by Noddings, caring requires that the one-caring must exhibit engrossment and motivational displacement toward the cared-for, and the cared-for must exhibit response to the caring (1984, 69). It is only when one has established such a relationship with another that one can truly understand the other to the degree necessary to determine how the practical joke would be received. Thus, to better understand the humor of practical jokes, one must develop a deeper understanding of the nature of caring.

The Nature of the Practical Joke

Often used synonymously with "prank," providing a precise definition of the term "practical joke" is elusive. Dictionary definitions of the term vary, some emphasizing the original use of the term "to parade and dance," while other definitions suggest that they are intended to embarrass someone or cause physical discomfort. Some commenters suggest the use of the word "practical" is usually used to differentiate jokes that involve some form of action from those that are purely verbal. However, this definition would exclude many "April Fool's Day" jokes, such as telling a friend that one is pregnant, then, after a pause, yelling "April Fools!" Such a verbal exchange would seem to be consonant with the essence of a practical joke, despite the lack of physical action. Tallman suggests that in folklore, practical jokes involve two distinct parties, one that is aware of the planned action from the beginning, and one that must remain unaware until a pivotal moment in which it is too late for the action to change course (260). Thus, for purposes of this essay, we will assume that the primary distinguishing characteristics of the practical joke are those suggested by Tallman: there must be an element of surprise which relies on planning by one party and a lack of knowledge by a second party (we might also referred to this as information asymmetry).

In addition, most would agree that to qualify as a practical joke, the interaction must be funny. One can imagine many acts of sheer cruelty that meet the defining characteristics of information asymmetry and surprise, but most would not classify them as practical jokes because of the severity of the suffering caused. Indeed, if one were to describe such acts of cruelty as "jokes," one would probably be labeled as a sadist or a psychopath. However, determining which jokes are funny is problematic. Humor is often in the eye of the beholder. It is not clear that we could establish an objective standard for what is funny. For example, courts have struggled with developing an objective determination of humor (for example, see the U.S. Supreme Court's discussion of whether an alleged parody of the song "Pretty Woman" met the definitional requirement of having "comic effect" in *Campbell aka Luke Skywalker v. Acuff Rose Music, Inc.*). As E.B. White wrote, "Humor can be dissected, as a frog can, but the thing dies in the process and the innards are discouraging to any but the purely scientific mind." Nevertheless, in order for a practical joke to live up to its purported classification as a "joke," we must presume that it was at least intended to be humorous.

While the practical joke may superficially seem to primarily provide amusement to the perpetrator and annoyance to the victim, practical jokes often play a more complex role in transforming the relationship between these parties. In Mark Twain's novel *The Adventures of Huckleberry Finn*, the character Huckleberry Finn plays a series of three practical jokes on Jim, an African American slave seeking his freedom. In separate articles analyzing these practical jokes, Chadwick Hansen and James McIntyre highlight a shift in the character development of Jim as the novel progresses through these practical jokes, from a "sub-human type-character who is insensitive to pain, to a well-rounded character of great dignity and depth of feeling." Told in the first-person, this character development is concurrent with an apparent change in Huck Finn's understanding of and appreciation for Jim, and indicates the development of a richer and deeper relationship between the two characters. More than a mere literary device, this suggests that practical jokes may have the tendency to change relationships.

Determining whether one should perform a practical joke requires a careful ethical analysis. Practical jokes have the tendency to change human relationships, but not all of these changes are for the better. Subtle differences in the nature of the existing relationships and in the context of the actions can lead to differing interpretations of the meaning of the action and thus lead to different kinds of changed relationships. In some cases, the perception by the victim as being outside of the social group who are "in on the joke" might result in even greater feelings of exclusion. A key element in successful relationships is trust. Practical jokes can lead to a breakdown of trust between individuals, or it can build a sense of trust.

Thus, the potential dangers of practical jokes are real. The unethical practical joke could lead to physical suffering, emotional suffering, and/or a breakdown in harmonious relationships between individuals. One might suggest that, given this list of potential negative side effects, one should err on the side of prohibiting all practical jokes. However, this seems to go against human nature. Humor, in its various forms, seems to be a universal desire of our species, as it has been observed in all cultures and at all ages. Humor seems to break up monotony, to promote happiness, to buffer stress, as well as to gain intimacy. Psychologists have shown positive correlations between humor and increased feelings of emotional well-being and optimism (Crawford & Caltabiano). Thus, the question seems to be when and how we should use humor.

Utilitarianism: The Good Practical Joke

According to a utilitarian approach to ethics, a practical joke might be deemed "good" or "bad" based on the results produced. As stated by Mill, utilitarianism is "The creed which accepts as the foundation of morals, Utility, or the Greatest Happiness Principle, holds that actions are right in proportion as they tend to promote happiness, wrong as they tend to produce the reverse of happiness" (Mill). However, attempts to use a utilitarian approach to evaluate whether one ought to participate in a practical joke proves problematic and highlights two long-discussed shortcomings of utilitarianism.

The first of these shortcomings of utilitarianism, frequently referred to as the "utility ignores justice" problem, is often illustrated by hypotheticals in which an innocent individual is punished in order to promote the greater good. Not only is the practical joke analogous to the case of unjust punishment, but it might even be a better example. In the case of a cruel practical joke perpetrated purely for the amusement of a larger group, utilitarianism seems to require that one individual might be called upon to suffer pain or humiliation if the number of individuals receiving entertainment from watching the joke is large enough. In the case of unjust punishment, utilitarians such as McCloskey have suggested that the way around the problem would be the creation of a general rule, such as "do not punish an innocent person." But if such a rule is necessary to ensure that an act utilitarian analysis does not lead to an unjust result, what might be the comparable rule with respect to the practical joke? If one accepts the premise of this essay that some practical jokes are desirable, then a broad, sweeping rule such as "do not perpetuate practical jokes" would be inappropriate. Perhaps "do not perpetuate practical jokes against unwilling victims" would be better, but as we have defined practical jokes as requiring the element of surprise, no victim will be known to the perpetrator as willing or unwilling in advance of the action. Thus, the required element of surprise means that no rule of utility can be devised that would avoid the problem of circularity.

Next, assuming, arguendo, that the outcomes of a practical joke should be a basis of evaluating whether one should engage in the activity, the case of the practical joke illustrates a shortcoming of utilitarianism: the difficulty of predicting consequences. The aim of ethics should be to provide useful guidance for living. In Plato's dialogue, the *Gorgias*, Socrates said "For you see what our discussions are all about—and is there anything about which a man of even small intelligence would be more serious than this: what is the way we ought to live?" (*Gorgias*). Thus, even if we were to stipulate that the determination of whether a practical joke is good or bad should be determined by the maximization of utility, this would only be a valuable exercise if we are able to predict the outcomes of perpetrating the practical joke.

The problem of predictability is a challenge for utilitarianism writ large, but it is particularly highlighted by the case of the practical joke. In order to determine whether one ought to plan and execute a practical joke, one must be able to predict in advance how the object of the joke will feel about having been forced to be an unwitting participant. Predicting this reaction by the victim requires even more than the skill of ordinary prediction, because no two individuals will respond in the same manner. What is required is that one know the individual well enough to know how she will feel about being the subject of a practical joke. But, because the response to the joke is likely to be contextual, depending on the relationships involved, one must also know about the relationships between the object of the joke, the perpetrator of the joke, and all of the other observers whose presence might influence how the joke is received. Thus, even if knowing how one should act depends on predicting the amount of happiness that will be produced, this prediction will be ineffective unless one has the skill of empathy.

Deontology: Avoiding the Wrongful Practical Joke

A deontological analysis of practical jokes would seek to determine whether the act of performing a practical joke involves a wrongful act. German philosopher Immanuel Kant argued that we have an absolute duty to respect the humanity of others, or, alternatively, never to use others merely as a means to an end. From a Kantian perspective, there are a number of potentially problematic aspects of the practical joke.

First, by its very definition, the practical joke relies upon deception, thus it would seem that the practical joke might violate Kant's first categorical imperative, the formula of the universal law of nature. Kant argued that lying is prohibited under all possible circumstances (even, famously, the hypothetical in which there is a murderer at the door wondering if an innocent victim is in one's house). Although there may be an important distinction between lying and deception, Kant's analysis would treat deliberate acts of deception as morally equivalent to lying. This would probably be the case under the formula of the universal law of nature, but deliberate acts of deception would even more clearly violate the second categorical imperative, the humanity formula, by failing to respect the rationality of the subject of the practical joke. Kant would argue that one would only respect the rationality of the victim by giving full knowledge necessary to make an informed choice prior to the commencement of the practical joke.

One problem with this conclusion is the paradox that, in certain situations, humans often prefer not to know. Psychological studies have shown that people often choose ignorance. For example, in a recent study by Gigerenzer and Garcia-Retamero, between 85 percent and 90 percent of people did not want to know about upcoming negative events, and 40 percent to 70 percent preferred to remain ignorant of positive events, while only 1 percent of the participants in their study consistently wanted to know. In Western cultures in which gifts are given as a surprise, the individual receiving the gift would often prefer to be surprised by the gift, presumably because there is more happiness associated with the element of surprise. Assuming that "good" practical jokes exist, and that practical jokes depend on the ignorance of the object, the object of the joke must prefer not to know. This presents a paradox since we must respect the will of the individual who would have preferred not to know about the joke in advance.

Second, Kant also posited in the humanity formula that it is immoral to use another person merely as a means to an end, and that people must— under all circumstances—be treated as ends in themselves. Quite often a practical joke seems to provide more benefits to the bystanders than to the victim of the joke who might be considered a means to the end of others' amusement. Here, it appears that Kant's analysis would usually provide good guidance: when the primary purpose of the practical joke is to amuse the bystanders at the expense of the victim, then it is likely that we might deem the practical joke to be unethical. However, we might question whether this is always, or necessarily, the case. One might imagine an individual who would enjoy providing amusement for one's friends, thus even if the primary motivation of the practical joke is the amusement of the bystanders, it still might be the preference of the individual to have been permitted to be the butt of the joke. Thus, the same paradox exists with respect to Kant's "means to an end" formulation: it is possible that to respect an individual's choice to be treated as a means to an end might require that we violate the principle.

The Caring Practical Joke

While there is merit to considering the maximization of utility and the respect of the individual when deciding whether or not one should engage in the execution of a practical joke, neither of these are sufficient to give guidance as to how one ought to live. Missing from both of these are the necessary elements of empathy and caring. Instead, a better form of guidance would be to act in as caring a manner as possible, given the nature of the relationships involved.

As described in Nel Noddings' *Caring: A Relational Approach to Ethics & Moral Education,* ethics is not about abstractions, it is about relationships. Acting ethically does not mean always acting the same way toward all, but rather requires that the one-caring truly understand the cared-for. Acting ethically does not involve following universal rules applied generically to individuals without regard to the cared-for's individual situation, but rather requires that the one-caring know the cared-for well enough to understand the cared-for's needs and desires. Under this formulation of the ethical life, relationships are not irrelevant to ethics, but rather are at the foundation of ethics.

Furthermore, central to Noddings' explanation of ethics is the idea that our focus should not be on judgments of "right" or "wrong," but rather on acting in a caring manner toward those with whom we form relationships. Thus, for example, suppose one were to decide to give a surprise gift to another individual. Is this a good act or a bad act? Under the principle of utility, this would presumably be deemed a good act, although it is difficult to tell, because whether the gift is welcome might depend on the nature of the gift and the nature of the relationship between the individuals. It is possible that the gift might make the recipient less happy, because it might make one sense some undesired obligation. The kinds of information required to answer the ethical question are within the domain of empathy and require an understanding of human relationships. Under a Kantian, analysis, it is unclear whether the giving of a surprise gift is ethical because it is an act taken without the prior consent of the recipient. But, given Kant's desire to base ethical determinations purely on reason and universal principles and to remove "interest" from the equation, the answer would almost certainly not depend on the specifics of the relationship between the individuals.

Under a caring approach, the question should not be whether gift-giving is a good act or a bad act. As Noddings states, "it is important to understand that we are not primarily interested in judging, but in heightening moral perception and sensitivity" (90). The more appropriate questions under an ethic of caring would include the following: what is the nature of the current relationship between the one-caring and the cared-for, and how can an act such as gift-giving further the potential that exists within this relationship? If the focus is appropriately on understanding the relationship and further building it, the cared-for will likely have a clearer understanding not only of whether one should give the gift, but also understand the kind of gift most likely to enhance the existing relationship.

As in the analogy of the gift, a caring approach to the practical joke would focus on heightening moral perception and sensitivity, and on understanding and building of human relationships. Under an ethic of care, the question shifts from the "goodness" or potential wrongfulness of the practical joke to instead emphasize an understanding of the cared-for and a focus on the question, "how can I best build a stronger and healthier relationship among this group of individuals?" With that shift of focus, the question of whether one ought to plan and execute a practical joke should become evident. Without this shift of focus, the most relevant factors, the truly important ones, are all too likely to be overlooked or misunderstood.

Works Cited

Alcott, Louisa May. *Little Women*. Penguin Books, 1953.
Brontë, Charlotte. *Jane Eyre*. Broadview Press, 1999.

Luther R. Campbell a.k.a. Luke Skyywalker, et al., Petitioners v. Acuff-Rose Music, Incorporated. No. 510 U.S. 569. Supreme Court. 7 Mar. 1994.

Crawford, Shelley A., and Nerina J. Caltabiano. "Promoting Emotional Well-Being Through the Use of Humour," *The Journal of Positive Psychology,* 2011, vol. 6, no. 3, pp. 237–252.

Gigerenzer, Gerd, and Rocio Garcia-Retamero. "Cassandra's Regret: The Psychology of Not Wanting to Know." *Psychological Review,* vol. 124, no. 2, March 2017, pp. 179–196.

Hansen, Chadwick. "The Character of Jim and the Ending of 'Huckleberry Finn,'" *The Massachusetts Review,* vol. 5, no. 1, 1963, pp. 45–66.

Hunt, Alan, and Carol Hunt. "The Practical Joke in 'Huckleberry Finn.'" *Western Folklore,* vol. 51, no. 2, 1992, pp. 197–202.

Lee, Harper. *To Kill a Mockingbird.* Harper Perennial Modern Classics, 2006.

Marsh, Moira. *Practically Joking.* University Press of Colorado, 2015.

McCloskey, H.J. "An Examination of Restricted Utilitarianism." *The Philosophical Review,* vol. 66, no. 4, 1957, pp. 466–485.

McIntyre, James P. "Three Practical Jokes: A Key to Huck's Changing Attitude Toward Jim." *Modern Fiction Studies,* vol. 14, no. 1, 1968, pp. 33–37.

Mill, John S., and George Sher. *Utilitarianism.* Hackett Publishing Company, 1979.

Noddings, Nel. *Caring: A Relational Approach to Ethics & Moral Education.* University of California Press, 1984.

Plato. *Gorgias.* Teubner, 1909.

Shakespeare, William. *Twelfth Night.* Houghton Mifflin, 1928.

Smith, H. Allen. *The Compleat Practical Joker.* A. Barker, London, 1954.

Tallman, Richard S. "Generic Approach to the Practical Joke." *Southern Folklore Quarterly,* vol. 38, December 1974, pp. 259–274.

Twain, Mark. *The Adventures of Huckleberry Finn.* Penguin, 1986.

"Laughter is not our medicine"

Hannah Gadsby's Nanette *and the Balm of Comedy*

Grant Moss

Hannah Gadsby's Netflix special *Nanette* questions the ability of comedy to tell stories in a meaningful way. As she notes in her very powerful monologue, stories require three narrative parts—a beginning, middle, and end—whereas jokes only require two parts: a setup and a punch line. In a story, the tension created by the beginning and middle part of the narrative is resolved by the ending; in a joke, the tension created by the setup of the narrative is diffused by laughter, but it is not resolved. Gadsby notes that LGBTQ people (as well as other marginalized groups) learn at an early age to use this diffusion of tension through laughter as a survival strategy.

In this essay, I wish to explore the ideas Gadsby raises in a broader context, especially some of the implications of her comments about comedy and marginalized communities. I also wish to discuss whether political satirists such as Trevor Noah of *The Daily Show* are similarly hampered in their ability to tell meaningful stories; does the use of humor in current political satire actually make it more difficult to tell the story of the rise of fascism in the United States by diffusing tension through laughter? The larger ethical question to be considered is how the structure of the joke, as well as the social pressure to consider the joke in isolation from the privileged social position the comedians have benefited from in the past, undermines the social critique contained in the joke. At the same time, the success of comedians from alternative identities who use comedy as a way of critiquing the social injustices they endure must also be questioned if the formal characteristics of their critique render it impossible to begin with.

232

Jokes and Stories

Although Hannah Gadsby has been familiar to Australians and the British for over a decade, she was largely unknown to American audiences until her Netflix special, *Nanette*, premiered and became a sensation in 2018. Her special had significant insights into comedy and its impact on women, LGBTQ people, and politics. Gadsby's work has always dealt with social issues; as Corinna Burford notes, her previous work dealt with "her thoughts on sexuality, homophobia, gender, and stories about her family and childhood growing up in ... a small town in Tasmania" (*Vulture*). Her early material included numerous self-deprecating jokes about herself and her body; in 2010, for instance, Gadsby commented that "I never recovered from puberty. I didn't get visited by the breast fairy. I got a visit from the thigh fairy, and she had a trigger finger" (*Vulture*). However, Burford also mentions that *Nanette* "takes a very different approach to storytelling and highlights the problematic nature of comedy and joke construction itself." Most importantly Gadsby spoke both powerfully and eloquently about the limitations of jokes and comedy as vehicles for conveying significant stories. Gadsby could use her comedy to speak truth to power about life as a lesbian, sharing her experiences and perspectives with her audience. To do so, she had to create moments of tension and incongruity that would be resolved with the punchline. Gadsby's point is that the tension release went no further than that moment with that joke. At its core, Gadsby's critique of comedy is a critique of believing that the jokes have an effect beyond the laughter. While she may be telling stories about her life and how she has managed to navigate a heterosexist culture, the audience gets released from the ongoing tension that she experiences on a regular basis. In this way, her work raises interesting questions about the differences between using jokes to tell a story as opposed to treating jokes as stories in themselves. For comedians who speak from a marginalized point of view, the joke does not resolve or improve on that marginalization, it merely draws from it to provoke laughter.

In *Nanette*, Gadsby speaks persuasively about the ways that comedy is problematic for performers who are marginalized, including herself:

> I do think I have to quit comedy though. And seriously ... I know it's probably not the forum to make such an announcement, is it? In the middle of a comedy show. But I have been questioning, you know, this whole comedy thing. I don't feel very comfortable in it anymore. You know ... over the past year, I've been questioning it, and reassessing. And I think it's healthy for an adult human to take stock, pause, and reassess. And when I first started doing the comedy, over a decade ago, my favorite comedian was Bill Cosby. [Audience laughs] There you go, it's very healthy to reassess, isn't it? And I built a career out of self-deprecating humor. That's what I've built my career on. And ... I don't want to do that anymore. Because, do you

understand... [audience applauds] do you understand what self-deprecation means when it comes from somebody who already exists in the margins? It's not humility. It's humiliation. I put myself down in order to speak, in order to seek permission ... to speak. And I simply will not do that anymore. Not to myself, or anybody who identifies with me [audience cheers] [Gadsby, 2018].

Note that the audience applauds at her initial renunciation of self-deprecation, as if they are anticipating a standard narrative of empowerment and self-improvement. Instead of the punch-line being a moment of triumph it is a reiteration of the power structures that keep people marginalized. Gadsby goes on to make it clear that comedians such as herself are put in a double bind: first, their marginalization is justified by being fodder for her comedy; how bad can it be if she can joke about it? Second, speaking of all marginalized people, Gadsby points out that she has to ask the audience's permission to speak about her marginalization in the first place. If a woman, or a person of color, or a queer person, or any other marginalized person is speaking to a white audience, it is customary—if not obligatory in some circumstances—to perform this act of self-abasement before speaking. It is a metaphorical genuflection to the patriarchy thanking it for allowing a second-class citizen to speak. This sort of apology for one's existence is largely unknown among white, male, hetero, cis-gendered comedians, at least until (maybe) only recently. While other comedians might see value in these jokes because of their potential for consciousness raising, highlighting the ways that comedy can be a vehicle for social justice, Gadsby only sees further acts of debasement and reification of the social norms that perpetuate her marginalization.

A similar dynamic—the separation of the artist or problematic social facts from the art for sake of audience enjoyment—is at work in other artistic fields. Gadsby, who has a degree in art history, speaks to what every teacher of English Renaissance literature confronts: Renaissance literature is dominated by white, male, hetero, cis-gendered authors. In the late 20th and 21st centuries, scholars finally began to include more female and non-white authors in the canon; it is striking what a difference this makes to scholars and to students. In Tudor and Jacobean literature classes, for instance, students who were given nothing but Philip Sidney, Christopher Marlowe, William Shakespeare, Ben Jonson and so forth, were suddenly given access to Elizabeth Cary, Aemilia Lanyer, Aphra Behn, Jane Anger and many others. And those women writers had wildly different life experiences, ideas, and priorities than their male contemporaries (*quelle surprise*). Once those voices were available, students and scholars had to re-examine what value had been placed on male voices of the past. Or as one of my Tudor Literature students remarked when we were studying *Astrophil and Stella*, "oh goody, another guy trying to get laid." The old canon was filled with the musings of straight men trying demeaning women via the old Madonna/whore binary, a phenomenon Gadsby sums up memorably when discussing her degree in art history:

> Art history taught me there's only ever been two types of women. A virgin or a whore. Most people think that Miley Cyrus and Taylor Swift invented that binary, but it's been going on thousands of years. There's only ever been two options for a little girl to grow up into. A virgin or a whore. We were always given a choice. Take your pick! Ladies' choice! That's the trick. That patriarchy. It's not a dictatorship. Take your choice! And I don't fit very neatly into either of those categories. Virgin or whore? I mean, on a technicality, I'd get virgin. I know [Gadsby, 2018].

She goes on to lament that "The history of western art is just the history of men painting women like their flesh vases for their dick flowers," a striking metaphor for the objectification of women in western art. Similar moves are made in comedy when the joke is separated from the joke teller or the audience is not challenged to question the social factors that shape the set-up of the joke. The laughter might release the tension in the room but nothing else has been addressed or resolved. The audience will leave, however, having derived enjoyment from the mining of other people's marginalization or pain.

After complaining about this rampant sexism in art (with a particularly memorable tirade on Picasso), Gadsby says that she has been told that she has to "Separate the man from the art":

> "Separate the man from the art." That's what I keep hearing. "You've got to learn to separate the man from the art. The art is important, not the artist. You've got to learn to separate the man from the art." Yeah, all right. Let's give it a go. How about you take Picasso's name off his little paintings and see how much his doodles are worth at auction? Fucking nothing! Nobody owns a circular Lego nude, they own a Picasso!

This is a familiar refrain, not just in art, but any other discipline that has been unwilling to openly confront the misogyny of its subjects. However, in the wake of #MeToo, many scholars have had to reconsider what was once an unquestioned axiom of the western canon. By separating the art from the artist, we can include sexist, racist, and homophobic materials in the western tradition without grappling fully with the degradation that such works inflict upon the marginalized. It also compels us to recognize that separation of artist from art is a type of white privilege which is unavailable to the marginalized—note the ongoing frustration of artists who do not wish to be pigeonholed as a "woman painter," or a "black writer," etc. When we combine this with the introduction of other, previously stifled voices, we find that a reconsideration of both which works we consider worthy of study and what explicit and implicit criteria we use to evaluate such works. This change is slowly but surely forcing scholars to question what value there is in continuing to valorize the sexist performative masculinity of the past while trying to determine how best to incorporate the voices which were suppressed or

236 Part Four: Laughter and Ridicule

ignored. The inclusion of marginalized voices forces us to reconsider the principles by which we evaluate and determine "the greats" instead of blindly accepting a pre-existing canon and passing it on to the next generation of students and scholars.

The separation of art from the artist is an extremely complex issue which I cannot do full justice to in this work. However, there are also contextual issues which can be brought to bear on this problem. For instance, if we are studying a historical era in which sexism is a regrettable but near-omnipresent cultural norm, do we reject the works of Shakespeare, which largely tend to reinforce the patriarchy? As someone who teaches Shakespeare's works regularly, I do not yet have a comprehensive answer to this question—those of us who teach early literature are still grappling with how best to address this— but it may be possible to focus on the broader scope of an artist's work while acknowledging that the horrific sexism of a play such as *The Taming of the Shrew* renders this "comedy" largely unamusing to a twenty-first-century audience. By contrast, we may be able to acknowledge that a play such as *The Merchant of Venice*, although dreadfully anti–Semitic, is able to make some salient points about the disenfranchised (specifically, women and Jews), even if those points may not be part of the author's original intent. In other words, while *Taming* makes women the butt of an extended joke we no longer find funny, *Merchant* makes anti–Semitic jokes as part of a larger story about humanity, mercy and loyalty. A similar critique can be applied to comedians and comedy: do we continue to laugh at comedians who have proven problematic pasts (Cosby, Louis C.K.)? Do we continue to laugh at jokes that trade in sexist, racist, or homophobic attitudes (the nursery rhymes of Andrew Dice Clay)? And if the answer is no, how do we take seriously Gadsby's critique of comedy: that the very structure of the joke mines social inequities for laughs even as it does nothing to address them?

I mention this because I believe Gadsby's monologue in *Nanette* could have the same effect on comedy as unleashing the voices of sixteenth- and seventeenth-century women writers. Yes, there have been many female comedians before her, but Gadsby is doing something very different from most of her predecessors: she is able to speak forthrightly about the fact that comedy is problematic for all of us, but especially for the marginalized, because jokes are not stories. They can function as part of a story, but they are not complete stories in and of themselves. The joke may be part of the comedian's story, but even at its best, comedy is incomplete (and often fabricated or exaggerated) biography. The audience never gets to hear the whole story. I'll let her explain more clearly:

> Let me explain to you what a joke is. And when you strip it back to its bare essential … components, like, its bare minimum, a joke is simply two things, it needs two things to work. A setup and a punch line. And it is essentially a question with a sur-

prise answer. Right? But in this context, what a joke is is a question that I have artifi-cially inseminated with tension. I do that, that's my job. I make you all feel tense, and then I make you laugh, and you're like, "Thanks for that. I was feeling a bit tense." I made you tense. This is an abusive relationship. Do you know why I'm such a funny fucker? Do you? It's because, you know, I've been learning the art of tension diffusion since I was a children. Back then it wasn't a job, it wasn't even a hobby, it was a sur-vival tactic. I didn't have to invent the tension. I was the tension. And … I'm tired of tension. Tension is making me sick.

Gadsby, who identifies as lesbian, has elegantly identified a fact of LGBTQ life that few have addressed in comedy. She learned to diffuse tension as a child because, as a lesbian, she was the source of the tension. First and fore-most, she learned to do this in order to survive. Queer people learn to do this at alarmingly young ages, and as she notes, the purpose of this tactic is survival; as she notes in the many powerful and often disturbing anecdotes in *Nanette*, "Being different is dangerous." The fact that this diffusion amused other people, and that she has to continually perform this survival tactic in the performance of her comedy, is what Gadsby thinks is ethical problem of comedy writ large. In the beginning, there is the tension. The joke, lacking the middle of the beginning-middle-end structure of the story, skips over the source and lingering effects of the tension that is resolved in the punch-line. Because the middle is never explored, but is instead a well to be drawn from, its power over marginalized people never diminishes. Sadly, skipping over the middle reiterates it and comedians, Gadsby included, contribute to its perpetuation.

Gadsby's diffusion of tension is, I submit, connected to the disengage-ment required for humor to have an effect. As John Morreall states in *Comic Relief: A Comprehensive Philosophy of Humor*:

When we want to evoke anger or outrage about some problem, we don't present it in a humorous way, precisely because of the practical disengagement of humor. Satire is not a weapon of revolutionaries. Humor involves cognitive as well as practical disen-gagement. While something is making us laugh, we are for the moment not con-cerned with whether it is real or fictional [101].

In order to laugh at a joke, an audience requires a certain degree of cognitive disengagement, which Gadsby experiences as the audience distancing itself from the pain and sorrow which often underlie satirical and political humor. It is Gadsby's version of the relief theory of humor—that jokes release a "pres-sure valve," to quote Morreall (15). Although Morreall and other philosophers have found the relief theory inadequate to the task of explaining the workings of humor in the human mind (as well as in society), it clearly resonates for Gadsby, and is apropos for the type of comedy that Gadsby is discussing and performing. It is also a key element for comedy told by the disenfranchised since such comedians are often expected to perform a certain amount of self-deprecation (or self-abasement) as the price of being heard by a mainstream (i.e., straight, white, cis) audience.

But in addition to recognizing that comedy is a different experience for the marginalized, Gadsby also explores the limitations of humor itself, arguing that even if we make room for outsiders' voices, jokes are insufficient to tell many stories: "I feel that in a comedy show, there's no place for the best part of the story, which is the ending. You know, in order to finish on a laugh, you know, you have to end with punch lines." She gives a vivid and devastating example of this during her show. Early on, she tells a joke about being mistaken for a man by a drunk, angry man. Later on in the show, she reveals that the actual story resulted not in humor but in severe injury after the man, realizing that Gadsby was a woman and a lesbian, beat her severely. The joke version of this incident is incomplete—it's punch line allows the audience to feel relief. By contrast, when Gadsby reveals the real account of the incident, her audience is silent, at least in part because the tension has not been relieved. We as viewers have to live with the discomfort and anguish of hearing the true story, and are denied the safe purging of emotion that a punch line would have provided.

Gadsby rejects the notion that humor and satire can serve as anything more than a balm for societal ills, arguing powerfully that there are some stories that cannot be adequately conveyed with jokes. However, she is also rejecting the notion that there is any way for a comedian to make a critique both powerful and pleasant, which may be a rejection of earlier activist (or charged, to use Krefting's term from *All Joking Aside*) comedians. For Gadsby, the truth of her experiences—and by extension, the truth of the experiences of the marginalized—is too traumatic and alien for white, heterosexual audiences to internalize through humor alone. In this respect, she rejects the incongruity theory of humor, in which laughter is provoked by the recognition of something incongruous, as delineated by Morreall (12). Morreall's Zen-influenced take on the incongruity theory argues that "humor throws a monkey wrench into the cognitive processing of the rational mind, and thus prompts us to question its nature. That is why incongruity of all kinds is so useful in Zen.... Contradictions are used in the same way, to frustrate the rational mind, and thus call attention to it" (135). The presumption here is that the humorous realization of incongruity is an educational experience for the student, and that the pleasure makes it easier for the student—or the audience, in Gadsby's case—to question the assumptions underlying the supposedly rational discourse. But Gadsby, while acknowledging that the laughter brings pleasure (and relief of tension) to the audience, rejects the idea that the incongruity experienced through humor is ultimately educational for the audience. In other words, she does not believe that the recognition of the incongruity is going to result in a change in the way the audience thinks and behaves.

Late Night Comedy Is Not Your Friend

Toward the end of *Nanette*, Gadsby talks about comedy and politics, with numerous fascinating digressions along the way. She talks at length about how male comedians often target the victims of injustice rather than its perpetrators, since the victims often make easy punchlines (her example is Monica Lewinsky). I would counter that political satirists and comedians, despite their intentions, may actually make it easier for Americans to cope with hate groups, school shootings, police brutality and other injustices by allowing us to release our tension through laughter rather than resolving it through anger and action. Obviously, there are counter-examples: Morreall makes the point that Charlie Chaplin's film *The Great Dictator* made the threat of Hitler to American audiences who were not necessarily inclined to read world news reports about the rise of European fascism (119). But when we examine the current state of political satire in the United States—*The Late Show with Stephen Colbert*, *Full Frontal with Samantha Bee*, Trevor Noah's *The Daily Show*, and many others—what we start to see is a troublingly familiar pattern. These comedians are doing on a national level what Gadsby is talking about from an individual perspective: they are diffusing tension. The joke begins by the host telling the audience whatever horrific thing that Trump has said or done that day. They comment on it, and give us a punch line. The audience laughs, the tension is released, but nothing is changed or resolved. Trump persists. We chuckle at his idiocy, or at the foolishness of the media, and then we go about our day, an excellent example of Morreall's ideas on the disengagement of humor (101). In other words, humor causes us to separate and distance ourselves from whatever situation we are laughing about, as we can see in the following example from *The Daily Show*:

> NOAH: In case you were wondering, shutting down the US-Mexico border wouldn't just hurt the hombres down south, no. There will also be more painful consequences here in the US, because, economists have warned that a closed border could affect 5 million American jobs and over 600 billion dollars in trade. Yeah. And if you think a border shutdown won't affect you, because you don't live or work around the border, well, you might want to think again.
> MSNBC REPORTER: The US, listen to this, would run out of avocados in three weeks if President Trump shuts down the border with Mexico.
> NOAH: Do you hear that? That's the sound of yoga moms all over America freaking out right now. [imitates yoga mom] "Where will I get my healthy fats?" So once again, Donald Trump has shown there's no problem he can't make twice as bad.

We don't get resolution. Because the tension has been diffused, we avoid what bell hooks memorably calls *Killing Rage* in her book of the same title. We are thus able to cope with an increasingly fragmented government and society.

Gadsby, by contrast, wants more; her goal is for an audience to get angry, and to stay angry long enough to take political action. However, even Gadsby's audience, although apparently moved by her presentation, arguably remain complicit in allowing injustice to continue.

One could respond to Noah's short joke about avocados with one of John Oliver's long rants. In 2014, the show launched a successful protest movement to save net neutrality—a movement which resulted in FCC servers crashing due to a record number of consumer comments coming in (Oliver). In 2017, the FCC attacked net neutrality again, prompting a powerful satiric response from Oliver:

> The point is, everyone needs to get involved. Comment now, and then maybe comment again once the FCC makes this proposal official, even call your representative and your senators and do not tell me that you don't have time to do this. If the internet is evidence of nothing else, it is evidence that we all have way too much time on our hands. And yes, I'm talking to you, everyone who posted "May the fourth be with you" for Star Wars Day, this, and every fucking year. And I'm talking to you, everyone who posted on Facebook about Ten Concerts You've Seen and One You Didn't. And to you, everyone who did it ironically and added a clever joke twist, because, and this is important, you are exactly as bad. Because you cannot say that you are too busy when 540,000 of you commented on Beyoncé's pregnancy announcement, and 673 of you took time to review the Grand Canyon on Yelp, seven of whom gave it a one-star review—what the fuck is wrong with you? And I'm specifically looking at you, person on Amazon who gave *The Wolf of Wall Street* one star because and I quote "There were no wolves in the movie." And to you, the thirty-one people who took the time to say they found that review helpful. And finally, I'm looking at the frankly surprising number of people, who for some reason, keep tweeting "Choke me Daddy" at the pope. You're wasting your time! He's not going to choke you. The optics would be very bad. So come on [Oliver rises from desk], I'm calling on all of you, the internet, time wasters and troublemakers to join me once more, in just five minutes or ten minutes of minor effort. I need you to do this. Once more unto the breach my friends, simply go to this URL [gofccyourself.com] and tell the FCC to preserve net neutrality and Title II, once again commenters, America needs you to rise, or more accurately, remain seated in front of your computers, to this occasion. So please, fly my pretties! Fly once more! [Oliver].

Comparing the structure of this segment with the border closure segment from *The Daily Show* shows that while both are laden with jokes, the jokes are not the main point of the Oliver's rant. Noah's segment on the border crossing was primarily intended to make the audience laugh, and it is successful. Although it makes viewers more aware of the ramifications of Trump's attempts to close the border, it does nothing to suggest that anything can be done. Oliver's point is to get viewers to take action, something which is arguably antithetical to them, as watching TV is an inherently passive and sedentary activity. The targets of the satire are not just the FCC and its chairman, Ajit Pai; it also skewers the absurdity and pettiness of internet commentary. It also takes on the common twenty-first-century complaint of having no time for activism, noting that "if the internet is evidence of nothing else, it is evidence that we all have way too much time on our hands" and giving numerous examples of the more ludicrous examples of internet comments. That net-neutrality was repealed in 2017 shows the limits of activism inspired by satire and humor: once the energy has dissipated it is difficult to create it again. Satire and humor have limits on what they can achieve, just as Morreall argues on the philosophical level and Gadsby realizes on the personal level—they can release tension, but they cannot by themselves effect change.

If the first problem of comedic satire is that once the tension is released it is difficult, if not impossible, to recreate, then the second is the comedian's oft stated position that their goal is to entertain, not save the world. In an interview with David Tennant for his podcast *David Tennant Does a Podcast With...*, Samantha Bee tacitly acknowledged this phenomenon as one of the main effects of her show:

> Tennant: And what is that job? Is it to be entertaining, principally, or is it to be like the fool in King Lear, who tells truth to power?
> Bee: Well, I think it's principally to be entertaining. I hope it's entertaining, and then the second part of that is to be ... is to just ... speak.
> Tennant: And do you feel that satire has a power, or does it always feel a little bit like...
> Bee: I don't think it has so much ... well, I ... you know, I'm not sure if it has a ton of power, I don't know that it does, but I do think that it has ... I do think that it has the power of catharsis. I do think that people benefit from knowing that somewhere out there there's someone who shares a point of view. I think that's beneficial. I think people go ... they just get so tense, they just get so bound up and so it is beneficial to have someone say it all, and be rude about it, and be an asshole on TV, and then everyone goes, "Yeah! That's what I was thinking!" There's something to that. I don't know that there's so much more than that [Tennant].

The catharsis that Bee talks about is effectively the same as Gadsby's diffusion of tension. Earlier in the interview, she strongly disavowed any desire to become more politically active:

> Tennant: Currently you're spending all your days getting very worked up about how badly the country is run.
> Bee: It's terrible.
> Tennant: Is there any point where you feel, "Do you know what? I need to sort it out."?
> Bee: No. No.
> Tennant: But why not? You've got the skills, surely?
> Bee: No.
> Tennant: You can think fast, you understand the issues.

BEE: I'm a curator.
TENNANT: Do you have a duty?
BEE: No. I'm a curator of others. I think like I have good ideas for other people, but this is my work, this is my area [Tennant].

Bee thus acknowledges that although she is horrified by what she reads in the news, there are limits to what a satirical show like *Full Frontal* can achieve. As Dorothy Parker remarked about the 1927 executions of Sacco and Vanzetti, "I had heard someone say and so I said too, that ridicule is the most effective weapon. Well, now I know that there are things that never have been funny and never will be. And I know that ridicule may be a shield but it is not a weapon" (qtd. in The Algonquin Round Table).

That said, there are some instances in which satire can make a difference—in October 2004, then–*Daily Show* host Jon Stewart famously appeared on CNN's *Crossfire* and effectively cancelled the show by ruthlessly mocking its hosts. Although Stewart was apparently expected to make a few harmless jokes, he began by asking hosts Paul Begala and Tucker Carlson to "Stop, stop, stop, stop hurting America," and continued from there ("Jon"). Stewart went on to satirize both the hosts and the show itself, stating that calling *Crossfire* a debate was equivalent to "saying pro wrestling is a show about athletic competition" ("Jon"). After Carlson accused Stewart of being easy on 2004 Democratic presidential nominee John Kerry, this exchange ensued:

STEWART: You know, it's interesting to hear you talk about my responsibility.
CARLSON: I felt the sparks between you.
STEWART: I didn't realize that—and maybe this explains quite a bit.
CARLSON: No, the opportunity to...
STEWART: ...is that the news organizations look to Comedy Central for their cues on integrity.
(LAUGHTER) ["Jon"].

The entire episode continued in this vein, apparently to the surprise of the show's hosts and producers. Toward the end of the show, Carlson told Stewart to "Be funny," resulting in the following:

CARLSON: Wait. I thought you were going to be funny. Come on. Be funny.
STEWART: No. No. I'm not going to be your monkey.
(LAUGHTER)
BEGALA: Go ahead. Go ahead.
STEWART: I watch your show every day. And it kills me.
CARLSON: I can tell you love it.
STEWART: It's so—oh, it's so painful to watch.
(LAUGHTER)
STEWART: You know, because we need what you do. This is such a great opportunity you have here to actually get politicians off of their marketing and strategy.
CARLSON: Is this really Jon Stewart? What is this, anyway?

STEWART: Yes, it's someone who watches your show and cannot take it anymore.
(LAUGHTER)
STEWART: I just can't ["Jon"].

The reaction both by the studio audience and by the media coverage was powerful—Stewart had openly criticized both the premise of and the hosts of a widely-watched political program and revealed that the emperor(s) had no clothes. Or perhaps, more accurately, he was able to articulate something that most viewers felt about political coverage in the era of the 24-hour news cycle. Only a few months later, CNN President Jonathan Klein announced the cancellation of *Crossfire*, citing Stewart's critique as one of the reasons for ending the show, noting "I think he made a good point about the noise level of these types of shows, which does nothing to illuminate the issues of the day" (Kurtz C01). Ironically, Stewart ended *Crossfire* not with a joke, but with an earnest plea for it to be better.

The Tension Remains

Gadsby's plan after *Nanette* was to quit comedy. Her original plan was to "drop a bomb" before taking a long hiatus from standup, as she told Jimmy Fallon on *The Tonight Show*:

I thought, "I'll drop a bomb and leave." …And the plan's backfired…. I said I was quitting, and then if I quit, I'm an idiot now. If the show had gone as badly as I'd planned, it would have worked. But now I'm left with the choice. I'll either be an idiot or a hypocrite…. I'll be a hypocrite ["Hannah"].

So although we shall benefit from more of Gadsby's comedy in the future, it may be a while before we get to hear her tell her story properly, without tension-relieving jokes diluting the message. There are reports that she is writing a memoir entitled *Ten Steps to Nanette*, but it is unclear when it will be published (Wright).

One question raised by Gadsby's critique of joke structure and satire is whether a different type of joke structure would allow for an investigation of the absent middle that she thinks is important for addressing (and redressing) the sources of tensions marginalized comedians mine for laughs. This could take the form of more self-referential comedy, monologues punctuated with humor, or laughter interrupted with call backs to painful truths—as Gadsby does when she tells two different versions of being confused for a man. At the same time, the limits satire based on the release of that tension remain an obstacle to the types of social change that Gadsby would like to see. At the end of *Nanette*, Gadsby leaves the audience with a comment on what laughter can and cannot do, concluding that "Laughter is not our

244 Part Four: Laughter and Ridicule

medicine. Stories hold our cure. Laughter is just the honey that sweetens the bitter medicine." She may well be right on a personal level, but at the moment, our key sources of political comedy and satire are giving us plenty of laughter, but not much medicine.

WORKS CITED

"The Algonquin Round Table." *PBS*, Public Broadcasting Service, 7 August 2015, www.pbs.org/wnet/americanmasters/the-algonquin-round-table-about-the-algonquin/527.
Burford, Corinna. "A Guide to Hannah Gadsby's Pre-Nanette Work." *Vulture*, 28 June 2018, www.vulture.com/2018/06/a-guide-to-hannah-gadsbys-pre-nanette-work.html.
Cameron, Dell. "The FCC Will Terminate Net Neutrality on June 11." *Gizmodo*, 10 May 2018, gizmodo.com/the-fcc-will-terminate-net-neutrality-on-june-11-1825920287.
Gadsby, Hannah. *Hannah Gadsby: Nanette*. Guesswork Television/Netflix, 2018.
"Hannah Gadsby's Stand-Up Special Was Supposed to Bomb but It Backfired Big Time." *The Tonight Show*, NBC, 25 July 2018, www.nbc.com/the-tonight-show/video/hannah-gadsbys-standup-special-was-supposed-to-bomb-but-it-backfired-big-time/3767864.
hooks, bell. *Killing Rage: Ending Racism*. Holt, 1995.
"Jon Stewart's America." *CNN*, Cable News Network, transcripts.cnn.com/TRANSCRIPTS/0410/15/cf.01.html.
Kefting, Rebecca. *All Joking Aside: American Humor and Its Discontents*. Johns Hopkins UP, 2014.
Kurtz, Howard. "Carlson & 'Crossfire,' Exit Stage Left and Right." *Washington Post*, 6 January 2005, p. C01.
Morreall, John. *Comic Relief: A New Philosophy of Humor*. Wiley-Blackwell, 2009.
"Net Neutrality II." *Last Week Tonight with John Oliver (HBO)*. *YouTube*, uploaded by Last-WeekTonight, 7 May 2017, https://www.youtube.com/watch?v=92vuuZt7wak&t=60s.
Tennant, David. "Samantha Bee." *David Tennant Does a Podcast With...*, Overcast app, 8 April 2019.
Wright, Megh. "Hannah Gadsby to Bless Us with Wisdom in New Memoir Ten Steps to Nanette." *Vulture*, 14 August 2018, www.vulture.com/2018/08/hannah-gadsbys-ten-steps-to-nanette-lands-u-s-publisher.html.

About the Contributors

Steven A. **Benko** is a professor of religious and ethical Studies at Meredith College. He received a Ph.D. from Syracuse University. He teaches, researches, and writes on ethical subjectivity, focusing on comedy and ethics, particularly the moral dimensions of laughter and how laughter reveals and shapes individual identity and social dynamics. He is the coeditor of *The Good Place and Philosophy* and has published on ethics and *The Good Place*, *Monty Python's Life of Brian*, posthuman epistemology, transhumanism and ethics, and critical thinking pedagogy.

Shouta **Brown** is a doctoral student in the philosophy program at Emory University. His research interests include political philosophy, aesthetics and social epistemology. His research aims to articulate the conditions of political imagination both as existing conditions that function to limit our ability to imagine society otherwise and new conditions that can be developed to transform our imaginative practices for the sake of a better future.

Robert R. **Clewis** is a professor of philosophy at Gwynedd Mercy University, Pennsylvania, and is a visiting scholar at the Max Planck Institute for Empirical Aesthetics in Frankfurt. He is the author of *The Kantian Sublime and the Revelation of Freedom* (2009) and *Kant's Humorous Writings* (2020) and the editor of *The Sublime Reader* (2019) and *Reading Kant's Lectures* (2015). His contemporary philosophical work also engages with psychological research on awe and the sublime.

Caroline E. **Compretta** is an assistant professor in the Center for Bioethics and Medical Humanities at the University of Mississippi Medical Center. She received a Ph.D. from the University of Kentucky. As a medical anthropologist, she works to address the social determinants of health and health disparities. Her work focuses on the medical ethics of practitioner and patient interactions and the ways dominate socioeconomic narratives affect healthcare communication and treatment plans.

Ralph H. **Didlake** is a professor of surgery and the director of the Center for Bioethics and Medical Humanities at the University of Mississippi Medical Center. After practicing general and transplant surgery for 25 years, he developed an interest in the human context of health and disease and completed a master's degree in bioethics at Loyola University, Chicago. His interests include teaching medical ethics and professionalism, and research in the areas of social determinants of disease and medical humanities.

Shelly A. **Galliah** is a visiting instructor at Michigan Technology University and has just completed her dissertation, which combines popular culture, science communication, comedy studies and big data analysis. At Michigan Tech, she has taught composition, science fiction and popular culture. She has published on pedagogy, satirical comedy, science fiction, and American naturalism. Her main interest is in celebrity citizen science communicators, particularly their use of comedy and satire to critique manufactured scientific controversies.

Nicole **Graham** is a third year religious studies Ph.D. student at the University of Kent, where she also received a BA. She received an MA from the University of Exeter. She is a member of the Humour and Religion Network. Her research explores questions of gender and ethics in the study of laughter and humor in religion.

Erica A. **Holberg** is an assistant professor of philosophy at Utah State University. She completed a Ph.D. at the University of Chicago. Her research examines how pleasure matters for the development of individual character and for the development, transmission, and stability of the character and values of communities. In particular, she is interested in the development of moral agency and moral psychologies within the social context of sexist oppression.

Eleanor **Jones** is a graduate of Meredith College in religious and ethical studies and is pursuing an MA in environmental philosophy at the University of Montana in Missoula. Her areas of research include feminism, environmentalism, and culture and comedy. She has completed three separately funded undergraduate research projects and presented at three conferences.

Rebecca **Krefting** is the chair and an associate professor in the American Studies Department at Skidmore College. Her research specializations are studies in humor and performance; identity and difference; media representations; visual and popular culture; and American subcultures. She is the author of *All Joking Aside,* and has published journal articles in *Studies in American Humor, Comedy Studies,* and *Journal of Cinema and Media Studies,* as well as several edited collections. Her research examines major industry shifts impacting the business and economy of stand-up during the second comedy boom.

Jennifer **Marra** earned a Ph.D. in philosophy from Marquette University. She has published on comedy, the metaphysics of humor, practical and theoretical ethics, and philosophy of culture. She is serving her sixth year on the Executive Board of The Lighthearted Philosophers' Society, an academic organization specializing in the philosophy of humor and humorous philosophy. She also runs the LPS Facebook page.

David K. **McGraw** is a professor in the School of Integrates Sciences at James Madison University. He received a Master of Administrative Studies from Southeastern Oklahoma State University and a JD from Georgetown University. He primarily teaches undergraduate students in the integrated science and technology program to think about the ethical, social and legal dimensions of science and technology.

Olivia **Moorer** is a graduate student at Loyola University Chicago. She received a B.A. from Gonzaga University. She researches popular culture and film, with particular focus on horror and comedy. She is interested in "the return of the repressed" as shown through both comedy and horror, and how these genres reveal what is socially repressed. In addition to her research on comedy and ethics, she has presented on queerness in *House of Cards* and Black temporality in *To Pimp a Butterfly*.

Grant **Moss** is an associate professor of English and literature at Utah Valley University. He received a Ph.D. in English from the University of North Carolina at Chapel Hill. His academic focus is on the literature of early modern England, with a particular emphasis on how Elizabethan culture and history is represented in twenty-first-century culture and media.

Christophe D. **Ringer** is an assistant professor of theological ethics and society at Chicago Theological Seminary. His research interests include theological and social ethics, African American religion, public theology, religion and social sciences, religion and politics, critical theory and African American religion, and cultural studies. He is interested in African American religion as a site for understanding the relationship of self, society and the sacred as it concerns human flourishing.

Liz **Sills** is an assistant professor of communication studies at Northern State University. She received a Ph.D. from Louisiana State University. Her interests lie in rhetorics, philosophies and cultural consequences surrounding comedy. She has contributed to *Comedy Studies, Empedocles: European Journal for the Philosophy of Communication* and in 2013 the Eisner Award–winning volume *Black Comics: Politics of Race and Representation*. She is president of the Lighthearted Philosophers' Society, and president of the Speech Communication Association of South Dakota.

Cindy Muenchrath **Spady** adjunct teaches for several different institutions in both philosophy and religious studies. She earned a BA from Simpson College, an M.Div from Iliff School of Theology and a D.Min from Drew University. She is particularly interested in how popular culture shapes our beliefs and lives.

Jonathan Peter **Wright** is a graduate student in cinema and media studies at York University, Toronto. His research explores the experience of confusion in film viewing. He approaches the topic from the field of film-philosophy. His other research interests include Emerson, Gadamer, aesthetic evaluation in film and "aesthetic exploration." His work can be found in *Film Matters, Senses of Cinema* and *Trans-Humanities*.

Index